THE
OWNERS

All NBA, NFL & MLB Team Owners Since 1920

(Who Paid How Much & When)

Bill Beermann

THE OWNERS
All NBA, NFL & MLB Team Owners since 1920
(Who Paid How Much & When)

Copyright © 2017 by William F. Beermann
First Edition
Printed in the USA

Cover design: Keri Lamparter Communications
Cover photo: iStock.com/rramirez125

ISBN 978-0-692-87575-9

Published by BB Publishing
P.O. Box 792
Bridgehampton, New York 11932

www.billbeermann.com

Introduction

It has been said the NFL stole Sunday from God. The average NBA salary is hovering around $8 million a year, and MLB is grappling with technology to call balls and strikes instead of umpires. Sports, which used to be games, have evolved into a multibillion-dollar entertainment business, which has driven team values, according to Forbes valuations, to the sky. Who is making all the money? The owners? Who are these guys? Who were these guys?

As a writer, former athlete, and semi-retired small business entrepreneur, I was curious to learn more about those billionaires we see tucked away in their private owners' boxes. It seemed to me this was an overlooked group, one that garnered little attention compared to the players, coaches, and fans.

In my experience as a business owner and investor, success and profits were always attributed to the boss, or CEO. He is the one who runs or delegates the management and the acquisition of players. This curiosity led me to search for a book on the subject, but there wasn't one. Yes, I could Google an individual owner, if I knew who he or she was, or go to a team's website, or fish for articles, but it was not enough to gain a full picture of a team's financial history. I wanted to know who all the owners were, how they made their money, how they managed their teams, and if ownership was a good investment over the years. More important, I wanted to find out which owners made a difference in team performance and winning championships. I wanted to see which owners built winning dynasties and how long they lasted. Since I found no such information available in one place, I decided to compile it myself.

Here it is: a collection of brief biographies and anecdotes about America's "Big 3" (baseball, basketball and football) professional sports team owners. Each chapter, each team story stands alone so the reader can choose his or her city, team, or sport to read first. This history about who bought which team from whom begins nearly 100 years ago when Curly Lambeau and his associates founded the Green Bay Packers for the $500 cost of uniforms, and ascends with Steve Ballmer's record-setting purchase of the L.A. Clippers for $2 billion in 2014 followed by the 2017 sale of the Houston Rockets for $2.2 billion.

The owners represent a cross-section of American sports and business history. Most were entrepreneurs who worked hard to earn their fortunes and make their way into the sports world. Many brands associated with these owners, like Ford, CNN, Microsoft, Coors, Wrigley, Hilton,

McDonalds, and many others, are household names in America today. Some were rags-to-riches owners while others inherited their teams. Movie stars and known personalities like Gene Autry, Bing Crosby, Oprah, Donald Trump, Danny Thomas, Lamar Hunt, Michael Jordan, Bob Hope, Peyton Manning, Shaquille "Shaq" O'Neal, and many others were (or still are) owners or would-be owners.

In 2017, Forbes valued the Dallas Cowboys at $4.8 billion, their highest valuation of the 92 teams chronicled in this book. They, and most other teams, have become more than sports teams. They have become brands. Often, their brand value is not commensurate with their performance on the field, but that doesn't seem to make much of a difference in terms of attendance or viewership. Yes, the contending teams are going to do better than the cellar dwellers, but fans are, for the most part, loyal … even when their team is losing. This dedicated (often fanatic) fan support has driven team values and player compensation through the roof. Until TV revenues kicked in to sports some 50 years ago, most teams struggled for financial survival. Although the franchises maintained (or substantially increased) their capital value, they often couldn't make ends meet, which forced many owners to sell. Rarely did I see a team franchise sell for less than it had cost. The NFL and MLB owner histories go back to their origins in 1920. Although pro baseball has its roots dating back to Civil War days, I chose to start with its modern era.

There are several hundred (473) owners (or owner groups) portrayed herein. Some owners are covered in more detail than others. The length and detail depended on the number of owners of a team, the length of time the team was in existence, and whether an owner's story was colored with drama of one kind or another. In some cases, owners engaged in trickery or sleight of hand to either buy, protect, or relocate their franchise. Some owners faced bankruptcy and were forced to sell. Many became embroiled in difficult negotiations with stadiums and city governments. A few went to jail. For the most part, we see American entrepreneurship at its best.

Owners were and continue to be a brotherhood, a fraternity of people (mostly men) with one thing in common: the competitive spirit to compete and win. That is not to say all owners were buddy-buddy. Quite the contrary, there was often bad blood and back-stabbing like the time Texas oil heir Clint Murchison secretly acquired the rights to the Washington Redskins fight song so George Preston Marshall (the Redskins' owner) couldn't play it at Redskins games unless he agreed to approve Clint's bid for an NFL franchise in Dallas. (Marshall had been the only owner who voted against Murchison.) The dirty little bribe worked and the Dallas Cowboys were born. Murchison didn't fare so well himself, turning a fortune into a pile of debt.

And, there is the sneaky time when Robert Irsay moved the Baltimore Colts from Baltimore to Indianapolis in the dead of night to avoid the police and beat the city's next-morning vote to declare eminent domain over the Colts. There was Art Modell who finagled his way out of Cleveland to relocate to Baltimore, leaving angry Cleveland fans without a team for three years.

And who knew, even at the turn of the century, that sports would become the number-one product for live television broadcasting, the place where advertisers could best reach their audience. As ad rates soared, so did the coffers of the leagues and their players, not to mention the media. All in all, it's the millions of diehard fans like me (like us), who are paying the costly tab to see the action.

Real estate was once the industry where an overwhelming majority of owners earned their stake to buy a team. Lately, the investment bankers, smelling capital appreciation, have been getting into the act. Oil and gas saw some huge fortunes accumulated and invested in sports teams. Some owners bought their teams to sell tickets to support the stadium, field, or arena that they owned or rented. A few teams are still in the hands of the families who founded them, some going back to 1920.

Many owners were good athletes or devoted sports nuts who dreamed of owning a team one day. Owning a team presented a way to play and compete vicariously. There are certain themes that run throughout this fraternity: brains, balls, money, ego, identity, fame, fortune, greed, and competitive spirit. Most have the same lofty goal to bring home a championship to their city and fans, with all the money and recognition that comes with the trophy... and the "trophy investment."

As we can see from the Forbes valuation at the end of each chapter, the average value of a "Big 3" franchise is well over $1 billion, and growing. The average value of an NFL team is over $2.5 billion. Owners today are playing their own sport: "Billionaire Ball" -- the game of buying and selling professional sports teams ... *if* there is one for sale.

*In Memory of
Wendy*

Foreword

As a 17-year-old baseball fanatic, I was in a trance when I entered the Pittsburgh Pirates' dressing room in May 1960. The Pirates had been cellar dwellers most of the '50s but it didn't keep me from going to 20 to 30 games a season. I lived in Shadyside, two miles from Forbes Field, and could walk to the games. I would pass by the field where the Pitt Panthers practiced. In those days when college football was king, the Panthers, with star player Mike Ditka, were by far the football team in Pittsburgh. The Steelers played second fiddle.

My walk continued across the cobblestoned street (with rails for trolley cars), and through the University of Pittsburgh's urban skyscraper campus, past Shenley Park, and into the Forbes Field bleachers. For one buck, I could root for the "Bucs" and chow down on a 25-cent hot dog or a 15-cent Klondike bar, usually both. I longed to catch a foul ball, but few were hit to the left field bleachers. In those days, we avid fans would buy the Pirates' program, with a scorecard to record every play. In addition to showing player photos and stats, they always featured the photos of two men in business suits: John W. Galbreath, the team's owner, and Branch Rickey, the general manager. As a young fan, I wondered why they were pictured. What did they have to do with winning games? Wasn't it all about the players?

At home as a child, the voices of Bob Prince and Rosey Rowswell broadcasting the play-by-play were omnipresent. Sometimes I cried when my Pirates lost. I loved that team. My dream, like most Little Leaguers, was to be the player who hit the winning "walk-off" home run in the bottom of the ninth.

I had been invited to Forbes Field by Dick Groat, the Pirates' Captain and shortstop. Groat, a basketball great who some have credited with inventing the jump shot, had played basketball at Duke with Lefty Driesell, who was recruiting me to go to Davidson College on a basketball scholarship. Lefty said Groat could vouch for the great program he would be building at Davidson, a southern school about which I knew very little. He was right. Lefty, now a coaching legend, went on to be one of the winningest NCAA Division I college coaches of all time.

The Pirates dressing room behind the dugout was dark and cave-like with a dirt floor that had the same aroma as infield. The redolence of freshly cut grass drifted in from the outfield. The players were getting dressed, some smoking cigarettes while they put on their spikes and joked around. I listened to Groat's pitch about Lefty's coaching ability and stared in awe at all my heroes. He introduced me to the immortal Roberto Clemente, and Bill Mazeroski, who would hit the dramatic ninth-inning "walk-off" home run to beat the Yankees in the 1960 World Series. (I didn't get to go to any of those games because I was doing wind-sprints in North Carolina, getting ready for the start of the freshman basketball season).

A few weeks after meeting Groat and the Pirates, my boyhood dream of playing on the Pirates' infield came true. I was selected to the All-City baseball team and we were invited to a pre-game recognition ceremony that included taking infield practice. Nine of us, dressed in our high school uniforms, sat in the dugout waiting to be introduced over the loudspeaker. One by one, our names and schools were announced as we took our positions on the field. For some reason, I was put at first base, a position I had rarely played. A Pirates coach came to the plate with a "fungo" bat and began hitting hard grounders to the infielders. The grounder to me went right through my legs and on in to right field, to the sound of friendly boos from fans.

As I reflect on my past as a fan of baseball, basketball, and football, I never gave the credit for winning or losing where it was most deserved: to the owners.

— Bill Beermann

Acknowledgments

Many thanks go to the writer/researchers I hired to help me do the spadework. Rebecca Hermann, PhD, an ardent baseball fan and published baseball writer, manages her own "leadership/motivational" business (www.winningcultureleadership.com). Much credit must be given to researchers Vanessa Greaves and Lexi Beermann for their relentless digging for accurate information and compelling tidbits. And, of course, to Forbes, for its detailed reporting on the business of sports and its annual team valuations. A special thanks to Keri Lamparter for the book design and production coordination.

NOTE: Purchase prices listed before each chapter:

These prices were obtained from various published articles. They are meant to reflect what the owner paid. In many cases the owner acquired 100-percent ownership, which would reflect the value of the franchise at that time. Other owners bought a minority or majority share, which might not reflect the total value of the team because the percentage of ownership was not always revealed. I included these tables to provide the reader with a capsule view of the rising value over time in a quick glance. It is not written to be penny-perfect. At the end of each chapter, I included the Forbes most-recent valuation for comparison with previous purchase prices. Of course, the effect of inflation over time must be considered.

NOTE: Owners of more than one team:

Some owners bought and/or sold more than one team. These individuals are noted and/or described in more than one chapter. In a few cases, I refer the reader to another team's chapter for more information about an owner of multiple teams.

NOTE: Forbes valuations:

The Forbes valuations shown at the end of each team chapter represent the year in which they were published by Forbes, not on the team's financial year upon which the valuations were based.

Legend of League and Organization Initials

AAFL	All American Football League
AAU	Amateur Athletic Union
AFL	American Football League
AFL	Arena Football League
ABL	American Basketball League
AFC	American Football Conference
AL	American League
ALCS	American League Championship Series
APFA	American Professional Football Association
BAA	Basketball Association of America
LDS	League Divisional Series (baseball)
MLB	Major League Baseball
MLS	Major League Soccer
NBA	National Basketball Association
NBL	National Basketball League
NFC	National Football Conference
NFL	National Football League
NL	National League
NLCS	National Leagues Championship Series
PCL	Pacific Coast League (baseball)
USFL	United States Football League
WNBA	Women's NBA

Contents

National Basketball Association

Atlanta Hawks

Former names: Buffalo Bisons 1946; Tri-Cities Blackhawks 1947-51; Milwaukee Hawks 1951-55; St. Louis Hawks 1955-1968

Year	Owner(s)	Purchase Price
1946-1968	Ben Kerner	$2,500
1968-1977	Tom Cousins and Carl Sanders	$3.5 Million
1977-1996	Ted Turner	$7.27 Million
1996-2004	AOL Time Warner	
2004-2015	Atlanta Spirit/ B. Levenson	$208 Million
2015-	Antony Ressler	$730 Million

Ben Kerner was one of the early pioneers of professional basketball. He grew up in Buffalo, went to Canisius College and the University of Buffalo, and then founded a successful sports marketing firm in the early '40s. He and a friend purchased the original franchise, the Buffalo Bisons, from the then National Basketball League (NBL) in 1946 for $2,500. Kerner struggled with his franchise, moving it first to Moline, IL and changing the name to the Tri-City Blackhawks, then to Milwaukee as the Milwaukee Hawks in 1951. After four years, he realized he needed a larger market. He knew St. Louis was primarily a baseball town, but he felt the city was prime for a professional basketball team and moved the team there in 1955. Who did he bring with him? None other than one of the greatest (early) NBA legends of all time -- Bob Pettit. He named them the St. Louis Hawks.

Kerner's marketing skills became his trademark. He spent summers providing clinics to kids in surrounding towns and held post-game concerts with the likes of the Glenn Miller Orchestra. With the help of general manager Marty Blake, the Hawks traded for future Hall of Famers Cliff Hagan, Ed Macauley, Slater Martin, and Clyde Lovellette. They also hired coach Red Holzman, who went on to win two NBA titles with the N.Y. Knicks. Interesting to note: Ben Kerner hired legendary Hall of Fame coach "Red" Auerbach in 1949, but Red quit to join the Boston Celtics when he learned that Kerner made a trade without consulting him. Coach Auerbach went on to win nine NBA titles with the Celtics.

Kerner also chose Bob Cousey in the 1950 draft but traded him to the Chicago Stags when Cousey ask for more than Ben was willing to pay. Cousey, who ended up with the Celtics when the Stags went under, played in 13 consecutive All Star games. Beginning in 1956, the Hawks became a mini-dynasty, winning five Division titles, and playing in four NBA Finals.

And, in 1957-58, the Hawks defeated the mighty Boston Celtics to win the NBA Championship.

In 1960, he had special baskets designed that operated on a hydraulic lift and could be installed quicker than any produced at that time. The ultimate promoter, Kerner instituted the NBA Game of the Week and arranged that the All-Star game be played in St. Louis three times over a 10-year span. Ben Kerner's Hawks became the darling of St. Louis fans and made the playoffs 12 of 13 years.

In 1968, the team was sold to Tom Cousins for a reported $3.5 million. Cousins, a prominent Atlanta real estate developer, moved the team to Atlanta, renaming it the Atlanta Hawks. Carl Sanders, former governor of Georgia, was a minority owner. Cousins also owned the Atlanta Flames hockey team, which he sold for approximately $16 million in 1980, giving him extra cash to spruce up the Hawks' facilities.

Then came Ted Turner. The billionaire media mogul bought both the Atlanta Braves baseball team and the Atlanta Hawks in 1976. He paid $7.27 million for 95% ownership of the Hawks. Not only did the teams fit his ego, they fit nicely into his broadcast empire. His impact on global communications, philanthropy, massive land acquisitions, (not to mention actress Jane Fonda), have put him in the limelight for decades. Once known as "The Mouth of the South," Turner's accomplishments are undenied, except for one little tidbit: his Hawks never won an NBA title during the 20 years he owned the team.

In 1996, when AOL Time Warner acquired Turner Broadcasting, the Hawks came along with the merger. In 2004, the Hawks were sold to Atlanta Spirit, LLC, for $208 million. Bruce Levinson, the controlling owner, had to put the Hawks up for sale after he was charged with making racially tainted remarks about the team and its fan base. Levinson hired Goldman Sachs to fetch a buyer at a valuation of $1 billion. However, the final price, reported by Forbes, was $730 million. The NBA approved the sale in 2015.

The winning bidder was billionaire philanthropist Antony Ressler, the co-founder of private equity firms Apollo Global Management and Ares Management. Minority owners included former Duke and NBA star Grant Hill, Jerry Itzler and wife Sara Blakeley, the billionaire entrepreneur who founded Spanx. Michael Gearon and his Atlanta-based group, who were part of Atlanta Spirit, LLC, kept a minority stake.

At the time, Ressler's worth was estimated by Forbes at $1.4 billion. He was part of a group that tried to purchase the L.A. Clippers in 2014 with a bid of $1.2 billion but was foiled by Steve Ballmer's $2 billion bid.

NBA Finals Appearances: 4   Wins: 1
Forbes 2017 Valuation: $885 Million

Boston Celtics

Year	Owner(s)	Purchase Price
1946-1951	Boston Garden Arena Corporation	
1951	Walter A. Brown	$2,500
1951-1964	Walter A. Brown and Lou Pieri	$50,000
1964	Marjorie Brown and Lou Pieri	
1965-1968	Marvin Kratter	$3 Million
1968-1972	Ballantine Brewing Co.	$6 Million
1972-1975	Robert Schmertz	$4 Million
1975-1978	Irv Levin and Harold Lipton	$4 Million
1978	John Y. Brown and Harry Mangurian	Trade
1979-1983	Harry Mangurian	
1983-1993	Don F. Gaston, Allen H. Cohen, and Paul DuPee	$15 Million
1993-2003	Paul Gaston	
2003-	Boston Basketball Partners, LLC	$360 Million

If there is one franchise in the history of the NBA that stands above the rest, it must be the Boston Celtics, with the Los Angeles Lakers not far behind. (The Celtics own one more NBA title than the Lakers). If there is one NBA coach who stands above the rest, it must be Red Auerbach. Thanks to Red, the Celtics became a dynasty. In 1949-50, Ben Kerner, founder of the Hawks, let Red slip away to the Celtics, and the rest is history as Red created the first NBA dynasty.

In 1945, shortly after Walter A. Brown became president of the Boston Garden Arena Corporation, he took a mortgage on his house to help found the Celtics. In fact, he was responsible for building the very foundation upon which the Celtics reigned, the famous parquet floor that became so identifiable as a Celtic icon. That floor, which cost $11,000, was constructed in 1946 for the Boston Arena. It was moved to the new Boston Garden in 1952. The wood had been cut in Tennessee for World War II purposes. Leftover scrap strips were pieced together in an alternating pattern to get the most use of the existing wood. There were 247 5' x 5' blocks, 1.5 inches thick, held together by wood planks and brass screws that were joined together by 988 bolts. It took several men two to three hours to assemble. Over the years of Celtic supremacy, many opponents complained about the "soft" spots on the Garden floor. Red Auerbach would reply to those critics that it wasn't as bad as Madison Square Garden.

If ever there existed a home court advantage in the NBA, it was in the Boston Garden. The acoustics were such that the crowd noise was like a sixth player, and there was no air conditioning to cool those late spring playoff nights. In the 1984 finals, the heat and humidity was so bad they brought in oxygen masks.

In addition to spearheading the Celtics' dominance, Walter A. Brown helped found the BAA (Basketball Association of America) in 1946, and was a central figure in the merger of the BAA and the NBL (National Basketball League) into the NBA in 1949. After five losing years, the Boston Garden Arena Corporation sold the team to Brown for $2,500. Soon after, Lou Pieri became co-owner for $50,000. Pieri, a Brown University graduate and sports entrepreneur, was the person who convinced Brown to hire Red Auerbach, and to sign Bob Cousey. During their 15-year ownership, the Celtics won six NBA championships.

Walter A. Brown, a graduate of the elite Philips Exeter Academy, was also instrumental in the development of professional hockey. In 1951, he purchased his tenant, the financially strapped Boston Bruins. Brown, along with several other arena managers, including Lou Pieri, founded the Ice Capades in 1950. It was Brown, having great influence in the Boston area, who denied Koreans entry into the 1951 Boston Marathon, stating they should be preparing to fight for their country, not preparing to run in marathons.

Walter A. Brown was inducted into both the hockey and basketball Halls of Fame. His reputation earned him the honor of having the NBA Championship Trophy named after him. In addition, the Celtics retired jersey #1 in his honor. When Walter died in 1964, his share was taken over by his wife, Marjorie Brown, who co-owned the team with Pieri.

In 1965, the team was sold to the Ruppert Knickerbocker Brewing Corporation, a subsidiary of National Equities, for $3 million. Marvin Kratter, founder of National Equities, became the Celtics' chairman of the board. Kratter, Brooklyn-born, made his fortune in New York real estate. He had owned the St Regis Hotel for a period, and bought Ebbetts Field from Walter O'Malley, renting it back to him for use by the Dodgers until they moved to L.A. in 1957.

In 1968, the Celtics were sold to the Ballantine Brewing Co. for $6 million. In 1971, Ballantine was taken over by Investors Funding Company, which sold the team to Transnational Communications, Inc. for the same price. After falling behind on the payments, the company transferred the team back to Ballantine, which proceeded to search for a new buyer.

In 1972, Irv Levin, who had minority ownership in the Seattle Supersonics, and Harold Lipton, a successful businessman and lawyer, bought the Celtics for $3.7 million but were forced by the NBA to sell their shares because of a conflict of interest. Robert Schmertz, who had been a part-owner of the Portland Trailblazers, qualified to buy the team and paid

$4 million, with Levin and Lipton having an option to buy back 50 percent of the team. Embarrassing: Schmertz gets indicted for bribery in 1975. His business was building retirement communities and he got caught bribing a public official for permits. (Meanwhile…Levin and Lipton are still in the picture, wanting to acquire their 50 percent). Schmertz reneged on their option. After a series of lawsuits in 1975, Levin and Lipton acquired their 50 percent ownership for $2 million. Six months later, Schmertz died and Levin and Lipton bought the remaining shares for another $2 million.

In 1978, Levin (whose fascinating travels through the entertainment business and professional sports ownership are detailed in the L.A. Clippers' story), and Lipton traded the team to John Y. Brown and Harry Mangurian for their ownership of the Buffalo Braves (now the L.A. Clippers). In 1979, Mangurian, who made his fortune in the retail furniture business, obtained complete ownership of the team and, in 1983, he sold the team to Allen H. Cohen, Don F. Gaston, (the Celtics chairman) and Paul DuPee for $15 million. Mangurian went on to make a name for himself as a thoroughbred horse breeder and philanthropist.

Under Gaston's leadership, the Celtics went public in 1986, offering 40 percent ownership for 2.6 million shares at $18.50 a share, totaling roughly $120 million. Paul Gaston succeeded his father, taking over ownership of the team in 1993.

In 2003, the team was sold to Boston Basketball Partners (BBP) LLC, a local private investment group, for $360 million. There are four members of the executive committee: Wycliff Grousbeck, H. Irving Grousbeck, Steve Pagliuca, and Robert Epstein. As soon as BBP got hold of the reins, they made the brilliant decision to hire former Celtic star guard Danny Ainge as director of basketball operations. Ainge did not inherit a very good team. In 2006, they had the second worst record in Celtic history going 24-58. But Ainge made two bold moves in 2006. He acquired center Kevin Garnett from the Timberwolves and sharpshooter Ray Allen (who some call the greatest clutch outside shooter of all time) from Seattle. They joined the great Paul Pierce, creating the Celtics' "Big Three." In their first year (2007-2008), the Celtics produced the biggest turnaround in league history going 66-16, or 42 more wins than the previous season. They went on to defeat the Lakers in the NBA Finals, giving the Celtics their 17th championship. Had the Celtics lost, the Lakers could have claimed their 17th championship and been one-up in their series.

In 2017, BBP made more bold moves, acquiring two superstars who should put the Celtics on solid footing for years to come.

NBA Finals Appearances: 21   Wins: 17
Forbes 2017 Valuation: $2.2 Billion

Brooklyn Nets

Year	Owner(s)	Purchase Price
1967-1969	Arthur Brown	$30,000
1969-1978	Roy Boe	$1.1 Million
1978-1998	Alan Cohen, Joseph Taub	N/A
1998-2004	Raymond Chambers, Lewis Katz	$150 Million
2004-2010	Bruce Ratner	$300 Million
2010-	Mikhail Prokhorov	$200 Million

The Nets long ago established themselves as an NBA franchise, yet to this day grapple with something of an identity crisis brought about by their nomadic history. Having roamed the New York Metro area for six decades, from New Jersey to Long Island back to New Jersey and then back to New York, the team's relationship to its fan base is a zero-sum game with generations of Long Island fans feeling deserted, generations of New Jersey fans feeling deserted, and New York City fans wholly indifferent as their allegiance is to the New York Knicks. And no wonder: In total, the team has operated in eight different venues and locales -- four in New Jersey (Teaneck, Piscataway, East Rutherford, and Newark), and in Commack, West Hempstead, and Uniondale on Long Island. And while Brooklyn is a borough of New York City it is also geographically part of Long Island, so make Brooklyn their fourth stop on Long Island.

The team's original owner, trucking magnate Arthur Brown, founded the New Jersey Americans of the American Basketball Association in 1967. One year later, Brown would rename the team the New York Nets and move them to Long Island. The next year he would sell the team to Roy Boe, who'd made his fortune (with his wife), in a women's clothing company.

The New York Nets would achieve a measure of success on Long Island while in the ABA, winning championships in 1974 and 1976. Despite this, Boe would struggle financially. In 1976 the Nets were among four ABA teams to merge into the NBA (the others being the San Antonio Spurs, Denver Nuggets, and Indiana Pacers). Treating the merger more as an expansion model, each ABA team was to pay an expansion fee of $3.2 million to the NBA. The financially constrained Boe would be assessed an additional $4.3 million fee to be paid directly to the New York Knicks for "invading" their New York territory. To come up with the requisite amount of money, Boe would sell his star player, Julius "Dr. J" Erving, to the Philadelphia 76ers and one year later move the team from Long Island back to New Jersey. As Boe's fiscal situation worsened, he would sell the team in 1978 to a group of New Jersey real estate developers led by Alan Cohen and Joseph Taub, nicknamed by the local press the "Secaucus Seven."

After a long run ranging from middling success to mediocrity, the team would be sold in 1998 to another group of New Jersey realtors. It was led by Lewis Katz and Raymond Chambers, who called themselves the C.Y.O. (Community Youth Organization). It was their intention to make Newark the permanent home of the New Jersey Nets, whose centerpiece would be a brand-new showplace arena in downtown Newark. The C.Y.O. formed a partnership with George Steinbrenner, creating a holding company called YankeeNets, which owned the Yankees, Nets, and later the New Jersey Devils of the NHL. YankeeNets would go on to create a regional sports television network, YES. Ultimately, YankeeNets could not persuade Newark to fund the construction of the new arena and continuous friction within the partnership would lead to its dissolution.

With their dream of a Newark arena thwarted, C.Y.O. would in 2004 sell the team to New York real estate developer Bruce Ratner, who envisioned a new arena in Brooklyn as home of the Nets, the centerpiece for an ambitious $3.5-billion sports arena, business, and residential complex called Atlantic Yards. As the mega-project encountered one encumbrance after another -- controversy involving the use of eminent domain in acquiring the land, a slowing economy hampering the raising of capital, etc. -- Ratner would sell an 80-percent interest in the team in 2010 to multi-billionaire Mikhail Prokhorov, the third-richest person in Russia (according to Forbes). Included in the deal would be Prokhorov's funding ($700 million) and ownership of the new arena, the Barclay's Center. The Brooklyn Nets began play in their new arena in 2012 under the principal ownership of the first Russian owner of an American pro sports franchise.

For a franchise that has been around as long as the Nets, with an impressive array of players over the years ranging from Rick Barry to Julius Erving to Nate Archibald to Bernard King and Jason Kidd, the Nets finally seem in a stable position: an owner with deep pockets; a wonderful facility, and a locale in which to build a loyal following. The challenge, as has always been the case, will be to finally shed their migratory reputation, put down roots in one place, and build a generational fan base. A skeptic might point out that the New York Knicks have owned New York City (including Brooklyn) forever -- a neat trick considering their only two championships were in 1970 and 1973 and that, as such, the Nets will never insinuate themselves into the hearts and minds of Brooklynites. On the other hand, great players, a winning program, and championships tend to work wonders in professional sports and so the former New Jersey aka New York aka Brooklyn Nets seem well-positioned to carve out a niche of their own in the future.

The question looms: when? The 2016-17 Nets had the worst record in the NBA. Putin would be ashamed that a Russian Plutocrat could not make the grade. It has been reported that Prokhorov has been seeking to sell a significant minority share in the Nets.

NBA Finals Appearances: 2   Wins: 0
Forbes 2017 Valuation: $1.8 Billion

Charlotte Hornets

Former names: Charlotte Bobcats 2003-2014

Year	Owner(s)	Purchase Price
1988-2002	George Shinn	$32.5 Million
2002-2010	Robert L. Johnson	$300 Million
2010-	Michael Jordan	$275 Million

North Carolina has always been a hotbed for college basketball. No other state could boast as many powerful teams as those that emerged in the '50s and '60s including "The Big Four" of Duke, Carolina (UNC), Wake Forest, and N.C. State who led the most powerful NCAA conference in the country, the ACC (Atlantic Coast Conference). Three of the teams were clustered no more than 25 miles from the others in North Carolina's "research triangle" of Raleigh-Durham and Chapel Hill, with Wake Forest not far away. Not only was "Tobacco Road" a nickname for the rich red-soiled tobacco fields surrounding this area, it referred to the sweet smell of tobacco burning in the nearby factories that fans encountered on a trip to one of these teams' games. Remember the "Dixie Classic?"

Charlotte didn't emerge as a major American basketball city until Davidson College, 20 miles north, hired future Hall of Fame coach Lefty Driesell in 1960. Bold and brazen, Lefty created an extension to Tobacco Road that stopped in the tiny town of Davidson, NC. He did this by building powerhouse teams in the 1960s, teams that could compete with the mighty "Big Four." In 1962, Sports Illustrated in its pre-season predictions ranked Davidson College number one, an amazing accomplishment for a school of less than 1,000 men at the time. Many of the school's home games were played in the Charlotte Coliseum.

George Shinn founded the Hornets in 1988 with a partner, Cy Bahakel, a Lebanese-American. They raised the NBA's fee of $32.5 million. Shinn put in $8.7 million and Bahakel $6 million; the balance came from bank loans. Even though Shinn was the majority owner, it is Cy Bahakel, a former North Carolina state senator who made his fortune by launching radio and TV stations, who should get the credit for bringing pro sports to Charlotte, because Cy guaranteed the bank loans that gained the NBA's approval. Shinn had an option to buy Cy's share after one year and exercised it.

George Shinn, a native North Carolinian from Kannapolis, wasn't book-smart (graduating last in his high school class) but he was enterprising, street smart, and able to raise enough money to buy the business college he attended and several other small colleges. He consolidated them into a single entity, Rutledge Education Systems, and sold it for some $30 million, providing him the funds to finance the purchase of the Hornets. He was also successful investing in real estate and car dealerships.

The City of Charlotte was more than enthusiastic to have a professional sports team, especially an NBA team that would put the growing city even more on the national map. From 1988 to 1996, Charlotte led the NBA in attendance with 21,000 season tickets sold. Sellouts of 24,000 were common. The fan base was hot to trot. Unfortunately, so was George Shinn. In 1997, he was brought to trial on a kidnapping and rape charge by a Charlotte woman who accused him of forcing her to perform oral sex. The trial became a soap opera that was broadcast on Court TV and became national sensational news. Shinn claimed the sex was consensual. His lawyer voiced the famous line, "If she wasn't 'bitin,' she wasn't fightin'." The court ruled in Shinn's favor, but the trial not only busted Shinn's reputation, it also exposed Shinn for having an affair with one of the Hornet's cheerleaders. Shinn became an embarrassment to the proud citizens of Charlotte.

Attendance plummeted. The Hornets went from the best attendance in the league to the worst. The once avid and loyal fans stopped coming to Hornets games. It was a disaster of huge proportions and George Shinn and family looked to get out of town. Shinn applied to the NBA for approval to move the team to New Orleans. In 2002, the Hornets' relocation was approved and the city of Charlotte was left in the lurch. But not for long.

In late 2002, the NBA, anxious to keep the Charlotte market, awarded an expansion franchise to Robert L. Johnson, founder of BET (Black Entertainment Network). Johnson, who paid $300 million for the franchise, became the first African-American majority owner of an American sports franchise. Although Johnson was indeed a successful businessman and entrepreneur, he didn't turn out to be the owner the fans had hoped he would be.

Johnson, born in Mississippi in 1946, the ninth of 10 children, grew up in Freeport, Illinois, graduated from the University of Illinois, and went on to get a master's degree from the Woodrow Wilson School of Public and International Affairs at Princeton. He entered the television broadcasting business, worked for the Corporation for Public Broadcasting and the National Urban League, and became vice-president of government relations for the National Cable and Television Association. Having learned the ropes and made strategic contacts, Johnson launched BET in 1980, the first cable TV network focused on African-Americans. By 1991, BET became the first black-controlled company on the New York Stock Exchange. In 2000, Johnson and co-shareholder Liberty Media sold BET to Viacom for $3 billion. Johnson, who owned 42 percent, became the first African-American billionaire.

Alas, one year after the lucrative sale to Viacom, Robert and his wife, Sheila, who co-founded BET, divorced after 33 years of marriage. Sheila is reported to have received one of the largest divorce settlements in U.S. history. And get this: she subsequently married the judge who presided over their divorce case.

During his span as owner, Robert Johnson, despite his civic contributions and philanthropy, did not have much impact on the team. Their performance was mediocre. Johnson was a busy man, investing in business ventures and sitting on several prestigious boards, including the NBA Board of Governors. The first clue that Johnson might not be the owner the fans had hoped came when he decided to name the team after himself: "Bob-Cats." When queried, his response inferred he had 300 million reasons why he chose that name. Perhaps worse, the uniforms were ugly and kept changing but never hit the mark. Who were the Bobcats? Their identity and branding kept changing. But the straw that broke the fans' backs came after Johnson, who had the city build a new arena, had luxury boxes installed instead of more seating. Then it was learned he charged for community events, which were supposed to be free. His reputation was tarnished and Johnson decided to split.

In 2010, he sold majority ownership of the Bobcats to Michael Jordan, a minority owner of the Bobcats since 2006. Jordan's group paid $275 million. Johnson kept a minority share. The transaction made Jordan the first former player to become a majority owner of an NBA team; and, changing places with Johnson, the only African-American majority owner of an NBA team. Ownership was not all a bed of roses for the great Michael Jordan. The team stunk-it-up on the court. In 2013, when the New Orleans Hornets changed their name to the Pelicans, Jordan changed the Bobcats' name back to the Hornets. The original Charlotte Hornets were now the Charlotte Hornets again. In addition to regaining their name, they regained their original history and records from the 1988-2002 Hornet span in Charlotte. Hope mounted for a brighter future.

It will be interesting to observe if a great super-star player can become a great owner.

NBA Finals Appearances: 0
Forbes 2017 Valuation: $780 Million

Chicago Bulls

Year	Owner(s)	Purchase Price
1966-1972	Dick Klein	$1.6 Million
1972-1983	Arthur Wirtz	$5.1 Million
1983-1985	William Wirtz	N/A
1985-	Jerry Reinsdorf	$9.2 Million

There is only one pro team sport wherein an individual player can determine the fortunes of his team -- win a game, or a series, or a championship, solely by virtue of his ability, and his will.

Football is too dependent upon 11 players executing individual assignments in unison (on both offense and defense). The best hitter in baseball only gets up four times a game and the best pitcher only gets to pitch every fifth day. That is not to say that a Lawrence Taylor cannot singlehandedly wreck a game, or a Sandy Koufax cannot win a World Series by starting three games. Nor is it to say that complementary players are not essential (they are) or that competent coaching is not required (it is). Rather, it is to say that the very nature of a game that has 11 or nine players makes it more difficult for a single player to dominate. But basketball is different. There are only five players and they all simultaneously play both offense and defense. Roll a basketball onto the court, and if a Michael Jordan should pick it up ... history changes. Forever.

By the time the Chicago Bulls selected Michael Jordan of the University of North Carolina with the third pick of the NBA draft of 1984, they had been for 18 years a more than credible NBA franchise and in fact a winning franchise from their inception in 1966 -- the only expansion team in NBA history to reach the playoffs in their inaugural season by posting the best record ever for an expansion team: 48-33.

Where Chicago had always been one of the greatest pro sports towns -- the Cubs and White Sox in MLB, the Bears in the NFL, and the Blackhawks in the NHL -- basketball had always been problematic; three teams tried, and failed, to take hold in Chicago. The Chicago American Gears of the NBL folded in 1947, the Chicago Stags of the BAA/NBA folded in 1950, and the Chicago Packers/Zephyrs of the NBA in 1962 relocated east as the Baltimore Bullets. Why, then, would a fourth attempt in 1966 be any different?

The NBA was entering into a national television contract with ABC and a vital franchise in the Chicago market would of course be crucial to penetrating the Midwest region. Dick Klein, a former pro basketball player who became successful distributing promotional materials to banks and other businesses, led a group of investors who put up $1.6 million and were awarded the rights to the expansion franchise in Chicago. And by 1972, when Klein would sell the team to Chicago real estate mogul and sports entrepreneur Arthur Wirtz, the Bulls had already moved into Chicago Stadium, which he owned, along with the Chicago Blackhawks.

Upon his death in 1983, Arthur's son, William, would inherit his father's empire, retaining the Chicago Blackhawks, but selling the Bulls, in 1985, to another Chicago real estate mogul, Jerry Reinsdorf, who'd started out as a C.P.A. and lawyer, working as a tax attorney for the IRS.

Reinsdorf's Chicago Bulls would be to the 1990s what the Boston Celtics were to the 1960s and the Los Angeles Lakers were to the 1980s. Winning six championships in nine years by virtue of two "three-peats," (1991-'93 and then 1996-'98), interrupted only by Michael Jordan's temporary "retirement," it is entirely possible that the Bulls may well have won two more titles (1994-'95) had Jordan not left to try his hand as a professional baseball player. And while history records that the Chicago Bulls have never lost an NBA Finals, it is interesting to note that the first six years of Jordan's career were filled with consecutive playoff losses -- to the Milwaukee Bucks (1984), Boston Celtics (1985), Boston Celtics (1986), Detroit Pistons (1987), Detroit Pistons (1988), Detroit Pistons (1989), and Los Angeles Lakers (1990). Once the winning started, there would be a constantly evolving cast of great supporting players such as Steve Kerr and Dennis Rodman. But there were only two constants: head coach Phil Jackson, and Scottie Pippen, a highly skilled and rather unique talent in his own right -- voted one of the NBA's 50 greatest players, and inducted into the NBA Hall of Fame in 2010.

Jerry Reinsdorf remains the owner of the Chicago Bulls, who now play in the United Center and who have, since Michael Jordan and Phil Jackson left, been a lot like the rest of the teams in the league, sometimes good, sometimes bad, and sometimes mediocre -- with no more appearances in the NBA finals, which is, for lack of a better word, "normal." Today, when we think about NBA dynasties, we must consider Jordan's Bulls in the same class as the Boston Celtics and Los Angeles Lakers.

NBA Finals Appearances: 6   Wins: 6
Forbes 2017 Valuation: $2.5 Billion

Cleveland Cavaliers

Year	Owner(s)	Purchase Price
1970	Nick Mileti	$3.7 Million

1980	Louis Mitchell	NA
1980	Joe Zingale	$1.4 Million
1980	Ted Stepien	$2.3 Million
1983	George & Gordon Gund	$20 Million
2005	Dan Gilbert	$375 Million

The Cleveland Cavaliers are the only professional sports team that has been bought and sold four times in one calendar year, 1980 -- a dubious distinction to be sure but an interesting footnote in the history of professional team ownership.

Nick Mileti, a successful Cleveland attorney and businessman, led a group that founded the Cleveland Cavaliers, an expansion team, in 1970. In 1980, Mileti sold his 20-percent interest in the team to Louis Mitchell, a businessman from Columbus who in turn sold his interest to Nick Mileti's cousin, Joe Zingale, for $1.4 million, who one month later sold it to Ted Stepien, founder of Nationwide Advertising Service, for $2.4 million. Thus, in just one month, Zingale made a profit of $900,000.

Stepien's ownership, between 1980 and 1983, was turbulent and controversial and considered the nadir of the Cavaliers' history. Ted Stepien was a meddlesome owner and considered by many the worst in the NBA, at least until Donald Sterling (L.A. Clippers) competed for that distinction. Stepien thought he knew how to select or trade for good players but all he did was decimate the Cavaliers' talent base, which kept the team as one of the worst in the '80s. He alienated his players and often diddled them out of their per-diem meal money, or reimbursed them with checks that bounced. Fans hated him. He fired five coaches in three seasons and traded away all the team's first-round draft picks for mediocre players. To this day, there is a rule on the books in the NBA that prohibits a team from trading its first-round pick two years in a row, the "Ted Stepien Rule." He was also chastised for his racially tainted remarks. The NBA, fearing the franchise would be ruined, was forced to pressure Stepien to sell the team.

In 1983, Stepien did so, to brothers Gordon and George Gund III for $20 million, making a huge profit. The Gunds owned Richfield Coliseum, where the Cavaliers played, and they wanted to make certain the team remained in Cleveland. The Gund family patriarch, George Gunn II, sold the family beer brewery during Prohibition and bought decaf coffee maker Sanka, which he traded for shares in Kellogg's in 1927. The family still owns a nine-percent stake in Kellogg's. Patriarch George went on to become chairman of Cleveland Trust, the largest bank in Ohio at that time.

His sons, George Gund III and Gordon Gund, were obviously born with silver spoons but they didn't abuse privilege. One of their siblings, Agnes Gund, is an art patron and collector of international renown and a former president of the Museum of Modern Art. The Gund family could be called one of the most prominent in Cleveland's history.

Gordon Gund went to the prestigious Groton prep school and on to Harvard where he played ice hockey. He served in the Navy then, like his father, went into the banking business. Gordon, afflicted with retinitis pigmentosa for 10 years, was totally blind by 1970, but it didn't prevent him from continuing in business and remaining active as a philanthropist. His brother, George Gunn III, was first to enter pro sports team ownership, eventually controlling the San Jose Sharks of the NHL. During the Gunds' ownership of the Cavaliers, the team reached a level of respectability but never came close to a championship.

In 2005, the Gunds sold the team to Dan Gilbert, owner of Rock Ventures and Quicken Loans. After LeBron James's infamous television special, "The Decision," in which he announced his intention not to re-sign with Cleveland, Gilbert made news with his equally infamous, "The Letter," a public rebuke of James and his actions.

Ultimately, acrimony between the two dissipated to the point that James, after fulfilling his contract with the Miami Heat, chose to return to the Cleveland Cavaliers, with Gilbert welcoming him back with great fanfare. Alas, Gilbert and LeBron finally, after being down three games to one to the mighty Golden State Warriors, came back in dramatic fashion to sweep the next three games and win the NBA championship title. The long drought had finally come to an end, giving the city of Cleveland new life, and giving "King" James the return of his "crown." But not for long. One year later, the Warriors, who many dubbed "the greatest team of all time," beat the Cavs 4-1 to win the championship and regain the title.

NBA Finals Appearances: 3   Wins: 1
Forbes 2017 Valuation: $1.2 Billion

Dallas Mavericks

Year	Owner(s)	Purchase Price
1980-1996	Donald Carter & Norm Sonju	$12 Million
1996-2000	Ross Perot, Jr.	$125 Million
2000-	Mark Cuban	$280 Million

In terms of fan interest, support, and advocacy of professional sports, the state of Texas has few rivals, and no betters unless we want to call New England a state. At first blush, football always seems the first Texas association, given its deeply rooted cultural significance in both high school and college (not to mention the Dallas Cowboys and Houston

Texans). Baseball too, has two longstanding major league franchises: the Houston Astros and Texas Rangers. Texas basketball might be thought the redheaded stepchild if not for the fact that *three* NBA franchises have long thrived in the state.

Consider that the last to the party, the Dallas Mavericks, by 2016, held the longest consecutive sellout streak (618 games) of any professional sports franchise in North America. This streak began in 2001 and thus represents some 16 years of preeminence. However, when Cuban backed Hillary Clinton instead of Trump, both attendance and TV ratings dropped.

In 1980, NBA owners approved two expansion teams into the league: one in Minneapolis and one in Dallas. When the Minneapolis deal unexpectedly fell apart at the last minute, Dallas was left as the sole entrant. In the league offices, working under Commissioner Larry O'Brien (a former United States Postmaster General under President Johnson), NBA General Counsel, David Stern, determined the expansion fee to be $12 million. Stern would succeed O'Brien as NBA Commissioner and guide the league to unprecedented economic growth and worldwide popularity over the course of his 30-year tenure. The NBA championship trophy was renamed and is known to this day as the Larry O'Brien Championship Trophy.

Norm Sonju, President and GM of the Buffalo Braves in the NBA, was approved as an owner but had difficulty securing the requisite funds. His partner, Donald Carter, a wealthy businessman and investor, whose family fortune derived from his mother's company, Home Interiors and Gifts, a direct marketing business, guaranteed the $12 million fee. The team was named after the television character Maverick, played by James Garner in the popular western series "Maverick" (1957- 1962). Garner was also a minority partner in the ownership group. The Dallas Mavericks were the first NBA team to have a profitable debut season, averaging 7,789 tickets sold per game.

In 1996, Carter and Sonju sold the franchise to Ross Perot, Jr., scion of the wealthy Texas family whose patriarch, Ross Perot, had twice run for president of the United States as a high-profile third-party candidate, in 1992 and 1996, respectively. Interestingly, in 1982, Perot, Jr. took part in a circumnavigation of the globe by helicopter.

In 2000, Perot, Jr. sold the Dallas Mavericks to a season ticketholder and rabid Mavs fan, Mark Cuban, who the year before had sold his company, Broadcast.com to Yahoo! for $5.7 billion in Yahoo! stock. Cuban, a native of Pittsburgh, is a thoroughly self-made man. Growing up in a Jewish working-class family in the Pittsburgh suburb of Mount Lebanon, Cuban graduated from Indiana University and moved to Dallas in 1982. By 1990, he'd sold his first company, MicroSolutions, which was a software retailer and system integrator, to CompuServe for $6 million. In 1995, Cuban started AudioNet, which combined his twin passions for Indiana University basketball and webcasting. Just three years later, in 1998, AudioNet begat Broadcast.com, which one year later would auspiciously live-stream the Victoria's Secret fashion show for the very first time. It was that same year, 1999, at the height of the dot-com boom, that Mark Cuban became a billionaire by selling his company to Yahoo!.

Cuban is surely one of the most publicly conspicuous owners in professional sports -- a polarizing figure, beloved by his team's fans while notorious for receiving massive fines from the NBA league office for all manner of indecorous behavior directed at referees, opposing players, rival franchises, and so on. Cuban makes a practice of donating the exact amount of his fines to sundry charities and continues to happily and unapologetically live life on his own terms. But don't let his multimedia omnipresence -- television shows, movies, social media, print, etc. -- distract from the bottom line.

In their 20 years of existence prior to his acquisition of them, the Dallas Mavericks posted a regular season winning percentage of 40 percent, with middling post-season success and no championship(s). In the 10 years immediately following Cuban's purchase of the team, they had a regular-season winning percentage of 69 percent, one championship (2011), and continuous sell-outs. Under Mark Cuban's shark-like stewardship, the Dallas Mavericks have been a top-tier franchise and remain one of the more stable and profitable teams in the NBA.

Regardless, the Mavericks have lost their swagger over recent years and have become "bottom-feeders." In 2017, the Mavs were hovering near the cellar of their division. Let's see what the "Shark" Mark Cuban can do to turn his team around and climb back to the playoffs.

NBA Finals Appearances: 2   Wins: 1
Forbes 2017 Valuation: $1.45 Billion

Denver Nuggets

Former name: Denver Rockets 1967-72

Year	Owner(s)	Purchase Price
1967	James Trindle	$35,000
1967-1972	William Ringsby	$170,000
1972-1975	Frank Goldberg, A.J. Fischer	N/A
1975-1978	Carl Scheer	$1 Million
1978-1984	B.J. "Red" McCombs	$2 Million
1985-1989	Sidney Shlenker	$20 Million
1989-1997	Comsat Video Enterprises	$45 Million

1997-2000	Liberty Media	$755 Million
2000-	Stan Kroenke	$450 Million
2010	Josh Kroenke	Transfer
2015	Anne Kroenke Walton	Transfer

Another charter franchise of the ABA, the team was originally designated for Kansas City, Missouri. However, its original owner, James (J.J.) Trindle, could not secure an appropriate venue in Kansas City and at ABA Commissioner George Mikan's urging relocated to Denver. Also at Mikan's suggestion, Trindle would hire Vince Boryla as the team's general manager. Boryla, a collegiate star at the University of Denver, had gone on to a successful pro career in the NBA as an all-star player with the New York Knicks, which he later coached.

This begins the convoluted ownership history of the Denver Nuggets. As a franchise well into its fifth decade of NBA existence, the Nuggets have generally been a solid if unspectacular team with many post-season appearances, though none in the NBA finals, and only one in the ABA, where they lost to the New York Nets. Later that same year, 1976, they would be one of the four ABA teams to merge into the NBA, paying the standard $3.2 million entry fee like the other three ABA franchises. Across the decades and in both leagues the Denver Nuggets have had their share of star players such as David Thompson, Spencer Haywood, Dan Issel, Alex English, and Carmelo Anthony, and have always played a wide-open, fast-paced brand of offensive basketball, which would explain the sarcastic nickname given them by local sportswriters: the ENVER Nuggets (as in no "D"). As is the case in all team sports, prolific offenses are a flashy show but defense often wins championships. As such, the ownership history of the Denver Nuggets is more compelling than the basketball they've played.

Upon arriving in Colorado with his brand-new Denver Larks (named after Colorado's state bird) set to play in the Denver Auditorium Arena, Trindle, an owner with not especially deep pockets -- a fact not lost on Commissioner Mikan -- was presented with a $100,000 performance bond requirement by the league to retain the franchise. Unable to come up with the money, Trindle would sell a controlling interest in the team in 1967 to local trucking magnate William Ringsby for $170,000.

And how do the Larks become the Rockets even before the opening tip of that first ABA season? The name of Ringsby's company was Ringsby Rocket Trucking System.

From a historical perspective, the most notable event to occur under Ringsby's ownership was the signing of the first college underclassman to a pro basketball contract. Spencer Haywood would go on to win both Rookie of the Year and League MVP in 1969 -- as well as be at the center of several landmark lawsuits having not only to do with his initial entry into the ABA, but, one season later, his jumping to the NBA and signing with the Seattle Supersonics in 1970. The NBA had a rule that players had to be four years out of high school, whereas the ABA did not. Heywood sued the NBA and won.

In 1972, after five years of owning the team, Ringsby would sell the franchise to San Diego businessmen Frank Goldberg and A. G. (Bud) Fischer, whose eyes were squarely fixed on the new facility being constructed in Denver for the 1976 Winter Olympics, intended to be home to the NHL's expansion Colorado Avalanche as well as the NBA's expansion Denver Nuggets.

However, on the cusp of joining the NBA with a brand-new showplace, McNichol Arena, businessmen Goldberg and Fischer tired of operating at a loss and sold 33 percent of the team in 1974 to their GM, Carl Scheer. He put together a local ownership group that was named Nuggets Management, Inc., which one year later would purchase the remaining 67 percent to become sole owners.

From renaming the franchise (being well aware there had been a Denver Nuggets NBA franchise for one year in 1949 and '50), to inventing the slam-dunk contest, which first occurred in Denver during the ABA all-star game weekend of 1976, to recruiting his former head coach from Carolina, Larry Brown, Scheer is rightly considered the "Godfather" of modern-era Denver Nuggets basketball.

Eventually needing to raise more capital to keep the franchise running, Scheer's partners preferred to sell the team. Upon the advice of his head coach at the time, Doug Moe, Scheer would reach out to Billy Joe ("Red") McCombs of Texas, who in 1978 would agree to buy the team for $2 million, providing some cash to Scheer's partners as well as assuming its debt service and immediately negotiating very favorable terms with the Nuggets' creditors. McCombs would retain Scheer as team president and GM until replacing him in 1984 with Vince Boryla (a return Denver engagement). McCombs offered to reassign Scheer within the organization but Scheer would depart to run the Los Angeles Clippers.

The following year, McCombs would sell the Nuggets to a group headed by Sidney Shlenker, a Texas friend and former business associate who was then an executive in charge of booking and producing events at the Houston Astrodome -- perhaps his most notable was the famous 1973 "Battle of the Sexes" tennis match between Billie Jean King and Bobby Riggs.

Shlenker's tenure as owner was notable for its many failures, due in no small part to his more promotional background than executive experience in running a pro sports franchise. He first negotiated a new 15-year lease with McNichol Arena, which bound the team to that venue until 2001. He then set about renovating the arena to accommodate luxury boxes, three theme restaurants, a state-of-the-art scoreboard, a V.I.P. lounge, and a dinner club. Initially budgeted at $7.5 million, the cost for construction overruns and debt service soon reached $12.5 million, and he would ultimately put the team up as collateral for a $25 million loan.

By 1989, Shlenker would sell 67.5 percent of the team to Comsat Video Enterprises, a subsidiary of Comsat Corporation, and the remaining 32.5 percent to businessmen and partners Peter Bynoe and Bertram Lee, who would make history by becoming the first African-Americans to own a controlling interest in an American professional sports franchise. As per the agreement with Comsat, Bynoe and Lee would be general managing partners with Bynoe in charge of day-to-day operations. Almost immediately, tensions arose between the thrice-degreed Harvard-educated Bynoe and Comsat Video's CEO, Robert Wussler, former president of CBS, who'd started in the mailroom and worked his way up to become the youngest president (age 40) in the history of the "Tiffany" network. At this same time, the partnership between Bynoe and Lee ruptured, resulting in rampant dysfunction in the corporate suite that was also manifest on the court: the 1990-'91 Nuggets posted a league-worst record of 20-62.

Bynoe would recruit other partners and mortgage a 12-percent share of the team to Drexel, Burnham, Lambert, the junk bond investment firm. When Lee, who'd failed to provide his 10-percent cash when purchasing the team (with Bynoe) in 1989, missed another call for capital, he was forced out.

The team's fortunes would finally improve in 1991 and into 1992 with several major changes. First, Comsat hired Tim Leiweke as senior vice-president. At age 34, Leiweke was already a marketing star, having successfully launched the new Minnesota Timberwolves franchise. Next, Comsat Corp replaced Comsat Video's CEO, Robert Wussler, with Charlie Lyons, a Colorado businessman with extensive experience in the ski and hotel industries. Under Lyons, Comsat Video quickly bought out both Drexel, Burnham, Lambert as well as Peter Bynoe, thus enabling Comsat to assume 100-percent ownership under a new entity, Comsat Denver, Inc.

And finally, Bernie Bickerstaff was brought in to be the new GM. Bickerstaff fired head coach Paul Westhead after his second season, replacing him with Dan Issel, who despite never having coached, was a legendary player at the University of Kentucky (under Adolph Rupp) as well as for the Kentucky Colonels of the ABA, along with, of course, the Denver Nuggets (in both the ABA and NBA).

And during this early-mid '90s period the team improved and slowly revived fan interest. Comsat Corp., wanting to further diversify into sports franchises, entertainment, media production, and distribution -- in other words, producing content for broadcast by satellite -- would acquire other assets including the Colorado Avalanche NHL franchise and movie-maker Beacon Communications, and start construction on the new Pepsi Arena to replace the aging McNichol Arena, and organize all of them in 1995 under yet another corporate subsidiary, Ascent Entertainment Group.

Comsat would own 80 percent of Ascent and take the other 20 percent public, trading on NASDAQ. It seemed a sound strategy: owning two professional sports teams and their shared arena in the same city. The Avalanche had, after all, won the Stanley Cup in 1995, and the Nuggets were building towards sustained relevancy around Dikembe Mutombo at center and Mahmoud Abdul-Rauf at guard.

Yet prosperity was fleeting and ultimately short-lived, with Mutombo traded to the Atlanta Hawks in 1995 and Abdul-Rauf to the Sacramento Kings in 1996. By the first quarter of 1997, Comsat Corp. posted losses of $18 million due in large part to the mediocrity of the Nuggets and Avalanche in addition to construction costs attendant with the new Pepsi Arena. These factors would be the catalyst for Comsat's decision to divest itself of Ascent Entertainment Group.

In 1997, they sold Ascent Entertainment Group to John Malone's behemoth Liberty Media, which, having no interest in the sports assets (Denver Nuggets, Colorado Avalanche, and the Pepsi Arena), would immediately put them up for sale, retaining only the movie component. Unsurprisingly (this is the Denver Nuggets after all), things did not go smoothly for Liberty Media, which had no less than three separate transactions in place only to have each one fall apart.

Bill Laurie (whose wife Nancy is a Walmart heiress) offered $400 million, but the sale was blocked when Ascent shareholders sued, claiming all three sports assets (the Nuggets, Avalanche, and Pepsi Center) were severely undervalued and that $400 million was too low a sale price.

Next, Denver billionaire Donald Sturm, offered $461 million for the three assets. Sturm was willing to guarantee the City of Denver that he would not move the teams out of state for 25 years, but balked when they also insisted on the same terms in the event of Sturm's death prior to the end of the 25 years. Other prospective bidders who failed to close the deal included a group comprising John McMullen, Pat Bowlen, and John Elway, and Boston Celtics owner Alan Cohen, who partnered with Texas auto dealer David McDavid, who'd divested himself of his shares in the Dallas Mavericks in preparation for acquiring the Nuggets and Avalanche (and Pepsi Center).

Ultimately, though, it would be Stan Kroenke of Missouri who would purchase the Denver teams and Pepsi Arena. A well-known sports mogul and brilliantly successful entrepreneur, Kroenke had already purchased a share of the NFL's Rams when they relocated to St. Louis in 1995. The brother-in-law of Bill Laurie (their wives are sisters, daughters of Walmart co-founder James (Bud) Walton), Kroenke's net worth was pegged at $7.4 billion (Forbes 2016). He would go on, in 2010, to exercise his right of first refusal and purchase the rest of the St. Louis Rams from the estate of Georgia Frontiere, Carroll Rosenbloom's widow. That in turn would necessitate transferring ownership of his Denver teams to his son,

Josh, to comply with the NFL's requirement that none of their owners have professional teams in different cities at the same time.

He would in 2015 receive permission from the NFL to relocate the Rams back to Southern California and to transfer ownership of the Denver Nuggets, Colorado Avalanche, and Pepsi Center to his wife, Anne Walton Kroenke.

As for the Denver Nuggets, one can only presume that with the Kroenke family's vast resources, a foundation of stability is finally in place, which bodes well for a franchise that has been at times good, but never great.

NBA Finals Appearances: 0
Forbes 2017 Valuation: $890 Million

Detroit Pistons

Former name: Fort Wayne (Zollner) Pistons 1930s-1957

Year	Owner(s)	Purchase Price
1939-1974	Fred Zollner	$2,500
1974-2011	William Davidson	$8.1 Million
2011-	Tom Gores	$325 Million

Fred Zollner, along with his sister Janet, founded the Fort Wayne Zollner Pistons in 1939, which competed in the NBL (National Basketball League) in 1941. Zollner wanted a team not only because he loved sports but because he wanted a team to help promote his thriving piston business. Zollner Corporation manufactured pistons for the automotive industry, selling them to Ford, GM, John Deere and others. At one point, Zollner Corporation sold 70 percent of the world's heavy-duty aluminum pistons.

In 1944 and 1945, the Fort Wayne Zollner Pistons won the NBL Championship. Fred was very much the hands-on owner who recruited his own players and was the first to hire a head coach. In 1948, the name Zollner was dropped and they became the Fort Wayne Pistons.

Zollner was called "Mr. Pro Basketball" because, among other reasons, he was the main person who engineered the merger between the BAA & NBL. In fact, he gathered the owners around his kitchen table, where they hashed out the terms that created the NBA in 1949.

The Fort Wayne Pistons made the NBA Finals in '54 & '55. Zollner was the first owner to fly his players to road games on his private

DC-3. Some other NBA owners were irked (or jealous), claiming the plane gave the team a competitive advantage, so they reportedly finagled the schedule to the Pistons' disadvantage.

Although Fort Wayne named Fred the "Man of the Year" for his contributions as a civic leader and for bringing both sports (and industry) to Ft. Wayne, the city simply wasn't large enough to support the team financially. In 1957, Zollner moved the team to Detroit. For the next 17 years, Zollner's Detroit Pistons stunk it up on the court, having only two winning seasons. With the team having never made a profit, Fred, feeling the pinch, sold the team to William Davidson in 1974 for $8.1 million.

The NBA Western Conference Championship Trophy is named in Zollner's honor. In 1999, Fred was inducted into the Naismith Memorial Hall of Fame (commonly referred to as the NBA Hall of Fame).

William (Bill) Davidson, a college football player himself, would own and control the Pistons for 37 years. He took over his family's glass manufacturing business in 1957 just as it was entering bankruptcy due to a strike that crippled the glass industry. An aggressive risk-taker, Davidson went and bought his automotive glass products from Europe and sold them to American Motors. A year later, the company, Guardian Glass, exited bankruptcy and began to flourish. Eight years later, it went public. William became president and CEO of Guardian Industries, one of the largest glass manufacturers in the world.

It was under Davidson's leadership that his Pistons were nicknamed "The Bad Boys" when they won two consecutive NBA championships in 1989 and 1990. Isaiah Thomas, their number-one draft pick in 1981, led the offense as a prolific scorer but it was their defense, led by Bill Lambier and Dennis Rodman, that garnered them their mean reputation. The Boston Celtics president at the time, Red Auerbach, dubbed them "classic bullies."

In addition to owning the Pistons, Davidson was the principal owner of the Detroit Shock (WNBA), co-owner of the Detroit Fury (Arena Football League), and former owner of the Tampa Bay Lightning (NHL) and Detroit Vipers (IHL). To his credit as an owner, he amassed eight championships, including the Stanley Cup and NBA championship in 2004, the only owner to achieve such a feat.

He was also chairman of Palace Sports and Entertainment, which controlled the arena where the Pistons played. Built in 1988, and called "The Palace of Auburn Hills," it was the first NBA arena financed with private money. And it was the first to feature lower-level luxury suites. Davidson was the first owner to provide a private jet with spacious luxury seats for the team.

Bill Davidson served on the NBA Board of Governors as chairman and pushed for early NBA globalization. Like his predecessor (and neighbor in Florida), Fred Zollner, Davidson was named to the Naismith Memorial Hall of Fame, and was an inaugural inductee in the Jewish Sports

Hall of Fame. In recognition to his contribution to the Pistons, Davidson was given a banner next to the teams' retired numbers and his name, Bill Davidson, was placed on the Palace floor along with the great Piston stars who played during his reign. His net worth, at the time, was estimated by Forbes at $3.5 billion, making him the 68th richest man in the U.S.

When Davidson died in 2009, his wife, Karen, took control of the team. In 2011, despite Bill's vow never to sell the Pistons, and that the ownership of the team would remain in his family, she sold the Pistons and Palace Sports and Entertainment to Tom Gores for $325 million.

Shortly before Davidson's death, he transferred millions of dollars into trusts for his heirs, but, as generation-skipping tax avoidance schemes can result, this maneuver caused the IRS to claim the estate owed $2.7 billion in additional tax. They claimed the actual value of the shares of Guardian at his time of death, compared to the date of valuation of the "gifts" to his heirs, based on the estate's appraisal, was greatly underestimated.

In 2015, the estate settled by paying $457 million in additional taxes. The estate sued the accountants, Deloitte LLP, for $500 million, claiming malpractice and negligence. In 2016, a New York State judge dismissed the case against Deloitte.

Tom Gores, the third and current owner of the Pistons, was born in 1964 to a Greek father and Lebanese mother in Nazareth, Israel. In 1968, the family moved to Genesee, Michigan, where Tom excelled in high school sports, playing football, basketball and baseball, which earned him a scholarship to Michigan State.

After spending 10 years with his brother in the corporate buyout business, Tom founded his own private equity company in 1995, Platinum Equity. Since its inception, the company has acquired over 130 companies in a variety of industries including technology, manufacturing, distribution, transportation and equipment leasing.

In 2015, Tom purchased the minority share of the Pistons owned by his company, Platinum Equity, and became the sole owner. In 2016, Forbes estimated his net worth at $3.3 billion. Under Gore's reign, the Pistons have been competitive but remain several players short of becoming "the Bad Boys" again and winning the NBA Finals.

NBA Finals Appearances: 7   Wins: 3
Forbes 2017 Valuation: $900 Million

Golden State Warriors

Former names: Philadelphia Warriors 1946-1962; San Francisco Warriors 1962-1971

Year	Owner(s)	Purchase Price
1946-1952	Peter Tyrell	
1952-1962	Eddie Gottlieb	$25,000
1962-1963	Diners Club, Franklin Mieuli	$850,000
1963-1986	Franklin Mieuli	
1986-1995	Jim Fitzgerald	N/A
1995-2010	Chris Cohan	$119 Million
2010-	Joe Lacob, Peter Guber	$450 Million

There is an unusually symmetrical quality to the history of the Warriors franchise; they've won four NBA championships under four different owners in four different eras.

A charter member of the BAA (Basketball Association of America) in 1946, the Philadelphia Warriors won the championship in that inaugural season. Upon merging with the NBL (National Basketball League) in 1949, the newly formed NBA (National Basketball Association) would officially recognize the Philadelphia Warriors' 1947 BAA championship as the NBA's first championship.

The franchise was owned by Peter Tyrell, not a basketball man as such but rather a sports and entertainment entrepreneur closely aligned with the Philadelphia Arena, into which he booked all manner of events including basketball, boxing, rodeo, ice shows, etc. Tyrell was the principal founder and owner of the Ice Capades.

Tyrell did, however, hire as his first coach and general manager a man synonymous with basketball (especially Philadelphia basketball), Eddie Gottlieb. To this day, the NBA Rookie of the Year award is named the "Eddie Gottlieb Trophy," and Gottlieb was inducted into the NBA Hall of Fame in 1972.

One of a handful of professional basketball's pioneers dating back to the 1920s, Gottlieb's contributions to, and impact on, the modern NBA, was huge. "Mr. Basketball," as he was known, headed the NBA Rules Committee for decades, and was the NBA's singular schedule-maker for many years until giving way to computer software in 1978. Gottlieb would go on to purchase the Philadelphia Warriors from Tyrell in 1951. Under Gottlieb's ownership, the Warriors would win their second NBA championship in 1956.

One of the rules established during Gottlieb's tenure, as head of the NBA Rules Committee was the "territorial pick." With the new league intent on establishing solid fan bases in their respective home cities, the "territorial pick" allowed a team to forfeit its first-round draft pick to select any collegiate player within a 50-mile radius of its city. Perhaps not un-coincidentally, Gottlieb would in 1959 use a "territorial pick" to select a Philadelphia native son who had played at Overbrook High School, then just two seasons at the University of Kansas, before leaving school to play for a short time with the Harlem Globetrotters. And that is how, in 1959, Gottlieb acquired Philadelphia's own Wilt Chamberlain for the Philadelphia Warriors.

Perhaps the most transformational player in the history of the NBA, "Wilt the Stilt," changed the pro game forever. While not the fiercest competitor, greatest team player, or winner (think Bill Russell and/or Michael Jordan), the sheer physical talent disparity between Chamberlain and every other player in the league was of historic proportions. In 1962, Gottlieb would sell a 33.3-percent minority interest in the franchise to the Diners Club credit card company and the majority to a group of San Francisco Bay-area investors headed by Franklin Mieuli -- a colorful character very much of the time and place: San Francisco in the 1960s. Shunning business attire -- nobody ever caught Mieuli in a suit and tie -- he had a full beard, wore an omnipresent "deerslayer" cap (think of a Sherlock Holmes-style hat), and favored the motorcycle as his primary mode of transportation.

Born and raised in San Jose, Mieuli's professional background was in media. He produced radio and television broadcasts of local sports (both the 49ers and Giants), owned a San Francisco FM radio station with a jazz format called KHIP, and eventually formed a successful radio and television production company, Franklin Mieuli & Associates, which provided (and still does to this day), broadcast engineering for NFL, NBA, MLB, and college games, etc. Buying out both Diners Club and all the other investors, Mieuli would become the sole owner of the now San Francisco Warriors, having moved them west from Philadelphia after the 1961-'62 season. Playing in the Cow Palace (located in Daly City just south of San Francisco) for just two years, the team moved into the San Francisco Civic Auditorium, playing there from 1964-'66 before settling into what would become their permanent home city of Oakland in 1966, playing in the Oakland Coliseum Arena.

In 1971, the team re-branded itself the Golden State Warriors to reflect statewide appeal as well as its new exclusive and permanent home in Oakland. Mieuli was known to be a leading figure in encouraging minority hiring -- not only in assembling his roster, but in the front office as well.

The Warriors' third NBA championship in 1975 certainly reflected this imperative: other than their one superstar, Rick Barry (who is

Caucasian), 11 of the other 12 players on the team were African-American, as was head coach Al Attles, and his assistant, Joe Roberts.

Led by Finals MVP Barry, the series is remembered as one of the greatest upsets in NBA Finals history as the Warriors not only beat the heavily favored Washington Bullets, but also did so in a four-game sweep.

Franklin Mieuli would sell the Warriors in 1986 to the former owner of the Milwaukee Bucks, Jim Fitzgerald, who brought with him into an ownership position Dan Finnane, who had worked with him in Milwaukee. Widely respected as a sportsman and gentleman, Fitzgerald hired Don Nelson on a handshake as his head coach in Milwaukee, and later in San Francisco. Over their many years together, Fitzgerald and Nelson never had a contract, only that handshake agreement.

This would augur an extended down period for the franchise, one of pedestrian teams and continual rebuilding through two ownership cycles.

The Fitzgerald and Finnane regime would eventually sell the team in 1995 to Chris Cohan, owner of Sonic Communications, one of the largest independently owned cable outlets in the country. Cohan did much to renovate the Warriors' home, Oakland Arena, which eventually became the Oracle Arena. But his Warriors remained a mediocre team throughout his 15-year tenure as owner. When Cohan finally sold the team in 2010 to a group headed by Silicon Valley venture capitalist Joe Lacob and Hollywood film producer Peter Guber, the Golden State Warriors would almost immediately assume an upward trajectory that would culminate in their fourth NBA championship in 2015.

The latest and most current trend in professional sports ownership is perfectly represented in the person of majority owner Joe Lacob. A prominent venture capitalist, Lacob brings with him a different methodology and operational model that represents a major shift in the endeavor of owning a pro sports team. It made absolutely no sense to any of the so-called experts when he paid an exorbitant price for a moribund franchise that hadn't won a championship in 35 years and was more or less noncompetitive for just as long. Assembling an ownership group comprising like-minded finance people, but each with their own discrete area of expertise (different from his own), Lacob changed not only the culture of running a team but the business paradigm as well.

From physical infrastructure of the workplace to the hiring of critical personnel, the Warriors' mentality and perspective was "out-of-the-box" and just seemed smarter and sharper than the rest of the league. Of course, it is easy to be smarter and sharper when your point guard is the incredible Stephen Curry -- who was already on the team when Lacob came on board.

In a short five years, the Golden State Warriors won their fourth championship in 2015 and backed that up by compiling the best regular season record in NBA history the following year, going 73-9, though losing in the NBA finals (in seven games) to LeBron James's Cleveland Cavaliers.

In 2014, the Warriors purchased a 12-acre site in Mission Bay, San Francisco, and their new self-funded arena, Chase Arena, is scheduled to open for the 2018-19 season. At this writing, a full 25 percent of the teams in the NBA are now owned by venture capitalists, private equity investors, and hedge-fund managers, and that trend continues across all professional sports.

An interesting factoid about Mr. Lacob: as an undergraduate at UC Irvine in 1962, he took a class with a professor named Edward Thorpe, who wrote a book called "Beat the Dealer." Professor Thorpe was the originator of "card counting" as a means of just slightly tilting the odds when playing blackjack in a casino. He was banned from all casinos in Las Vegas. Several of his students would play in his stead using his system and they would all split the winnings.

Lacob reckons that he is today one of the 10 best blackjack players in the world and stated that he has won over $1 million, in one sitting, nine times. In the off-season after their Finals loss, the Golden State Warriors won the Kevin Durant sweepstakes, with the free agent choosing to sign with them. As any blackjack-player will attest, they like their odds and will double down with two aces against a king (even one named James). Lacob and his Golden State Warriors are "all-In." We would not bet against him.

In 2017, the Warriors regained their NBA Championship crown, defeating the Cavaliers 4-1, with Durant becoming MVP.

NBA Finals Appearances: 8   Wins: 4
Forbes 2017 Valuation: $2.6 Billion

Houston Rockets

Former name: San Diego Rockets 1967-1971

Year	Owner(s)	Purchase Price
1967-1971	Robert Breitbard	$1.7 Million
1971-1972	Texas Sport Investment	$5.6 Million
1972-1976	Texas Pro Sports, Inc.	N/A
1976-1979	Kenneth Schnitzer	N/A
1979-1982	George Maloof, Sr.	$9 Million
1982-1993	Charlie Thomas	$11 Million
1993-2017	Leslie Alexander	$85 Million
2017-	Tilman Fertitta	$2.2 Billion

The well-known saying "everything's bigger in Texas" certainly applies to the state's three NBA franchises. In their respective histories, each Texas franchise has revolved around star "bigs" who have delivered championships: Dirk Nowitzki in Dallas, the incomparable Tim Duncan (and earlier in tandem with David Robinson) in San Antonio, and of course, the most center-centric team of them all, the Houston Rockets, with Hakeem Olajuwon, Ralph Samson, Moses Malone, and Yao Ming.

The Houston Rockets were the first NBA franchise in Texas, moving to Houston from San Diego in 1971. Prior to that, the San Diego Rockets came into being as an NBA expansion team in 1967 (along with the Seattle SuperSonics). Founder and owner Robert Breitbard was a most atypical owner and may well be unique amongst the hundreds of owners profiled in these pages. Breitbard did not come from generational wealth or even family wealth, nor was he a self-made man in terms of acquiring a fortune. In fact, he was not a wealthy man, ever. His family owned a local dry cleaning business and eventually a laundry that Breitbard would own, California Linen and Industrial Supply.

A classmate of Ted Williams, the two graduated from Hoover High School in 1936 and remained lifelong friends. Brietbard's first love was athletics and for a short time he coached freshman football at San Diego State College (his alma mater). He was also a high school line coach for varsity football and the head coach for the baseball team. Ultimately, he chose to give up all coaching to run the laundry business.

In 1965, with four partners, Breitbard leased 80 acres of land in San Diego and built the San Diego Sports Arena. It required the issuance of $6.4 million in municipal bonds, to be repaid from future arena revenues. With the new arena, Breitbard was able to acquire an NBA expansion team in 1967, which was named the San Diego Rockets, the result of a public naming contest.

Breitbard's very first draft pick that year was a guard from the University of Kentucky named Pat Riley, and their debut record was 15-67, the worst ever in the history of the NBA (to that time).

The Rockets would do better with their next pick. After winning a coin flip with the Baltimore Bullets and securing the overall first pick in the 1968 draft, the San Diego Rockets selected Elvin "Big E" Hayes. Hayes would lead the league in scoring his rookie year and lead the Rockets into the playoffs despite a losing record (37-45) where they would be dispatched in the divisional round, losing to the Atlanta Hawks 4-2.

In 1971, the county assessor would impose a significant increase in Breitbard's property tax for the arena. He'd been paying $35,000 annually, but the figure ballooned to $142,000, which was untenable. With no viable alternative available to him, Breitbard sold his team to three Houston businessmen, Wayne Duddlesten, Billy Goldberg, and Mickey Herskowitz, who called themselves Texas Sport Investment, and who immediately relocated the team to Houston.

In 1972, Texas Sport Investment sold the Rockets to Texas Pro Sports, Inc., through which the team would pass from principals Ray Patterson to Irving Kaplan to James Talbot, Inc. in three consecutive years during which the Rockets would hopscotch around to various venues before taking up temporary residence at the University of Houston's Hofheinz Pavilion.

But they did have a few things going for them: a popular hometown superstar (Hayes had been a legendary college player at the University of Houston), and the fact that their team name finally made sense -- with NASA's close proximity, there were actual rockets in Houston. After just one season, Hayes would force a trade out of Houston because of his incompatibility with Tex Winter's offensive philosophy and system -- the so-called "triangle offense," which he would later bring with him to the Chicago Bulls as an assistant under head coach Phil Jackson.

The volatility of the team's ownership would stabilize in 1976 with the sale of the Houston Rockets to real estate developer Kenneth Schnitzer, a third-generation Houstonian, who'd built Greenway Plaza, a sprawling and meticulously designed urban development situated on 127 acres that featured a 400-room hotel, underground shopping mall, 10 office towers, and a brand new sports arena, The Summit, which became the Rockets' permanent home beginning with the 1975 season.

Schnitzer would in 1979 sell the Houston Rockets to George Maloof, Sr. of Las Vegas. The son of a Lebanese immigrant, he became the distributor of Coors Beer in the southwestern United States in 1937, the source of his initial wealth. George would eventually expand into the hotel, trucking, and banking businesses. Maloof, Sr. died one year after buying the team and was succeeded by his 24-year-old son Gavin, who would sell the franchise in 1982 to Houston's Charlie Thomas, owner of the largest automotive dealership group in Houston.

Having finally established the Rockets as consistently competitive post-season performers, Charlie Thomas would in 1983 make the difficult decision to trade away the best player in Rockets history, Moses Malone. Coming off another MVP award the year before, Malone would be an expensive re-sign and, for all of his greatness, had not led the team to a championship. Without Malone, the Rockets were an abysmal team, finishing dead last two seasons in a row.

That was the bad news. The good news: they received the overall first draft pick two years in a row, choosing Ralph Samson of the University of Virginia in 1983 and then the University of Houston's Hakeem Olajuwon in 1984.

The "twin towers" alignment of the two would signal the beginning of a resurgence that despite the immediate boost of reaching the NBA Finals in 1986 (which they again lost to the Boston Celtics) would falter thereafter and never fulfill its promise. Sampson would win Rookie of the Year and be a respectable player but chronic knee problems would prevent him from ever realizing the NBA greatness predicted for him and he would be traded away in a few years.

However, hometown hero (by way of Lagos, Nigeria) Olajuwon, after finishing second to Michael Jordan for Rookie of the Year, would steadily develop and blossom into what many considered the most nimble and athletically gifted offensive center in the history of the NBA. "The Dream's" patented offensive move, nicknamed the "dream shake," was as virtually unstoppable as Kareem Abdul-Jabbar's "skyhook," and infinitely more multifaceted: spinning right or left or going over or under his opposition, Olajuwon's footwork has never been equaled by any big man to ever play the game.

With that said, while Olajuwon would ascend to elite status as an individual player, the Rockets teams for the next several years would be mediocre -- usually losing in the first round or on occasion missing the playoffs altogether. In 1993, Schnitzer would sell the Houston Rockets to Leslie Alexander, an attorney who transitioned into a Wall Street bond trader, eventually opening his own Wall Street firm.

In sports, as in life, timing is everything: a neophyte owner, Mr. Alexander won consecutive NBA championships in his first two seasons of owning the Houston Rockets. Winning NBA Finals MVP in both 1994 and 1995, Hakeem Olajuwon, at the pinnacle of his career, thoroughly outplayed and dominated two of the top-50 players of all time: Patrick Ewing of the Knicks and then Shaquille O'Neal of the Magic.

As for their last "big," the Houston Rockets would in 2002 draft 7-foot, 6-inch Yao Ming of Shanghai, China -- the perfect centerpiece with whom to move into their new arena, the Toyota Center. Despite public pronouncements from the likes of Bill Simmons, Dick Vitale, and Charles Barkley that he would fail miserably as an NBA player, Yao would in fact be a more than credible player, becoming a five-time all-star. He also exhibited unusual dignity, grace, and good humor when encountering harsh and impolitic treatment such as when the Miami Heat passed out 8,000 fortune cookies at Yao's very first game, or with Shaq's supposedly humorous taunting of continually mispronouncing his name, which O'Neal later regretted as unfortunate rookie "hazing."

After his auspicious beginning, Leslie Alexander has yet to come close to another championship. Over the last 21 seasons, his teams have been winning and losing in fits and starts. However, in 2017, bolstered by the Rockets recent rise to prominence, Leslie sold the team to celebrity billionaire-restauranteur, Tilman Fertitta, for $2.2 billion, the highest price paid to date for any team in this book, and $550 million more than the valuation below.

NBA Finals Appearances: 4   Wins: 2
Forbes 2017 Valuation: $1.65 Billion

Indiana Pacers

Year	Owner(s)	Purchase Price
1967-1975	Charles DeVoe	$30,000
1975-1979	Arena Sports, Inc.	$650,000
1979-1983	Sam Nassi	$8 Million
1983-	Herbert Simon	$11 Million

Charles (Chuck) DeVoe and his brother John joined a group of Indianapolis businessmen who scraped together the $30,000 ABA (American Basketball Association) franchise fee and founded the Indiana Pacers in 1967. Chuck served as the team's president from '68 to '74, during which time the Pacers won three ABA championships, better than any other ABA team. Sadly, John DeVoe, who was team president in 1968, died of a heart attack while attending a game.

Chuck DeVoe was a great athlete. In fact, he may have been the best athlete of all the owners in this book, excepting of course Michael Jordan and perhaps George Halas. Chuck was a pro-level tennis player who won 11 Indiana State singles titles and played in two U.S. Opens in the '50s, when it was called the U.S. Nationals. He later won several senior national singles titles.

The ABA fought a long, nine-year battle with the NBA to gain attendance and attract franchise players, like they did by signing "Dr. J" (Julius Erving) and "Ice Man" (George Gervin). All ABA teams struggled for financial survival. This was an era before significant TV revenues paid the way. The ABA owners even agreed to pool their resources in hopes of signing UCLA's Lou Alcindor, offering over $1 million and allowing Lou to play for whatever ABA team he chose.

They hoped Alcindor could do for the ABA what Joe Namath did for the AFL. In the end, they didn't land him but they sent a message to the NBA that they meant business. To offer a more exciting product, the ABA used a red, white, and blue ball and changed the game forever by instituting the three-point shot.

In 1975, the Pacers were sold to Arena Sports, Inc. for $650,000. Tom Binford, one of Indianapolis's most influential men, led the acquisition. He was also instrumental in bringing the Colts to his city and served as chief steward of the Indianapolis 500.

The Pacers would be one of only four ABA teams that would be merged into the NBA in 1976, the others being the Spurs, Nuggets, and Nets. Arena Sports would have to shell out $3.2 million for the NBA entry fee, and would have to cough up another $1.6 million to compensate the two remaining ABA teams that were left out in the cold, the Spirits of St.

Louis and the Kentucky Colonels. To make financial matters worse, the ABA teams would not share in TV revenues for four years. The Pacers, who felt the financial pinch before the merger, were forced to sell off players to stay alive. The result: for the next 13-years the Pacers had only three winning seasons and only two playoff appearances.

In 1979, Sam Nassi paid $8 million to buy the Pacers (some called it a steal). At the time of the purchase, it was said the Pacers were losing $2 million annually. Nassi didn't mind. He was a professional liquidator of distressed assets, a self-proclaimed surgeon for companies going down the tubes. He claimed it was much more lucrative to bury a company than to build one. But he loved sports and basketball, so squeezing the blood out of this turnip would be fun. Nassi was no dope. He had a substantial interest in the arena where the Pacers played and could absorb the Pacers' losses until he found a buyer. In 1983, Herbert and Mel Simon bought the team for $11 million.

Herb Simon made his fortune in commercial real estate, specializing in the development of shopping malls. He is currently chairman emeritus of Simon Properties, one of the world's largest REITs with close to 230 properties. The best thing that happened during the Simonses' ownership was Larry Bird. Although his entire Hall of Fame career was spent with the Boston Celtics, he was welcomed back to his home state and became head coach of the Pacers from 1997 to 2000. In 2003, Bird became president of basketball operations, a post he still holds at this writing. During Bird's reign and the Simonses' ownership, the Pacers made NBA Finals once, but remain one of 12 NBA teams to never have won a championship.

Mel Simon died in 2009. Months before his death, Mel and Herb signed an agreement that transferred full ownership of the Pacers to Herb. Mel's wife, Bren, who has been in litigation with Mel's children since 2009, has sued for recovery of $21 million she claims was rightfully hers.

NBA Finals Appearances: 1   Wins: 0
Forbes 2017 Valuation: $880 Million

Los Angeles Clippers

Former name: Buffalo Braves; San Diego Clippers

Year	Owner(s)	Purchase Price
1970	Phillip Ryan and Peter Crotty	$3.7 Million
1970-1976	Paul Snyder	$1.1 Million

1976-1978	John Y. Brown	$6.7 Million
1978-1981	Irving Levin and Harold Lipton	NA
1981-2014	Donald Sterling	$13.5 Million
2014-	Steve Ballmer	$2 Billion

Throughout their history, the Clippers have engendered a bit more hatred and ridicule than they deserve. From a competitive standpoint, they have not been unlike a lot of other pedestrian NBA franchises in the fat part of the bell curve: a little below or a little above .500 with a few post-season appearances sprinkled in amongst perennially losing seasons. So ... what's so special about the Clippers to merit such notoriety? What's the worst-run franchise (and ownership) in professional sports? For years, sportswriters' shorthand punchline was ... the Los Angeles Clippers.

From their very beginning, the Clippers' history is dotted with unusual and off-kilter intrigues. Founded in 1970 as an expansion team (along with the Cleveland Cavaliers and Portland Trailblazers), the Buffalo Braves were originally owned by Neuberger-Loeb, a New York investment firm. This group was led by Phillip Ryan and Peter Crotty, who sold the franchise to local Buffalo businessman Paul Snyder before play began in its inaugural season. As is the typical profile for an expansion team, the Buffalo Braves were not very good for their first few years.

This might have been more palatable in a different locale than western New York, where whatever interest there was in basketball was collegiate, with the so-called "Little Three" rivalry between Canisius College, St. Bonaventure University, and Niagara College. Not to mention that Buffalo was football and hockey country. Even so, in the early years the Buffalo Braves were drawing near league average in attendance, turning a profit, and being modestly successful -- even though they had to share their home arena (Buffalo Memorial Auditorium) not only with various college teams but with the expansion Buffalo Sabres hockey team, which joined the NHL in 1970 as well.

By 1976, though, Snyder was finding it increasingly difficult to secure good home dates because of the less-than-accommodating stances taken by his co-tenants. Furthermore, he was receiving pressure from the NBA to resolve the issue. Snyder's first resolution was to sell the team for $6.2 million to hotel owner Irving Cowan, who wanted to move the team to Miami. However, the city of Buffalo filed a $10 million lawsuit to block the move and the sale fell apart. Snyder would then sign a new 15-year lease with the Buffalo Memorial Auditorium with a provision that the lease could be voided if the Buffalo Braves failed to sell 5,000 tickets in any year.

His second (and better) resolution was to sell a 50-percent stake of the team to John Y. Brown of Kentucky. Brown had bought Kentucky Fried Chicken from Colonel Tom Sanders in 1964, built it into an empire, and sold it in 1971 for a huge profit. Later that same year (1976), Brown would purchase the remaining 50 percent of the team from Snyder and sell that portion to businessman Harry Mangurian, Jr. And then partners Brown and Mangurain set about dismantling the team by any means necessary to break the lease -- selling and trading off star assets such as Bob McAdoo (to the New York Knicks for players and cash) and Moses Malone (who they'd recently acquired in a trade with Portland to Houston for two draft picks). Their head coach, Dr. Jack Ramsey, (a future NBA Hall of Famer), wanting to distance himself as much as possible from the team's decline, headed to Portland to coach the Trailblazers.

In the next two years, the now woeful Buffalo Braves would have four head coaches. In 1978, the current owners of the Boston Celtics, two Southern Californians from the film industry, Irving Levin and Harold Lipton, yearned to relocate back to Southern California, having had their fill of New England weather in the winter. Of the two partners, Mr. Lipton maintained the lower public presence -- ironic in that his daughter Peggy had been a major television star of the late '60s and early '70s, as the female lead of the hit series "The Mod Squad." She would retire from acting and marry legendary music producer, Quincy Jones.

John Y. Brown, who by this time had successfully engineered his team's descent below the 5,000-tickets-sold threshold, would effectuate an even-up swap of franchises with Levin (and Lipton) with no cash involved: Brown (and Mangurian) acquiring the Boston Celtics; Levin (and Lipton) acquiring the Buffalo Braves, a brilliant strategy for both parties (enthusiastically endorsed by then NBA general counsel David Stern). Levin knew that the NBA would never consider letting the Celtics leave Boston but be quite amenable to relocating the Buffalo franchise to Southern California, and NBA owners approved the relocation with a 21-1 vote.

As for Brown, who was not averse to a higher profile (he would go on to marry former Miss America Phyllis George and be elected Governor of Kentucky), swapping the Buffalo Braves for the Boston Celtics was a no-brainer. As part of the terms and conditions of the swap, rosters and draft picks were included, with one notable exception: Red Auerbach, who never met anyone in basketball who could get the better of him, insisted that his number-one draft pick of 1978 (who decided to return to school for his senior year) not be part of the deal. And so, after his senior year at Indiana State, the "Hick from French Lick," otherwise known as Larry Bird, joined the Boston Celtics in 1979.

Upon assuming ownership of the Celtics, John Y. Brown would quickly make a few player moves without consulting Red Auerbach, which distressed both fans and local media and did not endear him to either. Within one year, Brown's unpopularity in Boston was such that he sold his interest in the team to Harry Mangurian. With the Buffalo Braves now relocated to Southern California and doing business as the San Diego

Clippers, Levin's club got off to a promising start, finishing its first season with a record of 43-39, two games shy of the final playoff spot.

The next season, the Clippers signed San Diego native Bill Walton, two years removed from a championship campaign with the Portland Trailblazers. Chronic and devastating foot injuries caused Walton to miss 68 games in his debut season, and the entire next season. He would subsequently be traded to the Golden State Warriors.

In 1981, Levin began looking for a buyer and secured one in Phil Knight, the legendary founder and owner of Nike. The negotiations between Levin and Knight ultimately became contentious; the deal fell apart, and degenerated into a lawsuit.

To find another buyer, fate was neither kind nor solicitous to Irv Levin. Donald Sterling, an attorney and real estate developer from Los Angeles purchased the San Diego Clippers in 1981. Amongst Mr. Sterling's first actions was a public declaration stating that he would never move the team from San Diego. Behind the scenes, Sterling began lobbying the NBA for permission to move the team to Los Angeles, which the NBA rejected. In 1984, Sterling moved the Clippers to Los Angeles without NBA permission, for which he was fined $25 million by the league. Sterling then countersued for $100 million but agreed to drop the suit when the NBA reduced the fine to $6 million.

In Sterling's first 24 years of owning the Los Angeles Clippers, the team would have one winning season and compile the worst winning percentage in any major sport. It certainly did not help that they were now sharing the town with the glamorous Los Angeles Lakers, whose winning and championship pedigree was second to none.

This "little brother" syndrome would only worsen once the Clippers began sharing the new Staples Center with the Lakers, as their home arena, in 1999. After many years of ignominy, the Los Angeles Clippers would improve and even make the playoffs on occasion. In yet another unusual move, in 2013 they would trade two future first-round draft picks to the Boston Celtics for coach Doc Rivers.

In 2014, TMZ would release taped telephone conversations between Donald Sterling and an alleged mistress, on which Sterling was heard making reprehensible racist comments. Public outrage and condemnation was swift and severe. Within four days, the NBA issued Sterling a lifetime ban and a $2.5 million fine (the highest allowable), and prohibited him from attending NBA games and practices.

Adam Silver, the newly installed NBA commissioner, appointed Richard Parsons, former chair and CEO of Time Warner, as interim CEO of the Clippers. Sterling would soon thereafter sell the Los Angeles Clippers to former Microsoft CEO Steve Ballmer for $2 billion, nearly double the expected purchase price. In Ballmer's first year of ownership, the Los Angeles Clippers compiled a record of 56-26.

In summary, the Clippers do not have on their resume any dysfunctional action that is unique: other teams have purposely tanked seasons; other owners have swapped franchises; other teams have traded for coaches and had owners banned for life (for repulsive comments and actions); stolen away to other cities without permission, and been mediocre or worse for decades at a time. It's just that no one single team has done them all! But as of this writing, the Los Angeles Lakers are at their nadir -- Kobe Bryant has retired, their roster is ordinary, their uninspired play reflecting mediocre won-loss records, and their future anything but bright. On the other hand, the Los Angeles Clippers seem to be in the once inconceivable position of claiming Los Angeles as their own.

With a billionaire owner, a nucleus of elite players such as Blake Griffin and Chris Paul, and a top-tier head coach in Doc Rivers, the team that has been a laughingstock for so many years may well have, after all is said and done, the last laugh … if, and only if, their stars can remain healthy.

NBA Finals Appearances: 0
Forbes 2017 Valuation: $2 Billion

Los Angeles Lakers

Former name: Minneapolis Lakers 1947-1960

Year	Owner(s)	Purchase Price
1947-1957	Morris Chalfen and Ben Berger	$15,000
1957-1965	Bob Short	$150,000
1965-1979	Jack Kent Cooke	$5.175 Million
1979-2013	Dr. Jerry Buss	$67 Million
2013-	Jeanie Buss & siblings	Inherited

There are a few things about the Los Angeles Lakers that make them unique in the history of the NBA. From their earliest origins, the Lakers seem always to have had on their roster at least one superstar, and usually two. From the league's first superstar, center George Mikan, to Jerry West, to Elgin Baylor, to Wilt Chamberlain, to Kareem Abdul-Jabbar, Magic Johnson, Shaquille O'Neal, and Kobe Bryant, there is an unbroken lineage of resident Laker superstars spanning 1949 to 2016 that no other franchise can even approach -- kind of a remarkable phenomenon considering their 16 championships, which guarantees low draft picks and limited access to the best players.

Another unique and paradoxical characteristic of this franchise is that, for all of their success, the Los Angeles Lakers are as well known for losing as they are for winning. For a stretch in the 1960s, the Lakers appeared in six NBA finals and lost each time to the Boston Celtics (who were in the middle of winning 11 championships in 13 years). Finally, the Lakers hold the consecutive win streak of 33 games in 1972. And, unlike a few other professional teams in various sports that put up historic regular season winning records but fail to win championships (think, 18-0 New England Patriots; 116-win Seattle Mariners, and 73 - 9 Golden State Warriors), the Los Angeles Lakers closed the deal in 1972 by also winning the NBA championship.

In 1947, at the urging of local sportswriter Sid Hartman, Morris Chalfen (creator and owner of the "Holiday On Ice" ice show) and Ben Berger (owner of several movie theatres and cafes), both of Minneapolis, Minnesota, purchased the Detroit Gems of the NBL (National Basketball League) for $15,000. Relocating the team to their home state of Minnesota, known as the "Land of 10,000 Lakes," Chalfen and Berger renamed the team the Minneapolis Lakers.

Led by center George Mikan, they would win the NBL championship in their debut season. Joining three other NBL teams in jumping to the newly created rival BAA (Basketball Association of America) the very next season, the Minneapolis Lakers would repeat as champions in 1948.

In 1949, the NBL and BAA would merge to form the NBA (National Basketball Association) we know today. The Lakers would go on to dominate the nascent NBA of the early 1950s, winning three consecutive championships, defeating the New York Knickerbockers in 1951 and 1952, and the Syracuse Nationals in 1953.

With Mikan's retirement after the 1954 season, the Lakers would struggle both competitively and financially for the rest of the decade and Chalfen and Berger would sell the team to local attorney and trucking magnate Bob Short in 1957 for $150,000.

With the worst record in the league, the Lakers were awarded the first draft pick in 1958 and selected small forward Elgin Baylor of Seattle University. Considered an all-time NBA great, Baylor was the first "above the rim" scoring forward with an array of acrobatic moves that would presage all who would follow such as Connie Hawkins, Julius "Dr. J" Erving, et al.

In 1960, two events would occur that augured dramatic changes for the still-struggling franchise: Bob Short would move the team to Los Angeles, and with the second pick of the draft, the Lakers would select Jerry West of the University of West Virginia. Upon their arrival in Southern California, playing in the L.A. Sports Arena, the now Los

Angeles Lakers would build a championship-caliber team around two of the best young players in the sport: Baylor and West.

In 1965, Short would sell the team to legendary sports entrepreneur and team owner Jack Kent Cooke for $5.2 million. A Canadian, Cooke amassed his fortune in the media industry. owning radio stations, newspapers, and television stations. After becoming a U.S. citizen, he would buy several cable television systems, eventually forming TelePrompTer, a company that he would sell for $646 million in the late 1970s. He would go on to purchase New York City's iconic Chrysler Building in 1980, and the Los Angeles Daily News in 1980.

Cooke had also purchased a 25-percent interest in the Washington Redskins of the NFL in 1961. By 1974 he would become majority owner, and then sole owner in 1985. He'd also owned the Toronto Maple Leafs baseball team earlier in his career. Known for having a sharp eye and a special gift for recognizing managerial talent, Cooke gave first opportunities to the likes of Jerry West, Joe Gibbs, and Sparky Anderson.

As a native Canadian, Cooke had a special affection for ice hockey and brought the expansion Los Angeles Kings of the NHL to Los Angeles. It was also under Cooke's guidance that both the Los Angeles Forum and what is now called FedEx Field in Landover, Maryland, were constructed. To round out his resume and indelible imprint on the sporting world, Jack Kent Cooke was also the financial backer of the first heavyweight championship fight between Muhammad Ali and Joe Frazer, which took place in Madison Square Garden in 1971.

But it would be under the next owner, Dr. Jerry Buss, that the Los Angeles Lakers would experience their greatest prolonged success and highest profile. Buss accumulated a vast fortune in real estate and paid $67 million for the Lakers in 1979. Purchasing the Los Angeles Lakers, Los Angeles Kings, and the Los Angeles Forum in 1979, Buss would oversee the Lakers' greatest renaissance to date (a two-part affair). Part 1 was seemingly always Lakers and Celtics: the classic 1960s rivalry was revisited and reimagined in the 1980s NBA of Bird and Magic, the Pat Riley-led "Showtime" teams amassing five championships in the decade, in 1980, '82, '85, '87, and '88. And after a brief respite of the 1990s, dominated by Michael Jordan's Chicago Bulls, Dr. Buss would celebrate five more championships, in 2000, '01, '02, '09, and 2010.

Upon his death in 2013, Dr. Buss left the Los Angeles Lakers equally divided among his six children: Jeanine, Jim, Johnny, Jess, Joey, and Janie. At this writing, the Lakers find themselves in an unfamiliar position, not unlike the Minneapolis Lakers of the late 1950s immediately following Georg Mikan's retirement. With Kobe Bryant's retirement in 2016, the cupboard is bare: no superstars to speak of and a decidedly mediocre roster. It will be interesting to observe how the Lakers reinvent themselves yet again. If one can look to the past to predict the future, the Lakers' history of 50-plus years of excellence should hold them in very good stead going forward, but if the 2016-17 season is any indication, the wait may be more years than we think.

Hold on: Jeanie Buss recently hired Magic Johnson to head Laker Management. This move should accelerate change.

NBA Finals Appearances: 31   Wins: 16
Forbes 2017 Valuation: $3 Billion

Memphis Grizzlies

Former name: Vancouver Grizzlies 1994-2000

Year	Owner(s)	Purchase Price
1994-1996	Arthur Griffiths	$125 Million
1996-2000	John McCaw	NA
2000-2012	Michael Heisley	$160 Million
2012-	Robert J. Pera	$377 Million

If you can get past the fact that Grizzly Bears do not inhabit the state of Tennessee, the NBA's Memphis Grizzlies make perfect sense. Formerly the Vancouver Grizzlies, one of two teams that marked the 1995 NBA expansion into Canada (along with the Toronto Raptors), the Memphis Grizzlies are the first, and only, professional franchise (of the "big three" sports) to reside in Memphis.

The Vancouver Grizzlies came into existence in 1995 as Arthur Griffiths (owner of the Vancouver Canucks of the NHL) was awarded the new franchise. In the succeeding years, as his umbrella organization, Orca Bay Sports and Entertainment, encountered financial struggles, Griffiths finally sold his interest in the company to his business partner, John McCaw; the terms of the deal were never publicly disclosed.

Four years later, McCaw had a deal in place to sell the Memphis Grizzlies for $200 million to Bill Laurie, owner of the St. Louis Blues NHL franchise, whose wife was Nancy Walton, a Walmart heiress. When the NBA refused to allow him to relocate the Grizzlies to St. Louis, Laurie walked away from the deal. McCaw eventually sold the team to Chicago businessman Michael Heisley in 2000.

There is no small amount of controversy as to what transpired next. Conjecture abounds and there is no definitive "truth" as to the circumstances of Vancouver's relocation. One version is that as a condition of the purchase of the team, Heisley promised to keep the Grizzlies in

Vancouver. Another version implies that Heisley immediately started the process of relocation upon acquiring the team. Yet another version suggests that Heisley had made a good-faith effort to keep the team in Vancouver but that a combination of soft Canadian currency (at the time), lackluster fan support, resistance from talented players coming to the team because they did not want to live in Canada (an example being the second overall draft pick in 1999, Maryland point guard Steve Francis, refusing to sign and forcing a trade), and so on, dictated the move simply as a matter of survival.

On the other hand, Griffiths would later accuse Heisley of intentionally mismanaging the team in order to justify the relocation -- a charge vehemently denied by Heisley, with Griffiths countering that the Toronto Raptors were proof of the viability of NBA basketball success in Canada.

In any event, during his tenure as owner, Heisley effected a culture change that elevated the team to its greatest success to that point. Doubtless, his best decision was in hiring Jerry West as GM in 2002. An all-time NBA great as a player, West had fashioned a second auspicious career as a general manager and talent evaluator, winning a second NBA Executive of the Year award in '03-'04, his second season with the Vancouver Grizzlies. It is surely no coincidence that the Golden State Warriors began their ascent when Jerry West joined that organization as an executive board member in 2011.

As for the relocation, there would be seven American cities seriously considered: San Diego, Las Vegas, Anaheim, Buffalo, Memphis, Louisville, and New Orleans. Ultimately, Memphis was selected as the ideal location. Ironically, the fact that Memphis was not a "pro town" worked in its favor. Among other factors: the team would garner the highest broadcast rights from Memphis and Louisville, along with interest and attention, because they would be the only game in town; Tennessee boasted a strong basketball culture and fan base with the University of Tennessee, Memphis University, and the University of Kentucky; it had both a temporary venue in which to play immediately (Pyramid Arena) *and* the need to have a new facility, which would be customized for basketball (the city would pay for it and receive $92 million for the naming rights from one of Memphis's biggest businesses, calling it the Fed-Ex Arena), and finally, there was a very strong local advocate in Pitt Hyde, the founder of AutoZone, who offered to buy 50 percent of the team. And so, in 2001, the former Vancouver Grizzlies debuted as the Memphis Grizzlies.

In 2012, Heisley would sell the team to Robert J. Pera, a Silicon Valley communications technology magnate who also happened to be *from* Silicon Valley, having grown up in San Carlos, California.

Mr. Pera, founder of Ubiquiti Networks, was, at the age of 34, named one of the 10 youngest billionaires in the world by Forbes Magazine. Amongst Mr. Pera's minority ownership group were two notable Memphis natives: actor Justin Timberlake and entrepreneur Ashley Manning, whose future Hall of Fame husband, Peyton, is arguably one of the top three quarterbacks of all time.

NBA Finals Appearances: 0
Forbes 2017 Valuation: $790 Million

Miami Heat

Year	Owner(s)	Purchase Price
1988-1995	Zev Buffman, Lewis Schaffel, Billy Cunningham, Ted Arison	$32.5 Million
1995	Micky Arison	$68 Million

Beginning in the early 1980s, Zev Buffman, an Israeli-born theater producer, concert promoter, and impresario, aspired to bring an NBA expansion franchise to Miami. As a producer of over 40 Broadway shows, Buffman was a leading figure and mainstay of South Florida entertainment, having owned and refurbished the famed Coconut Grove Playhouse, and serving as president of the Jackie Gleason Performing Arts Center in South Miami Beach.

Buffman needed to enlist basketball people for the endeavor and so Billy Cunningham and Lewis Schaffel were brought on board as minority partners to manage all basketball operations. Cunningham's resume and credentials were impeccable: the legendary New York City ballplayer nicknamed the "Kangaroo Kid" was a star at Brooklyn's Erasmus Hall High School, then played for Dean Smith at the University of North Carolina, and went on to fashion an NBA Hall of Fame career as a player for the Philadelphia 76ers. After his playing career, he was head coach of the 76ers with one championship (1982) and a career won-lost record of 454 - 196 (.698 winning percentage). Cunningham brought with him his childhood, and lifelong, friend, former sports agent Lewis Schaffel. Needing financial backing, Buffman turned to another Miami mainstay, fellow Israeli-born entrepreneur Ted Arison, who had cofounded Norwegian Cruise Line in 1966, and then was the owner and the founder of Carnival Cruise Line, in 1972.

And so, armed with the endorsement of the Miami Sports and Exhibition Authority, it came to pass. The NBA approved a two-phase expansion plan that would bring four new teams into the league: the Charlotte Hornets and Miami Heat, for the 1988-89 season, and the

Minnesota Timberwolves and Orlando Magic, for the 1989-90 season. As is most often the norm, the expansion Miami Heat struggled mightily in its emerging years and by 1995, the team was sold to Ted Arison's son, Micky.

In short order, Micky Arison made a decision that would forever change the fortunes of the Miami Heat -- he hired Pat Riley to become team president and head coach. At the time coach of the New York Knicks, Riley, unable to come to terms with the Knicks over issues of greater control of player personnel as well as an ownership stake in the team, famously resigned by sending a fax.

With one year remaining on Riley's contract, the Knicks accused Miami of tampering, which was ultimately resolved with the Heat sending the Knicks a first-round draft pick plus $1 million as compensation, thus freeing Riley to move on to Miami.

Pat Riley has been the architect of three Miami Heat NBA championships: his first, in 2006, when he was the head coach, and then the back-to-back, 2010 and 2011 wins with the "Big Three" LeBron James-led teams.

NBA Finals Appearances: 5   Wins: 3
Forbes 2017 Valuation: $1.35 Billion

Milwaukee Bucks

Year	Owner(s)	Purchase Price
1968-1977	Wesly Pavalon and Marvin Fishman	$2 Million
1977-1985	Jim Fitzgerald	Unknown
1985-2014	Herb Kohl	$18 Million
2014-	Marc Lasry and Wesley Edens	$550 Million

Milwaukee used to be known as the city of "3-Bs" (Bowling, Beer and Baseball). That was until Wes Pavalon and Marvin Fishman put up the $2 million NBA expansion fee and founded the Milwaukee Bucks in 1968. That would add a fourth "B" (basketball) to the city's identity.

Wes Pavalon was a tall, athletic street kid from Chicago who had to beg, borrow and steal to get ahead, and he did. Bold and aggressive, Pavalon scratched and clawed his way to financial success by founding Career Academy, an international company that produced educational textbooks and other learning programs.

Pavalon, who turned out to be an excellent writer, was a 10th-grade dropout who had to buy and forge a stationery-store high school diploma to gain admittance to Wright Junior College. The diploma was never questioned and Wes got his degree.

Wes and Marvin convinced the NBA to allow the Bucks to be owned by a public company, Milwaukee Professional Sports and Services, which offered shares to residents of Wisconsin to raise enough money to compete for star players. It was at the time that the struggling ABA was positioning itself to get Lou Alcindor (Kareem Abdul-Jabbar), the sensational UCLA star. They boasted a fee of $1 million, or more, the cost to be split between the 11 ABA teams, to get Alcindor and give him the choice to play for whichever ABA team he chose. They felt Alcindor could do for the ABA what Joe Namath did for the AFL.

The Bucks had a hold on last place in the east. Pavalon raised the money but he needed to win the coin toss with Phoenix, which held last place in the west. The Bucks won the toss and signed Alcindor for a record $1.4 million. After he chose Milwaukee, the Nets, who felt he could be lured back to the New York area where he had grown up, offered him a guaranteed $3.2 million, which he refused, saying a bidding war would make him look greedy. Besides, big Lou wanted to play in the NBA.

In the '70-71 season, the Bucks, having also obtained Oscar Robinson in '69, won the NBA Championship. The next day, Lou Alcindor changed his name to Kareem Abdul-Jabbar. After six years with the Bucks, Jabbar asked to be traded to either the New York Knicks or the L.A. Lakers. Kareem went to the Lakers and set nearly every record in the book. Some peers call him the greatest NBA player ever.

Pavalon's partner, Marvin Fishman, who made his money in real estate, sold his ownership in the Bucks to buy the Chicago Bulls (because one couldn't own two NBA teams). In fact, he had a signed deal to buy the Bulls in 1972 for $3.2 million. That agreement was contingent on Fishman's group getting a stadium lease. The stadium was controlled by Arthur Wirtz, a Bulls owner who also owned the Chicago Blackhawks and Chicago Stadium, where both the Blackhawks and Bulls played.

Fishman claimed Wirtz and other Bulls owners were in cahoots with NBA executives to prevent him from purchasing the Bulls by refusing him a place to play. The NBA turned him down twice. He sued Wirtz and other Bulls owners (and the NBA) for $50 million, claiming restraint of trade. The NBA, which claimed in its defense that it couldn't get 75 percent of the owners to approve Fishman's deal, settled out of court for $750,000. After 10 years of legal battles, Fishman won a judgment for $12.3 million in 1981, but he never gained control of the Bulls.

James (Jim) Fitzgerald, a Notre Dame graduate who made his money building gas stations and shopping malls, took over control of the Bucks (for an undisclosed amount) in 1977, which he held until he sold the team to former Senator Herb Kohl in 1985. Fitzgerald and partners went on to own the Golden State Warriors in 1986 and controlled that team until 1995. Fitzgerald hired coach Don Nelson, who coached both the Bucks and Warriors during Fitzgerald's ownership reign. Unique was the fact they never had a written contract, simply a gentleman's handshake.

Herb Kohl, a former U.S Senator from Wisconsin, bought the Bucks for $18 million in 1985. Kohl earned an MBA from Harvard and soon started his own investment firm. He and his brother inherited the Kohl's chain of 50 grocery and department stores. Herb became president in 1970 and built the business until it was sold in 1979. He was elected to the Senate in 1988, where he served with distinction for 25 years.

Kohl nearly sold the Bucks to Michael Jordan in 2003 but felt the team belonged to Wisconsin and didn't want to risk them being moved to another city. In 2014, Kohl sold the Bucks to hedge fund billionaires Marc Lasry and Wesley (Wes) Edens, who vowed to keep the team in Milwaukee, for $550 million.

Lasry was born in Marrakech, Morocco, but grew up in Hartford, Connecticut. He was tapped by President Obama, at Bill Clinton's behest, to become ambassador to France but turned it down to continue as CEO of Avenue Capital, the private equity firm he started in 1995. Lasry is or was a high-stakes poker player whose apparent association with other questionable high-stakes players tainted his image for such a visible government post.

Wes Edens co-founded Fortress Investment Group in 1998 and made billions as an investment banker. After the Great Recession, he became known as the "subprime-lending king." Marc and Wes might need their billions to achieve their goal of winning the NBA championship in a small-market city like Milwaukee … without another Kareem Abdul-Jabbar to lead the way.

Milwaukee has now become the city of "5-Bs," the fifth being billionaires.

NBA Finals Appearances: 2   Wins: 1
Forbes 2017 Valuation: $785 Million

Minnesota Timberwolves

Year	Owner(s)	Purchase Price
1989-1995	Marv Wolfenson and Harvey Ratner	$32.5 Million
1995-	Glen Taylor	$89 Million

Marv Wolfenson and Harvey Ratner brought pro basketball back to Minneapolis in 1988 by paying the NBA franchise fee of $32.5 million. It had been 28 years since the Minneapolis Lakers departed the city for the greener pastures of Los Angeles.

"Marv and Harv," as they were called, grew up together and made their money developing apartments and a chain of health clubs with indoor tennis courts. Sports nuts from an early age, they had bought a three-percent interest in the original Minneapolis Lakers for a reported $1,500 and made a decent profit when the team left for L.A.

In their zeal, they took on considerable debt for the construction of a new downtown arena, the Target Center. As no good deed goes unpunished, construction overruns put them behind the financial eight ball and, after five miserable losing seasons, they sold to a group led by former Minnesota State Senator Glen Taylor.

Prior to the sale to Taylor, a group from New Orleans, Top Rank, had a deal to buy the Timberwolves (for a hefty $152 million) and relocate them to New Orleans. But, in a rare move, the NBA nixed the deal because of Top Rank's shaky financial position, which, among other things, was based on unidentified investors and on bank loans that hadn't been approved. Pressure from the city and the fans, who the year before had lost their NHL team, to keep the team in Minneapolis was festering. The state chipped in and approved a bill to use public funds ($48 million) to pay the debt on the Target Center … as long as a buyer could be found who would keep the team in Minneapolis.

Glen Taylor, a billionaire who was born and raised in Minnesota, put together a group and saved the day for the Twin Cities, paying $89 million in 1995. In 1999, Taylor bought the Minnesota Lynx (WNBA) and later, in 2005, tried to acquire the Minnesota Vikings but was outbid by real estate developer Zigi Wilf.

Glen Taylor, with an executive MBA from Harvard Business School, worked for Carlson Wedding Service, a company that specialized in wedding invitation printing. When owner Bill Carlson wanted to retire, Glen offered him $2 million, payable over 10 years. That formed the basis of Taylor Corporation, a multinational printing and electronics business, which grew to be one of the largest privately-owned companies in America, with over 15,000 employees. The company is based in North Mankota, Minnesota, of all places. In 2015, Taylor stepped down as chairman and CEO, handing the reins to his niece.

Taylor has been chairman of the NBA Board of Governors since 2008. He must have cleaned up his act since 2000 when the NBA suspended him for nearly a year for surreptitiously signing a player, Joe Smith, in violation of the league's salary cap rules. In fact, Taylor had the distinction of being suspended longer than any other owner -- that is until Donald Sterling stuck his foot in his mouth and was banned from the league and forced to sell his L.A. Clippers for a paltry $2 billion in 2014.

In 2014, Taylor purchased Minneapolis's largest newspaper, the Star Tribune, for a reported $100 million. Forbes clocked him in with a net worth of $1.9 billion in 2016.

NBA Finals Appearances: 0
Forbes 2017 Valuation: $770 Million

New Orleans Pelicans

Former names: Charlotte Hornets 1988-2002;
New Orleans Hornets 2002-2012

Year	Owner(s)	Purchase Price
1988-2010	George Shinn	$32.5 Million
2010-2012	National Basketball Association	$300 Million
2012-	Tom Benson	$338 Million

The New Orleans Pelicans came into being as the result of two disasters -- one natural and the other man-made.

First, the man-made disaster: George Shinn. A "perfect-storm-like" character, George Shinn was granted the expansion Charlotte Hornets in 1988. The NBA had clearly identified Charlotte, North Carolina, as a very desirable market to penetrate: the city was rapidly expanding and booming with banking and tech-industry money and employment attracting an influx of people; the state of North Carolina was a renowned basketball stronghold given its collegiate legacy, and Charlotte just happened to have the Charlotte Arena, a state-of-the-art, basketball-specific venue. With no small touch of irony, North Carolina native George Shinn, who'd attended the Evans Business College after graduating last in his high school class of 293 students, would make his money by purchasing several similar 18 to 24-month college programs, consolidating them under the name of Rutledge Education Systems, and selling it for millions of dollars. To ice his deal with the NBA, Shinn enlisted North Carolina media magnate and politician Cy Bahakel, who would put in $6 million of his own money (added to Shinn's $8.7), and guarantee their bank loans for the balance.

It would only take a short 10 years for Shinn to become so disliked and distrusted in the Charlotte, NC, community, highlighted by a very public trial in which he was accused of kidnapping and sexually assaulting a Charlotte woman, that he simply needed to "get out of town." In 2002, he relocated the team to New Orleans, where they would play as the New Orleans Hornets for the next three seasons.

The natural disaster was Hurricane Katrina, which in 2005 would devastate not only New Orleans proper, but the entire region as well. The New Orleans Hornets would relocate to Oklahoma City and play there for the next two seasons as the New Orleans/Oklahoma City Hornets, returning to New Orleans for the 2007 season.

Under financial duress, Shinn would, in 2007, sell 25 percent of his Hornets franchise for $62 million to Gary Chouest, the Louisiana multi-billionaire owner of his family's shipbuilding company, Edison Chouest Offshore, which specializes in boats used in oil exploration, oil rig construction, and oil spill response. Nevertheless, by 2010, the New Orleans Hornets would be bankrupt, leaving the NBA no choice but to purchase and run the team after Chouest backed away at the last minute from a deal in place with Shinn to purchase the rest of the team outright. It took two years for the league to find a suitable buyer and owner for the beleaguered franchise in the person of Tom Benson, owner of the New Orleans Saints of the NFL.

Benson, a native of New Orleans, moved to San Antonio, Texas, in 1958. After successfully reviving a few automobile dealerships, Benson would go on to make his fortune owning car dealerships, and later by investing the profits in small banks, eventually forming Benson Financial.

Benson always seemed to have one foot in New Orleans, and the other foot in San Antonio. Thrice married, he and his first wife adopted three children. Benson would purchase the New Orleans Saints of the NFL in 1985. A popular owner, he would often do a dance on the field after Saints wins, which came to be known as the "Benson Boogie." Over the years, his local popularity would wax and wane as he wouldn't confirm nor deny his intention to relocate the Saints to San Antonio, often using that noncommittal stance to leverage favorable terms for a new practice facility, renovations to the aging Superdome, and higher annual payments from the state to the team.

Thus, in the post-Katrina year of 2005, when a temporary "home" schedule had to be put together between LSU's Tiger Stadium in Baton Rouge and the Alamodome in San Antonio, the talked-about move surprised nobody and worried everybody in New Orleans. This would also mark the beginning of the first peculiar episode of Benson's erratic behavior -- a public scuffle with a journalist and then camera crew in Tiger Stadium (in which he claimed that he feared for the safety of his family), which was ultimately resolved. The next five years would engender controversy surrounding the open question of whether Benson wanted to relocate the Saints to San Antonio.

But in 2010, with the NFL's Saints back home in New Orleans and then winning the Super Bowl, Benson regained his standing and popularity. And so, when he acquired the basketball team in 2012, it was seen by all as a positive development. Wanting to start fresh and anew, Benson would in

61

2012 change the New Orleans Hornets' name to the Pelicans (the brown pelican being Louisiana's official state bird).

And so just as the people of New Orleans (as well as the NBA) had reason to finally feel that the franchise had found stability and forward momentum to replace the inertia of Shinn's regime, the Benson family's roiling internal conflicts came to light. Benson had disinherited his adopted daughter, Renee LeBlanc, and grandchildren Ryan LeBlanc and Rita Benson LeBlanc, completely cutting them out of both the Saints and Pelicans, in favor of his (third) wife, Gayle, who was to be his sole beneficiary.

LeBlanc would first charge that Benson was mentally incompetent and that Gayle Benson was exerting undue influence, publicly citing that Benson's physical frailty was accelerating because of a diet of candy, soda, ice cream, and red wine. He was ultimately found competent, but his daughter would next bring a federal lawsuit against him for not adequately replacing the value of the Saints and Pelicans shares, taken from her original inheritance, with equal value.

Finally, in June 2016, it was reported that a settlement was reached. Turns out, that settlement did not "settle." The suit was ultimately settled on the courthouse steps in early 2017.

NBA Finals Appearances: 0
Forbes 2017 Valuation: $750 Million

New York Knicks

Year	Owner(s)	Purchase Price
1947-1973	Ned Irish	
1973-1977	Madison Square Garden	
1977-1989	Gulf + Western	
1989-1994	Paramount Communications	
1994	Viacom	
1994-1997	Cablevision, ITT	
1997-2010	Cablevision	$650 Million
2010-	Madison Square Garden Corp.	

One of America's first great writers, Washington Irving, was a bit of a jokester. His first major work, "A History of New York From the Beginning of the World to the End of the Dutch Dynasty," was a satirical and humorous accounting of New York City's 50 years under Dutch rule in the 1600s, written by a crusty old Dutch historian named "Diedrich Knickerbocker," who, Irving claimed, had suddenly gone missing! Irving took out ads in newspapers seeking his whereabouts, pleading for any information, and so on. The hoax gained attention and traction. The book became wildly popular and made Irving a literary star -- who would, of course, go on to write the classic short stories "Rip Van Winkle" and "The Legend of Sleepy Hollow." The name "Knickerbocker" (shortened to "Knick") caught on and became the popular term for any person living in Manhattan -- all based on a well-played hoax and one very good joke.

There is a lot more, and a lot less, to the story of the New York Knickerbockers than one might imagine. The Knicks have been bad far longer than good and great only once, all the way back in 1970. Yet the New York Knickerbockers are today the most valuable team in the NBA. Neat trick. Win nothing in 43 years and still be worth more than every other franchise in the sport.

For any professional league (the NBA included), the New York City team is a "tent-pole" franchise and the league always benefits when the New York team is financially healthy, through ticket sales, marketing, ratings, television contracts, digital platforms, merchandising, international profile, etc. Yet no matter how abysmal a product the Knicks have put on the floor, they continue to sell out Madison Square Garden: from "celebrity row" behind the bench to "blue heaven," the upper level seats that are the farthest away from the court, there's no tougher ticket in town. One can readily understand when the PA announcer welcomes fans to "the world's greatest arena." But what exactly have the Knicks accomplished to validate the Garden's other nickname, the "Mecca of basketball"? Not surprisingly, the answer is ... absolutely nothing.

The term is a college basketball reference dating back to the 1930s and '40s when New York City was a central hub and hotbed of college basketball -- a fact lost on contemporary sports fans whose perception of college basketball in New York City as a wasteland, (rightly so), reaches back only so far as the glory days of the Big East conference of the 1980s into the '90s that produced the likes of Patrick Ewing and Alan Iverson (Georgetown); Chris Mullen and Ron Artest (St. John's); and Derrick Coleman and Pearl Washington (Syracuse). In fact, a full five decades earlier, the history of modern college basketball, as well as that of professional basketball, traces back to a New York City man named Ned Irish.

Never an athlete himself, Irish covered prep and amateur sports for three New York City daily newspapers while still a student at Brooklyn's Erasmus Hall High School. In 1928, upon graduating from the University of Pennsylvania, Irish began working as a $60-a-week sportswriter for the New York Telegram covering local college basketball: NYU, Fordham, Manhattan College, St. John's, CCNY, and Long Island University, among others.

By 1933, Irish felt certain that college basketball had outgrown all the local school gyms, as he continually encountered sold-out and overflowing crowds that hampered him from covering the games. In 1934, Irish approached Madison Square Garden to host a college game he'd set up between New York University and City College of New York, but the Garden did not have an open date and the game never came to pass. Later that same year, though, Irish successfully promoted a college basketball double-header at Madison Square Garden -- NYU vs. Notre Dame and Westminster vs. St. John's. At the height of the Depression, 16,180 fans attended, and Irish pocketed six months' worth of his salary as a sportswriter in one night. Irish summarily quit his newspaper job, deciding to promote college basketball full time.

The Garden, struggling for money, as was everyone else during this time, charged Irish $4,000 for use of the venue, a sum that he easily covered (with a lot left over for himself). The next year, Irish promoted eight college basketball double-headers, attracting approximately 100,000 fans, which enabled not only himself but Madison Square Garden, and the colleges as well, to turn a profit. Thus, the model was established: basketball programs from across the country would vie for the privilege of playing before huge crowds in the biggest and best city in the world at the one and only Madison Square Garden, which quickly became known as "the Mecca of College Basketball."

In today's world where the NCAA Tournament, March Madness, and "Bracketology" is a billion-dollar cottage industry and one of the biggest events on the sports calendar, where the NIT is an afterthought, something of a consolation prize for those not among the 68 teams invited to "the dance," it is interesting to note that there was a time when the exact opposite was true.

Ned Irish was a pioneer and seminal figure that at the end of the 1937-38 invited college teams to compete in Madison Square Garden. The NCAA tournament would not even be created until 1939 and it would long be thought of as the "other tournament" in contrast to the more glamorous and prestigious NIT.

In 1946, Madison Square Garden averaged 18,196 college basketball fans per game. Because of his long and profitable association with the Garden, Ned Irish wielded power on the business side of college basketball that has perhaps never been equaled. Also in 1946, Irish would be a major and influential figure in the creation of a new 11-team professional league, the Basketball Association of America, which just three years later would merge with the more established National Basketball League to form the modern-day NBA. Always a tough and hard-edged negotiator, Irish exploited his cozy relationship with Madison Square Garden as his rationale for being awarded ownership of the New York franchise. He further insisted that in the new league, the home team would keep all gate receipts -- advantageous only to him, as Madison Square Garden was his home venue.

In 1940s New York City basketball's golden era, Ned Irish was "king bee," and he would remain so until 1951, when an infamous game-fixing and point-shaving scandal involving seven colleges, four of them New York City schools -- CCNY, NYU, Manhattan College, and LIU -- proved to be catastrophic.

At the center of the scandal was the CCNY squad, both the 1950 NCAA and NIT champions. Frank Hogan, New York City's District Attorney, who prosecuted the case, famously remarked that "blatant commercialism which had permeated college basketball" was a contributing factor to an environment that attracted gamblers to the sport. Irish, the man single-handedly responsible for commercializing college basketball, publicly rejected that notion, instead placing blame only on the players and coaches. In any event, the scandal and its aftermath was a deathblow to big-time college basketball in NY City.

As for the New York Knicks, Irish's first move was to hire the St John's legendary coach, Joe Lapchick, as his head coach. And in typically heavy-handed fashion, Irish strong-armed the league into letting him break existing rules by acquiring two highly touted college players, Vince Boryla and Ernie Vandewegh, in addition to signing an undergraduate star who'd completed just two years of college, Harry Gallatin. Irish would also go on to sign the first non-Caucasian player, Wataru Misaka, as well as the first African-American, the Harlem Globetrotters' Nat "Sweetwater" Clifton, to professional basketball contracts.

The Knicks then, under Irish's control, had winning records in their first nine years of existence, making the playoffs every year until 1955. They would then enter a fallow period, making the playoffs only once in the next 11 years. That would change when Ned Irish, in the middle of the 1967-68 season, hired William "Red" Holzman, who was voted one of the top 10 coaches in NBA history and inducted into the Naismith NBA Hall of Fame in 1986. Holzman's coaching would lead the 1970 Knicks squad to the first of three NBA finals appearances in four years, winning championships in 1970 and 1973.

The 1970 New York Knicks are a historically important team considered by NBA aficionados as one of the best starting five units ever. Surely not amongst the most athletic or physically gifted, a compelling case can be made that the 1970 New York Knicks were the most intelligent, balanced, and complementary roster ever assembled, featuring four Hall of Fame players, including three "top fifty of all-time" players: center Willis Reed, guard Walt "Clyde" Frazier, and power forward Dave Debusschere. Rounding out the starting five were all-star guard Dick Barnett and Bill Bradley, who'd been considered the nation's top high school player, and was a member of the 1964 gold medal-winning Olympic basketball team, and a Rhodes Scholar. Also a member of that team was Phil Jackson (a

Hall of Fame coach), who credits Red Holzman as one of his most important coaching influences and mentors.

Nineteen-seventy-three would be a watershed year in that not only would it be their last championship, but it would also signal the end of Ned Irish's ownership, as well as his 40-year-plus relationship with Madison Square Garden. The New York Knicks, from their very inception, have been synonymous with the iconic name of their venue -- no matter that there have been four Madison Square Gardens, the first two (in 1879 and 1890) in the actual area of Madison Square in Manhattan, East 26th Street and Madison Avenue; then another at Eighth Avenue and 50th Street, the so-called "old" Madison Square Garden of the 20th century, Ned Irish's Garden; and finally the present-day Madison Square Garden, erected atop Pennsylvania Station. As much a New York City landmark as Central Park, the Empire State Building, the Statue of Liberty, and Yankee Stadium, Madison Square Garden is in the DNA of the New York Knickerbockers. The identity (and value) of the New York Knicks franchise is inextricably linked to its venue and it is simply inconceivable that one would ever be purchased without the other.

Thus, when Ned Irish, part and parcel of Madison Square Garden, having served over the years in a variety of positions -- president, basketball director, executive vice president, president of the Knicks, and member of the MSG board of directors -- left in 1973, he would leave as the only individual entity who ever owned and operated the franchise. A basketball man, through and through, he was inducted into the NBA Hall of Fame in 1964.

From 1977 forward, the New York Knicks (as well as Madison Square Garden) would become highly valued "assets" absorbed by one corporate conglomerate after another in a series of mergers and acquisitions: by Gulf + Western, which would change its name to Paramount Communications, which would be sold to Viacom, which would sell to ITT and Cablevision.

Charles Dolan, a visionary who in the mid-1960s built a cable television system in Manhattan, and created HBO, would sell both to Time Life, Inc. He would then start another cable system on Long Island, eventually expanding into New York City, then the metro area, and finally into Cleveland and Boston. He named this new company Cablevision.

Dolan would buy out ITT three years later. Succeeded by his son, James, the Dolans would eventually sell Cablevision to a European conglomerate called Altice for $17.7 billion but retain their sports and entertainment assets: Madison Square Garden, the Knicks and Rangers, MSG television network, Radio City Music Hall (including the Rockettes) and the Beacon Theater, amongst others, organized into a new corporate entity, the Madison Square Garden Company.

Corporate ownership of a professional sports team is not by definition inherently disastrous; there are examples where quite the opposite is true. But with the New York Knicks, there seems a causal relationship between their ownership and their decades-long competitive dysfunction and incompetence. Since 1994, when a Dolan has owned them, the New York Knicks have hired and fired 14 head coaches and eight general managers. That's more regime changes than the combined countries of the Middle East.

In 22 years of Dolan ownership, the New York Knickerbockers have had 22 different people running their front office and coaching their team. And they are the most valuable franchise in the NBA. That's no joke. Or maybe it is. Rest assured that, somewhere, Washington Irving is smiling.

NBA Finals Appearances: 8   Wins: 2
Forbes 2017 Valuation: $3.3 Billion

Oklahoma City Thunder

Former name: Seattle SuperSonics 1967-2008

Year	Owner(s)	Purchase Price
1967-1983	Sam Schulman	$1.75 Million
1983-2001	Barry Ackerly	$21 Million
2001-2006	Howard Schultz	$200 Million
2006-	Clayton Bennett	$350 Million

The Oklahoma City Thunder, originally the Seattle SuperSonics, were founded in 1967 by a syndicate headed by Eugene Klein and Sam Schulman, who paid the then NBA expansion fee of $1.75 million. Schulman, who earned a Harvard MBA, started his career by taking over a bankrupt Brooklyn bookbinder and turning it into a profitable enterprise. Klein made a fortune selling used cars, then built National General into a powerhouse. In 1965, they led a group of investors to purchase the San Diego Chargers for $10 million, the highest price paid for an NFL team at the time. Apparently, Schulman sold his interest in the Chargers to Klein, at an unreported price, and Klein sold his interest in the Sonics to Schulman for an unknown price.

Schulman is best known around NBA circles as the owner who took the NBA to the Supreme Court over the Spencer Haywood issue, and won. The issue: Spencer Haywood signed with the ABA's Denver Rockets as a college sophomore but left the team due to money issues. Schulman signed Haywood for the Sonics, defying the NBA rule that players had to be four years out of high school to be NBA-eligible. The court's decision in favor of Haywood and Schulman prompted the NBA to relax that rule.

In 1983, Sam sold the Sonics to Barry Ackerley, owner of Ackerley Communications, Inc., for $21 million, a nice profit for Sam. Ackerley, a media man once known as the "baron of billboards," owned the team for 18 years before selling the Sonics (and the WNBA's Seattle Storm) to the owner of Starbuck's, Howard Schultz, and a group of investors. Barry Ackerley was not the most popular owner in Seattle. Not only did he spend a lot of time at the courthouse, sometimes being sued by unpaid suppliers, he made enemies with the press, which tarnished his image with the Seattle fans. He was called an enigma, loved and hated at the same time.

Despite the controversies Ackerley created, his stubborn demeanor, and seeming need for perpetual discord, the SuperSonics performed well under his ownership, making the playoffs 13 out of 18 years, and the NBA Finals once. Regardless, the discord got to him, not to mention the work stoppage of '99, which caused financial woes, and the dilapidated building where the Sonics played. It all convinced him it was time to sell the team to Schultz for $200 million, again yielding a decent profit.

Howard Schultz, with his sense of civic responsibility, rode in on his coffee-colored horse and came to the rescue. He wanted to make sure the team remained in Seattle. He wanted to fix the problems and make Seattle proud of its team. However, he soon ran into a brick wall when he proposed that taxpayers should share the cost to renovate the building. After only two years, Schultz learned that owning a sports team wasn't as easy as brewing coffee and, when a group led by Clayton Bennett offered $350 million in 2006, Schultz, convinced they would keep the Sonics (and the Storm) in Seattle, sold. Bennett did not stay true to his word, and two years later agreed to cough up another $75 million to the city as compensation for relocating the team to Oklahoma City. He named them the "Thunder," and that is exactly what they became ... in more ways than one.

Clayton Bennett's cohort in the latent "conspiracy" to move the Sonics to OKC was Aubrey McClendon, a 19-percent Sonics owner, and the co-owner of the controversial Chesapeake Energy Company. One caveat behind Bennett's "promise" to keep the Sonics (and the Storm) in Seattle was securing a viable place to play. When the Washington legislature voted against the $500 million taxpayer-funded construction cost for a new arena in Renton, WA, Bennet's group plotted to split. Lawsuits prevailed: In 2008, Schultz sued Bennett and McClendon's group to rescind the 2006 sale so the franchise could be taken over by an owner who would keep the teams in Seattle (like a Steve Ballmer who could have been waiting in the wings). The State of Washington sued to force the team to play two more years in Seattle.

Although these lawsuits did not prevail in stopping the relocation, they did expose an incriminating series of emails between the plotters: Bennett, McClendon, and his cohorts. One of the emails suggested praise to the State of Washington for declining the arena funding, the excuse they used to get the team to OKC. Worse, McClendon said in an interview with the Oklahoma Journal- Record, "We didn't buy the team to keep it in Seattle; we hoped to bring it here...."

NBA commissioner David Stern was pissed and warned Bennett there would be a fine if McClendon's statement were true. Bennett played innocent with Stern, and lied. This was later exposed in the discovered emails, but it was too late. The Thunder were already entrenched in OKC with $120 million in public funding for arena improvements approved. The city threatened to sue Schultz for trying to block the sale. Schultz, knowing it was too late, but having exposed Bennett's lies to the public, dropped his suit. The NBA fined McClendon $250,000.

After a horrible 2008-09 season, the Thunder began to roar, making the playoffs in 2009-10 and every year since, with one trip to the NBA finals. Alas, their star and best player, Kevin Durant, bolted for the team that defeated them in the 2016 playoffs, the Golden State Warriors, leaving the Thunder without its best lightning bolt.

NBA Finals Appearances: 4   Wins: 1
Forbes 2017 Valuation: $1.025 Billion

Orlando Magic

Year	Owner(s)	Purchase Price
1989-1991	James Hewitt, Pat Williams, etc.	$32.5 Million
1991-2007	Richard M. DeVos	$85 Million
2007-	Bob Vander Weide	Inherited

The Orlando Magic were founded in 1989 by a group led by James L. (Jimmy) Hewitt and Pat Williams, who paid the NBA expansion fee of $32.5 million. They were one of four NBA expansion teams (along with Miami, Minnesota, and Charlotte) and the first professional sports team in Orlando, Florida.

Jimmy Hewitt was a successful banking entrepreneur who founded and managed various financial institutions in Florida. "If it weren't for Jimmy Hewitt's drive, personality and perseverance, the Magic wouldn't be in Orlando," said Mike Bianchi of the Orlando Sentinel. Jimmy convinced his friend Pat Williams, who was then general manager of the Philadelphia 76ers, to help him pitch the NBA on Orlando, a city without an arena or even a modern airport at the time. Their pitch convinced the NBA to add a fourth city to its expansion plans. The Magic made the playoffs in 14 of their first 27 seasons, not bad.

Before Pat Williams turned his focus to basketball, he was a budding minor league baseball player until, as a pitcher, his arm went dead and he entered the team management side of sports, where he proved to be one of the best. During his NBA career, he took his teams to 23 playoff appearances and five NBA finals. Twelve of those years were spent as general manager of the Philadelphia 76ers, where he traded for the great Julius Erving. The 76ers won the NBA title in 1982-83.

Prior to that, Williams had brief stints as GM of the Chicago Bulls and the Atlanta Hawks. Nineteen of Williams's former players went on to be NBA head coaches. In addition to his talents in sports team management, Williams is a gifted motivational speaker and author of some 100 books. He also hosts radio shows in Orlando and has received numerous awards for his contributions to sports. Added to Williams's accomplishments in the sports arena, he has 19 children, 14 of whom were adopted.

The Magic pulled one out of the hat when they won the first pick in the 1992 NBA draft lottery and landed Shaquille O'Neal (Shaq). That's when the Magic started to roll into the winning column.

Two years after Jimmy Hewitt and Pat Williams founded the Magic, they sold the team to Amway co-founder Richard DeVos for $85 million. DeVos, who grew up in the Depression, and his childhood buddy, Jay Van Andel, formed Amway in 1959. As adventurous young men, they attempted to sail to South America in 1949 but had to be rescued near Cuba because their boat was sinking. Their first real business venture was a drive-in diner. Next, they began selling all-purpose cleaners door-to door, which eventually became Amway (for American Way), a direct-sales "pyramid-style" business from which they made a fortune. Renamed Alticor, the company now operates in nearly 100 countries around the world with sales in the $10 billion range. DeVos retired in 1993 and turned the reins over to his four children.

DeVos, a deeply religious Christian, has written several books and is a strong supporter of the Republican Party. He contributed to the 2016 presidential campaigns of Jeb Bush and Scott Walker and has been known to contribute to other conservative Republican causes. DeVos philanthropic endeavors helped revitalize the city of Grand Rapids, Michigan, the city of his birth. Likewise, he and his family have invested heavily in the Orlando's future. On the other hand, DeVos has been criticized for his outspoken stance against gay marriage. Because of this, Rolling Stone magazine listed him as one of the 15 worst owners of a major sports franchise. Fortune pegged his net worth at $5.4 billion in 2016.

The state-of-the-art Amway Center, which boasts the tallest center-hung scoreboard in the NBA, opened in 2010 and is considered one of the most advanced arenas in the world. It cost nearly $500 million to build and was financed primarily with public money that took years of haggling to get approved. The Magic had to cough up a minimum of $50 million toward the cost of the arena and agreed to pay rent of $1 million per year for 30 years. Amway bought the naming rights for 10 years for $40 million.

In 2007, Richard DeVos turned over the leadership of the Magic to his son-in-law, Bob Vander Weide, although the shares are divided evenly among Richard's children. Since Bob took over, the Magic's performance has not been stellar.

In 2017, Richard's daughter, Betsy DeVos, was nominated by President Donald Trump for the position of Education Secretary. Her appointment was narrowly approved.

NBA Finals Appearances: 2   Wins: 0
Forbes 2017 Valuation: $920 Million

Philadelphia 76ers

Former name: Syracuse Nationals

Year	Owner(s)	Purchase Price
1946-1963	Danny Biasone	$5,000
1963-1976	Irv Kosloff, Ike Richman	$500,000
1976-1981	Fitz Eugene Dixon, Jr.	$8 Million
1981-1996	Harold Katz	$12 Million
1996-2011	Comcast Spectacor	$130 Million
2011-	Joshua Harris	$280 Million

When it comes to basketball, the city of Philadelphia (and the team that bears its name) is something of an anomaly. In recent years, the franchise has been dreadful and authored some truly epic losing seasons. And for 60-odd years before that, interspersed amongst three championships (1955, 1967, 1983), the franchise history ranged from run-of-the-mill ineptitude, to nondescript losing years, to a historically bad year (in 1972-73, with a 20-game losing streak en route to the worst-ever regular season record, at the time, of 9-73), to, finally, upon returning to respectability, a series of gut-wrenching post-season failures.

But at the same time, this basketball-proud city that is the hometown of Wilt Chamberlain, Earl Monroe, and Kobe Bryant, has a franchise that, if one looks a little deeper, enjoys a long and distinguished history of teams and rosters of great players across the decades that rival any in the history of the sport -- not only Chamberlain but players like Al Cervi, Dolph Schayes, Hal Greer, Billy Cunningham, Chet Walker, Julius Erving, Moses Malone, Charles Barkley, and Allen Iverson. Hall of Famers, all.

In 1956, Daniel Biasone, born in Italy and an immigrant to America, founded and owned the Syracuse Nationals of the NBL (National Basketball League). The NBL was a Midwest-centric league with franchises in smaller markets rather than big cities. Syracuse represented the easternmost team in the league. When, three years later in 1949, the rival BAA (Basketball Association of America), which comprised more major market teams, would merge with the NBL to form the NBA (National Basketball Association) we know today, the Nationals would nonetheless remain in Syracuse under Biasone's ownership, even while other former NBL teams now in the NBA, like the Fort Wayne Pistons and Rochester Royals, would move to Detroit and Cincinnati in 1957.

Biasone was a strong advocate of quickening the pace of the game and successfully lobbied the league to institute a shot clock. According to Biasone, the pace of the game of basketball was at its best in terms of an ideal balance of defense and offense when each team attempted 60 shots. In the 48-minute professional game, then, his calculation was rather simple: 48 minutes = 2880 seconds ÷ 60 (number of shots) = 24 seconds. While Biasone did not invent the concept of the shot clock, the 24-second shot clock first instituted in the NBA in 1954, and still in use to this day, is credited to him.

Biasone would sell the team in 1963 to Irv Kosloff, who'd made his fortune as a paper merchant. Kosloff would co-own the team with his good friend from high school, attorney Ike Richman, who would become responsible for day-to-day operations while Kosloff would focus on running his Roosevelt Paper Company, one of the largest paper companies in the country. Philadelphians Kosloff and Richman would move the team to Philadelphia in 1963 with the NBA's blessing, as it had just lost its Philadelphia franchise the year before with the Warriors' move to San Francisco.

Tragically, in 1965, while attending a Sixers game against the Celtics in Boston Garden, Ike Richman suffered a heart attack and died courtside. Kosloff would eventually hire Dr. Jack Ramsay as general manager. Philadelphia born and bred, a local standout college coach at St. Joseph, Ramsay would win an NBA championship in 1967, his first year on the job.

In 1976, the year of the NBA/ABA merger, Kosloff would sell the Philadelphia 76ers to Fitz Eugene Dixon Jr. of Philadelphia's Widener family, one of the wealthiest families in America. The Wideners' first patriarch, Peter Widener, originally supplied meat to the U.S. Army during the Civil War. He would use that first fortune to invest in Philadelphia trolley cars and public transit, going on to form the Philadelphia Traction Company. He would further use his great wealth to become one of the original founders of both U.S. Steel and the American Tobacco Company, and acquire substantial holdings in Standard Oil. At the time of his death, Widener was listed as one of the hundred wealthiest Americans.

Shortly after buying the 76ers, Dixon would execute a brilliant transaction. The cash-strapped New York Nets of the ABA, upon merging with the NBA, had been assessed a $4.3 million fee for "invading" the territory of the New York Knicks -- this in addition to the standard $3.2-million expansion fee. When Dixon offered $6.6 million for the New York Nets' one superstar asset, the Nets owner, Roy Boe, made the deal. And that is how the "Doctor" made his first house call in Philadelphia. Julius "Doctor J" Erving's arrival would augur an immediate reversal of the team's recent bad fortunes by leading them all the way to the 1977 NBA finals, where the Sixers would jump out to a 2-0 lead before dropping four straight to Bill Walton's Portland Trailblazers (coached by Dr. Jack Ramsay) in a classic NBA finals series.

Dixon would in 1981 sell the team to another Philadelphian, Harold Katz, the creator and founder of Nutri/System, which he built into 700 owned and franchised centers nationwide. When Katz sold Nutri/System in 1986, it was the largest medically supervised weight control company in the world. The Philadelphia 76ers' last (and most recent) championship was in 1983 under Katz's ownership.

In 1966, Edward Snider (a six-percent minority partner of Jerry Wollman, who owned the Philadelphia Eagles), upon learning that Philadelphia was to be awarded an NHL expansion team, put into action a plan to build a new sports arena, which would house both the new hockey team (the Philadelphia Flyers) as well as the 76ers. As owner of both the Philadelphia Flyers and the Philadelphia Spectrum, Snider created a holding company called Spectacor to run both. In 1996, Snider would sell a 66-percent stake in Spectacor to Comcast, creating Comcast Spectacor. Spectacor would in turn partner with the Philadelphia Phillies to form Comcast SportsNet. Comcast Spectacor would also purchase the Philadelphia 76ers from Harold Katz. Snider knew the team well as it had been his tenant at the Philadelphia Spectrum since 1971.

After the '83 championship, the Philadelphia 76ers would enter an extended losing period -- for the rest of Katz's tenure through the Comcast Spectacor years to the present ownership of Joshua Harris, a private equity investor and co-founder of Apollo Global Management, one of the world's largest alternative investment firms, whose personal net worth is estimated to be $2.5 billion.

It has been a unique period in that during this 34-year championship drought, the 76ers have experienced two distinctly exciting eras with singularly gifted talents at the fore, each undersized for the position he played and oversized in every other aspect -- their game, their personality, and their charisma. For eight seasons (1984-1992), "Sir" Charles Barkley, the "Mound of Round," was pretty much a force of nature -- a power forward playing so much bigger than his 6-foot, 4-inch height would suggest. Incredibly popular if not always politic, Barkley's teams were consistently competitive in the post-season but could never make it all the way.

After he was traded to Phoenix, the 76ers would descend into a four-year abyss not so affectionately referred to as "The Dark Ages" by 76ers fans. And then the second era would begin, with the arrival of a barely six-foot-tall guard from Georgetown University. Allen "The Answer" Iverson played both point and shooting guard and for the 10 years he was in Philadelphia (1996-2006) he pretty much owned the fans and city, although, like Barkley, was unable to deliver a championship.

Despite not having the championship pedigree of some other teams, the Philadelphia 76ers are as embedded in the history of the league as any team.

NBA Finals Appearances: 9   Wins: 3
Forbes 2017 Valuation: $800 Million

Phoenix Suns

Year	Owner(s)	Purchase Price
1968-1987	Richard Bloch	$2 Million
1987-2004	Jerry Colangelo	$44.5 Million
2004-	Robert Sarver	$401 Million

Richard Bloch, even by the standards of fellow team owners in professional sports, was particularly forward thinking in addition to being something of a renaissance man. Starting out in real estate development in California and Arizona, Bloch's interests and accomplishments would stretch from developing and owning the iconic Gulf + Western skyscraper in New York City, to a Hyatt Hotel in Los Angeles, to media, politics, financial services, entertainment, philanthropy, and arts patronage. Oh, and for a time, professional sports -- Bloch was the original owner of the Phoenix Suns.

A combat veteran of the Korean War, Bloch would build his first fortune in real estate development and construction on both coasts (New York City and Los Angeles) before leaving perhaps his biggest footprint in the American Southwest, owning one television station in Tucson and two others in Santa Fe, New Mexico. Known to be a close friend of Bill Clinton, Bloch has also been a major donor to the Democratic Party for decades. Formerly the CEO of Filmways, a film and television production company best known for classic "rural television comedies" like "The Beverly Hillbillies," "Petticoat Junction," and "Green Acres," Bloch's commitment to and support of the performing arts is both broad and diverse. Over the years, Bloch has sat on the boards of trustees of prestigious performing arts institutions such as the American Ballet Theater, La Jolla Theater, and American Film Institute.

A somewhat star-crossed franchise, the Phoenix Suns have the highest all-time win-loss percentage of any team that has never won an NBA championship. Things did not get off to a good start prior to the 1968-69 season for the expansion Suns who lost the coin flip for the rights to draft Lew Alcindor of UCLA (later known as Kareem Abdul-Jabbar) to the other expansion team that year, the Milwaukee Bucks. The man who lost that toss for the Phoenix Suns, GM Jerry Colangelo, is the continuous thread running through the history of the Phoenix Suns and indeed professional sports in Phoenix (and the entire state of Arizona).

Credit Richard Bloch's eye for talent and the future in hiring a then 28-year-old Colangelo from the Chicago Bulls' marketing and scouting departments to become the youngest GM in the history of the NBA. He would go on to one of the most esteemed and distinguished careers as a sports executive and businessman in American sports over the next 50-odd years (including earning *four* NBA Executive of the Year awards).

Coming a long way from his arrival in Phoenix with his young family and $200 in his pocket, Colangelo would eventually become the owner of the Phoenix Suns and bring major league baseball to Arizona as founder and owner of the Arizona Diamondbacks. He was also instrumental in bringing the Winnipeg Jets of the NHL to Phoenix as the Phoenix Coyotes (later renamed the Arizona Coyotes). Colangelo would always field competitive teams, playing an exciting up-tempo brand of basketball. With no shortage of centerpiece superstars over the years such as Charles Barkley, Kevin Johnson, and Steve Nash, the Phoenix Suns reached the NBA finals twice but could never cash in.

Colangelo would head a group that would acquire the Phoenix Suns from Bloch in 1987 but ultimately find no better luck in securing a championship despite deep playoff runs and conference title losses. With various other sports endeavors on the horizon, Colangelo would in 2004 sell the Suns to Arizona native Robert Sarver.

Born to a Jewish family in Tucson, Robert founded the National Bank of Tucson. He expanded it statewide into the National Bank of

Arizona, the largest independent bank in Arizona, then sold it in 1994 to Zions Bancorporation. Colangelo has had the second longest-running tenure leading the same NBA franchise, behind Red Auerbach of the Boston Celtics. In 2005, Colangelo accepted the position of director of USA Basketball, his teams winning the Gold Medal in the 2008 Olympic Summer Games in Beijing and the 2012 Olympic Summer Games in London.

Colangelo returned to the NBA in 2015 as the chairman of basketball operations for the Philadelphia 76ers before stepping back shortly thereafter and hiring his son, Bryan, as president of operations. Bryan had worked for his father in a similar capacity with the Phoenix Suns. Colangelo is affiliated with the 76ers as an "advisor."

NBA Finals Appearances: 2   Wins: 0
Forbes 2017 Valuation: $1.1 Billion

Portland Trail Blazers

Year	Owner(s)	Purchase Price
1970-1975	Herman Sarkowsky	$3.7 Million
1975-1988	Larry Weinberg	Unknown
1988-	Paul Allen	$70 Million

Harry Glickman, a journalist by trade and sports entrepreneur, was awarded the NBA Portland franchise subject to raising the funds necessary to satisfy the NBA expansion committee. Glickman, in very short time, spearheaded the formation of a syndicate headed by Herman Sarkowsky, and included real estate developers Larry Weinberg and Robert Schmertz. The group put up the NBA expansion fee of $3.7 million and the Portland Trail Blazers were born. Glickman, although not an owner, served as the team's president for 1987 to 1994.

Herman Sarkowski, who also co-founded the Seattle Seahawks, was born to a Jewish family in Germany in 1925. When Hitler came to power in 1934, the family immigrated to America and settled in Seattle. After serving in the U. S. Army during World War II, Sarkowski graduated from the University of Washington and began his business career as a real estate developer. He founded United Homes Corporation in the '60s, which became the largest homebuilder in the Northwest.

Sarkowski became president and managing partner of the Trail Blazers and, two years after their founding, increased his ownership stake when he bought-out Schmertz who had to sell to be eligible to buy the Boston Celtics in 1972. In 1975, Sarkowski, whose heart was in Seattle and needed to focus on the Seattle Seahawks, sold his share of the team to Larry Weinberg for an unknown amount.

Sarkowski, a prominent businessman, civic leader and philanthropist, went on to make a name for himself as a breeder who had great success in the horse racing world, winning a 1993 Breeder's Cup competition. He bought his first horse in 1960 and now owns a collection of some 50 thoroughbreds.

Two years after Sarkowski sold the Trail Blazers to Weinberg, they won the NBA championship behind the play of former UCLA star Bill Walton. Weinberg was born in 1926 to a Jewish family in New York City. During World War II, he served in the infantry and was seriously wounded in France where he had to spend a year recovering in a military hospital. He attended Cornell, the University of Arizona, and UCLA. In 1948, he formed the Larwin Company, a real estate concern that became one of the largest home building companies in the country. It merged with CNA Financial and Weinberg served on their board of directors from 1969 to 1980.

In 1988, Larry sold the Blazers to Microsoft co-founder Paul Allen for $70 million. In 1992, Weinberg was honored by the Trail Blazers with the retirement of the Trailblazers' jersey #1, which bore his name.

Paul Allen is one of the wealthiest men in the world. He was born in Seattle and went to the same private school (Lakeside) as Bill Gates, who was three years younger. As young men, both were mesmerized by computers and their potential. Paul Allen went to Washington State University but dropped out after two years to take a job as a computer programmer with Honeywell in Boston. Living in Boston, near Gates at Harvard, he convinced Gates to drop out of Harvard to launch Microsoft in 1975. It was Allen who came up with the name "Micro-soft." Seven years later, Allen left Microsoft when he was diagnosed with Hodgkin's disease, a form of cancer. He beat the cancer using radiation therapy. Much has been said about Allen's genius, his business savvy, and his extensive philanthropic endeavors.

Since he acquired the Trail Blazers in 1988, he spearheaded and financed the development of the Moda Center where the team plays. During his ownership, the Trail Blazers reached the playoffs 19 times, making the finals twice, but without a win. Allen also bought the Seattle Seahawks in 1997 (ostensibly to keep them in Seattle) for $288 million, and he owns an interest in Major League Soccer's Seattle Sounders, one of the most valuable teams in the league.

As a two-time cancer survivor, Paul Allen began living large, buying an enormous yacht on which he throws a lavish party during the Cannes Film Festival. He is also an accomplished musician (guitar) and plays in a band, The Underthinkers, which is said to be quite impressive with Allen performing.

In 2016, Forbes ranked Allen the 40th richest person in the world with a net worth just shy of $19 billion.

NBA Finals Appearances: 3   Wins: 1
Forbes 2017 Valuation: $1.05 Billion

Sacramento Kings

Former names: Rochester Royals 1946-1957; Cincinnati Royals 1957-1972; Kansas City Kings 1972-1985

Year	Owner(s)	Purchase Price
1946-1958	Jack and Lester Harrison	$25,000
1958-1966	Thomas Woods	Unknown
1966-1973	Max and Jeremy Jacobs	Unknown
1973-1982	10 Kansas City Businessmen	Unknown
1983-1992	Joseph Benvenuti, Frank and Gregg Lukenbill, and partners	$10.5 Million
1992-1998	Jim Thomas	$140 Million
1998-2013	Joe and Gavin Maloof	
2013-	Vivek Ranadive	$545 Million

The Sacramento Kings franchise is the oldest in the NBA. It has also been the most nomadic. They started in 1923 as a semi-pro team, the Rochester Seagrams. (For extra money, men played basketball part-time, often for the companies for which they worked.) The Seagrams joined the NBL (National Basketball League) in 1945 as the Rochester Royals and jumped over to the BAA (Basketball Association of America) in 1948. The BAA then merged with the NBL in 1949 to form the NBA.

Jack and Lester (Les) Harrison paid $25,000 for the team in 1945. Jack managed the business while Les coached the team. That year they won the NBL championship thanks to a team that included Naismith NBA Hall of Famer Bob Davies; Cleveland Browns star quarterback Otto Graham, and actor Chuck Connors, who went on to star in the popular TV series, "The Rifleman," a more lucrative career than football could ever be in those days.

Les Harrison was a legend in the NBA. As a coach, he had a .620 win-rate and was elected into the 1980 Hall of Fame in the same year as

Oscar Robertson, Jerry West, and Jerry Lucas. He helped break the color barrier by signing African-American Dolly King in 1946, and he helped institute the 24-second clock for the 1954-55 season.

The original NBA boasted 17 teams but by the 1953-54 season there were only nine teams still alive: the N.Y. Knicks, Boston Celtics, Philadelphia Warriors, Fort Wayne Pistons, Minneapolis Lakers, Milwaukee Hawks, Baltimore Bullets, and the Syracuse Nationals. Interesting to note: today, only two of those teams (Knicks and Celtics) remain in their original city. Pro basketball was in its infancy stage. Capturing and keeping fans was no cinch and most teams struggled for financial survival. In those days, college basketball was, pardon the pun, "king."

In 1957, due to tight finances, the team was moved to Cincinnati and re-named the Royals. In 1958, the team was sold to Thomas Woods for an unknown amount. Little information can be found about Woods other than that he died in 1961, and the team ownership went to his estate. During his ownership time, another new league was launched, the ABL (American Basketball League), which was started by none other than Abe Saperstein, founder, owner, and coach of the Harlem Globetrotters for 39 years.

Abe was a good athlete, playing baseball, basketball, and track in high school. Regardless, at a height of only five feet-plus, Abe's playing days were as short as he was. He was a better promoter than player. Many of his players were from Chicago but he called them the Harlem Globetrotters because he wanted it known the players were black, and that they travelled the world. He created a circus atmosphere to the game and had the talented players to make it entertaining. Who can forget Meadowlark Lemon, Goose Tatum, and Marcus Haines for the incredible moves they could make with the ball? Underneath it all, those black players, prostituting themselves as clowns, knew damned well that given the chance they could beat any team in the NBA.

By the late '40s, the Globetrotters were unbeatable and Saperstein got his chance to prove it. In February 1948, he and Max Winter, owner of the Minneapolis Lakers, orchestrated a game with the NBA's best team, which turned out to be Max's Lakers with star George Mikan. The game was played under the tense atmosphere of strong racial divide in Chicago. The crowd was huge. On a last second shot, the Globetrotters won by two points.

That game loosened the black-white divide and opened the door for African Americans to enter the NBA. In 1950, Chuck Cooper became the first black player to be drafted by the NBA, one year after Jackie Robinson broke the color barrier in baseball.

Abe Saperstein felt betrayed by the NBA. He had helped the NBA gain attendance by playing his Globetrotters in NBA doubleheaders to help the financially struggling teams. The NBA led him to believe he would be awarded a franchise in Los Angeles, but Laker owner Max Winter moved his team to L.A., trumping Abe's expectation.

That's when Abe decided to form his own league, the American Basketball League (ABL). The ABL went and signed players that otherwise would have gone to the Royals, namely Jerry Lucas and Larry Siegfried. A co-conspirator in the ABL was the infamous George Steinbrenner, who owned the Cleveland Pipers, an AAU (Amateur Athletic Union) team. George, a not-to-be-denied competitor, went and signed Jerry Lucas for a record $40,000 contract, snagging him from the Royals and the NBA. Behind Abe's back, Steinbrenner, who now had Lucas in his stable, was in secret talks with then NBA commissioner, Maurice Podoloff, to merge his Pipers with the Kansas City Steers of the NBA.

It all went for naught as the ABL played only one complete season and folded its tent for good in 1962. The only remnant was the three-point shot, which would re-surface when the ABA started a few years later. Abe Saperstein was inducted into the Naismith NBA Hall of Fame and will go down as one of the most influential men in the history of professional basketball.

In 1966, the Royals were bought from the Thomas Woods estate by Max and Jeremy Jacobs for an unknown amount. They moved the Royals to Kansas City and in 1973 sold the team to a group of 10 Kansas City businessmen, and they were renamed the Kings. There they remained until a group from Sacramento, led by Joseph Benvenuti and Gregg and Frank Lukenbill, real estate developers, purchased the team for $10.5 million in 1983, then moved it to Sacramento in 1985.

In 1992, the team was again sold, to a group led by Jim Thomas. They reportedly paid $140 million for 53 percent of the team and the ARCO arena. Jim, a Los Angeles real estate developer, pleaded with the city for a new arena but was turned down again and again. The best he could do was get a $70 million loan from the city to keep the team afloat while negotiations for a new arena continued. A minority investor, the Maloof Family of Albuquerque and Las Vegas, had an option to buy controlling interest and did so in 1998, buying Jim's interest for $156 million. (It included the ARCO arena).

The Maloof brothers, Joe and Gavin, are of Lebanese descent. In the 14-years they owned the team, they fought the city tooth and nail for help in financing a new arena. Despite that discord, the team performed well during their ownership, making the playoffs seven times and boasting five consecutive 50-win seasons.

The Maloof family started building its fortune in New Mexico in 1937 by distributing Coor's Beer in the southwest, founding a distribution empire. In 1994, the Maloofs expanded their holdings by opening the Fiesta Hotel and Casino in Las Vegas. They sold it in 2000 and tried to press their gain by developing the Las Vegas Palms Hotel & Casino and Palms Towers, but got in over their heads and had to sell their distribution business to satisfy their debt obligations. The Palms has never quite taken off as the Maloofs had envisioned.

In 2013, the Maloofs sold their 65-percent ownership of the team for $347 million (valuing the team at $545 million) to a Sacramento group led by Vivek Ranadive. Prior to that, an agreement to purchase the team was reached with Steve Ballmer (Microsoft) whose intention was to move the team to Seattle. The NBA nixed that relocation deal and approved the Ranadive sale because he agreed to build a new arena in downtown Sacramento.

The Maloofs had owned the Houston Rockets (1979-1982) during which time (1981) they won the NBA championship. During their ownership of the Kings, they ventured into the entertainment business, producing music and shows for television and movies. In 2008, they created the Maloof Money Cup, a skateboarding competition.

Vivek Ranadive, born in Mumbai, India, was the first person of Indian descent to own an American professional sports team. It wasn't the Kings. He had become a co-owner of the Golden State Warriors in 2010 but, to purchase the Kings under NBA rules, he had to sell his interest in the Warriors.

When Vivek left India at age 16, he landed in Boston with $100 in his pocket. He earned a master's degree in electrical engineering at M.I.T. and an MBA from Harvard. Vivek built his fortune developing computer software. In 1985, Teknekron Software Systems gave him $250,000 in seed money to develop innovative software for the financial industry. His work was brilliant and he is credited with helping to "digitize" Wall Street in the late '80s. In 1997, he formed TIBCO Software Systems, which he grew to nearly $1 billion in revenues by 2011. In 2014, the company, having gone public, was sold to Vista Equity Partners for $4.3 billion. Vivek has written three successful business-oriented books and has earned a black belt in Tae Kwon Do.

As brilliant and successful as Vivek was in the tech world, his tactics with the team have been a dismal failure. He has alienated his players, fired numerous coaches, made some dumb trades and, to make matters worse, has his minority owners wanting to impeach him. (He once suggested at 4 on 5 defense with a "cherry-picker" perched under the basket). But he did bring a state-of-the-art arena to Sacramento.

The Kings remain one of the most dysfunctional teams in the NBA. Vivek Ranadive might need his black belt if things don't turn around for the nomadic Kings pretty soon.

NBA Finals Appearances: 1   Wins: 0
Forbes 2017 Valuation: $1.075 Billion

San Antonio Spurs

Former names: Dallas Chaparrals; Texas Chaparrals

Year	Owner(s)	Purchase Price
1967-	John Klug and James Peters	$30,000
1967-1973	Robert Folsom, James Embrey, David Bruton, Jr, Joseph Geary, Graham R.E. Koch, Lawrence Pollock, Jr.	NA
1973-1988	B.J. "Red" McCombs, Angelo Drossos, John Schaeffer, Art Burdick	$1.6 Million
1988-1993	B.J. "Red" McCombs	$47 Million
1993-	Peter M. Holt	$75 Million

Not only is San Antonio the smallest pro sports town in Texas, where Dallas and Houston between them have the Big Three pro sports covered, San Antonio only has the one -- basketball. Every February the Spurs are forced to take an extended road trip because their home arena, the AT&T Center, hosts the San Antonio Stock Show & Rodeo. When they have victory parades, the players are loaded onto boats for a trip down the river alongside the San Antonio River Walk. But there is absolutely nothing provincial about the San Antonio Spurs when they step onto the court.

The San Antonio Spurs are an elite franchise: fourth all-time in NBA championships; first in winning percentage among active NBA franchises; a head-to-head regular season winning percentage against every active NBA franchise; the most consecutive 50-plus win seasons in NBA history (17 and counting), and have made the playoffs in 24 of the last 25 seasons -- quite a resume for one of the original 11 ABA franchises and one of the four ABA teams to merge with the NBA in 1976. As for the other three -- the Denver Nuggets, Brooklyn Nets, and Indiana Pacers -- their next NBA championship will be their first NBA championship. By any metric, one would be hard-pressed not to consider the San Antonio Spurs as the model franchise of the NBA.

Founded in 1967 as a charter franchise of the ABA, the Dallas Chaparrals never quite took hold in Dallas. After purchasing the team, John Klug and James Peters quickly sold it again that same year to a group of wealthy Dallas businessmen comprising Robert Folsom, James Embrey, David Bruton, Jr, Joseph Geary, Graham R.E. Koch, and Lawrence Pollock, Jr. Although their aggregate worth has been estimated to be in the

$750 million range, the group was loath to put a lot of money into the Chaparrals. Almost immediately, the team was plagued by low attendance as well as meager fan interest and media coverage. Within the first three years, the ownership group would attempt to disengage from Dallas-centrism by rebranding as the Texas Chaparrals and playing home games in both Fort Worth and Lubbock to become a more regional franchise.

It did not work and they would return to Dallas full-time before the '71-72 season. Billy Joe "Red" McCombs, a Texas billionaire -- he'd made his fortune in car dealerships, energy, and media (he was one of the founders of Clear Channel Communications), had been keeping an eye on the struggling Dallas franchise from its inception. Anxious to bring a pro sports franchise to San Antonio to raise the city's profile and cache, McCombs was receptive when he received the phone call from the desperate Dallas ownership group looking to sell. McCombs enlisted his good friend and former employee, Angelo Drossos, and together they negotiated a "lend-lease" agreement, the terms of which stipulated that within three years they would either return the team from San Antonio back to Dallas or purchase it outright. In what may well be the slickest negotiation and transaction in the history of pro sports ownership, McCombs and Drossos paid exactly $1 for the "lend-lease."

At first renaming them the San Antonio Gunslingers, McCombs and Drossos quickly thought better of it and settled on the "Spurs" before the first game. In that debut season in San Antonio, the Spurs averaged 6,303 fans, surpassing the Chaparrals' season total in just 18 games. A key acquisition was the offensive juggernaut George "The Iceman" Gervin, assuring the Spurs the requisite superstar around which to build a team. McCombs and Drossos tore up the "lend-lease" agreement after season one and bought the team outright, taking up permanent residence in San Antonio. Although never winning a championship, the San Antonio Spurs became an ABA powerhouse in very short order.

From the merger of 1976 (when they paid a $3.2 million NBA entry fee) through the 1980s, McCombs and Drossos' San Antonio Spurs would be a competitive and representative team, making the post season several times while also having their fair share of down years -- especially after trading George Gervin after the '84-85 season. In what would prove to be the first of two distinct watershed years, the '89-90 season marked an upward trajectory for the franchise. First, Red McCombs bought out Angelo Drossos and assumed full control. Second, their number-one draft pick of 1987, David "The Admiral" Robinson, having fulfilled his commitment to the United States Navy, came aboard. The San Antonio Spurs' 1989 season affected the single biggest one-season turnaround in NBA history (at the time), going from a record of 21-61 to 56-26, with Robinson being selected the unanimous NBA Rookie of the Year.

The early 1990s would see the Spurs continually make the playoffs only to come up short in later rounds. After acquiring sole ownership of the team, Red McCombs would hire and fire five head coaches: Larry Brown, Bob Bass, Jerry Tarkanian, Rex Hughes, and John Lucas, before selling the team in 1993 to local businessman Peter M. Holt. Under the leadership of Peter Holt upstairs and Coach Popovich on the sidelines, the San Antonio Spurs show no signs of relinquishing their position of eminence anytime soon and will happily continue to vacate the AT&T Arena every February for the Stock Show and Rodeo and float down the River Walk for their victory parades.

In March 2016, Peter M. Holt announced that he was stepping down as chairman and CEO and that his wife, Julianne Holt, would be assuming those duties.

NBA Finals Appearances: 6   Wins: 5
Forbes 2017 Valuation: $1.18 Billion

Toronto Raptors

Year	Owner(s)	Purchase Price
1995	John Bitove/A.Slaight	$125 Million
1996-1998	Allan Slaight	$65 Million
1998-	Maple Leaf S&E, Ltd.	$179 Million

When James Naismith first wrote the rulebook for basketball in 1901, there were only 13 rules written in 600 words. Today, there are more than 30,000 words in the rulebook. Because basketball was invented in America (Springfield, MA) many assume the inventor of the game was American but Naismith was born in Ontario, Canada, in 1861. Orphaned at age nine, he was raised by his aunt and uncle and obtained a degree in Physical Education (PE) from McGill University in Montreal where he taught until going to Springfield to teach at the YMCA International Training College in 1890. His assignment was to create a physical indoor game to provide exercise and competition for students during those long cold winter months. His game used a soccer ball; there were nine players on each side, there was no such thing as a dribble, there was a "jump-ball" after each basket, there were 13 basic rules and peach baskets at both ends of the court. Naismith named it "Basket-Ball."

In 1898, he earned a medical degree from the University of Colorado. That same year, Dr. Naismith was hired by the University of Kansa to teach PE, coach basketball, and serve as chaplain. Naismith brought basketball to Kansas with him. Basketball is just as ingrained in

Kansas's roots as is corn and it's no wonder the University of Kansas Jayhawks always have successful teams, often making the Final Four in the NCAA tournament.

In 1915, Naismith became a Presbyterian minister. In 1936, he was invited to Hitler's 1936 Olympics, the first year that basketball was played, to present the winning medals: Gold to USA; Silver to Canada, and Bronze to Mexico. It was there he was named Honorary President of the International Basketball Federation. Naismith lived to see the first NIT and NCAA tournaments before his death in 1939. He was the first member of the Naismith Memorial Hall of Fame, founded in Springfield where he invented the game.

In the mid-'90s, when the NBA decided to expand to Canada, they chose Toronto and Vancouver as their expansion cities. The Toronto Raptors were founded by two successful Canadian businessmen, John Bitove and Allan Slaight, each owning 44 percent, with the Bank of Nova Scotia owning 10 percent, and two minor investors with 1 percent each. In 1995, they paid the NBA expansion fee of $125 million. Bitove, a restaurateur who made his big money in wireless communications, was the person responsible for spearheading the development of a new arena, the Air Canada Center (ACC) in downtown Toronto. Allan Slaight, who could have been named Allan "Sleight" for his incredible sleight-of-hand talent as a young magician, made his fortune in broadcasting. Their first order of business was to hire former Detroit Piston star, Isiah Thomas, as general manager. Part of Isiah's deal included an option to purchase a share of ownership. In 1995, Thomas bought 9 percent, 4.5 percent from Bitove and 4.5 percent from Slaight.

When Bitove and Slaight bought the Raptors, they must have sensed a latent dislike for one another because their shareholder's agreement included an option, a shotgun clause, to buy out the other. And that's exactly what happened in 1996. Allan Slaight went out on a financial limb and bought John Bitove's share for $65 million.

Their shotgun clause was triggered by Slaight because they disagreed about where the Raptors should play. Bitove wanted the Raptors to have an arena dedicated solely to basketball. Slaight, who felt two arenas was overkill, wanted to share the expenses of the new arena being constructed for the Toronto Maple Leafs hockey team.

Isiah Thomas wanted to gain majority control of the Raptors but when he and his group couldn't meet Slaight's $88 million price tag, he up and quit. Perhaps that was a good thing for the Raptors as Thomas eventually went on to the Knicks where, as GM, he made decisions that helped keep the team mediocre, at best.

Unlike in the USA, betting on NBA games was legal in Canada, as it was and is in many other British Commonwealth countries. But it nearly cost the Raptors their franchise when the NBA put its foot down. However, the Raptors agreed to compensate the provincial lottery corporation for its lost revenues. Hence, future bets on the Raptors were "off the board." To this day, the Raptors continue to pay the lottery corporation $1 million annually.

In 1998, Slaight and the Bank of Nova Scotia decided it was time to get out and sold the Raptors and the Air Canada Center to Maple Leaf Sports & Entertainment, Ltd (MLSE) for $467 million, $179 million for the team and $288 million for the arena. MLSE also owns the NHL's Toronto Maple Leafs and the Major League Soccer team, Toronto FC, as well as several minor and junior league teams.

The fans in Toronto are as avid as any. In 2015-16, the Raptors won a record 57 games and, for the first time, made it to the Eastern Conference Finals, losing to LeBron James's Cavaliers in six games. In 2017, they reached the playoffs again, but were swept by the Cavaliers.

NBA Finals Appearances: 0
Forbes 2017 Valuation: $1.13 Billion

Utah Jazz

Former name: New Orleans Jazz

Year	Owner(s)	Purchase Price
1974-1985	Sam Battistone	$6.15 Million
1985-1986	Sam Battistone and Larry Miller	$8 Million
1986-2009	Larry Miller	$14 Million
2009-2015	Greg Miller	Inherited
2015-	Gail Miller	Inherited

Regarding the history of the Utah Jazz, there is a definite "if only…." quality that permeates the franchise. But let's start at the beginning. If you think about it, jazz has about as much to do with Salt Lake City as, say, lakes do with Los Angeles, but there you have it. The Utah Jazz are one of those teams who have retained their original name, which was perfectly logical from whence they came, but has no connection to where they presently reside. As, for example, "Lakers" having everything to do with Minnesota and nothing to do with Los Angeles, so too, "Jazz" has everything to do with New Orleans and nothing to do with Salt Lake City.

They are also one of those basketball teams whose resume and history would be completely different if not for one Michael Jordan, and his Chicago Bulls in their dynastic heyday. Consider that with Karl Malone and John Stockton in their respective primes, one of the greatest power forward-point guard combinations in NBA history, and playing under head coach Jerry Sloane, another all-time great NBA coach, the Utah Jazz might well have won back-to-back NBA championships in 1997 and 1998 and be viewed by history in a much better light ... but Michael Jordan was always in their way.

Sam Battistone, Jr., whose father founded the Sambo's restaurant chain, was the principal owner in the group that founded the New Orleans Jazz in 1974. As is the case with most expansion teams, the New Orleans Jazz experienced losing seasons and long-term mediocrity while also dealing with venue issues, playing in Municipal Auditorium and then Loyola Field House and finally in the New Orleans Superdome -- all within their first four years of existence. But lack of a permanent and suitable facility pales in comparison to two trades that would haunt the franchise forever. As in judging all trades, the benefit of 20/20 hindsight must always be considered.

Right away, the Jazz acquired "Pistol" Pete Maravich from the Atlanta Hawks for two first-round picks, three second-round picks, and one third-round pick over the next three years. An exorbitant price to be sure but given that Maravich had started at LSU and was one the flashiest ball handlers and most prolific scorers in the history of college basketball, a not unreasonable price. Had he not developed chronically bad knees that would shorten his career, the trade might well have been worth the price.

The second trade, though, is far less defensible. In 1977, the New Orleans Jazz traded three first-round picks for Los Angeles Laker guard Gail Goodrich -- a great player, no doubt, but aging and becoming gradually, and then increasingly, ineffective. The ramifications of the trade are mindboggling: had the New Orleans Jazz never made that trade and retained their picks, they would have acquired both Magic Johnson *and* Moses Malone.

By 1979, with the team struggling financially and with no relief in sight, Battistone relocated the Jazz to Salt Lake City. Despite being the smallest market in the NBA, the Jazz did indeed fit in Utah, and found a home. Battistone would sell a 50-percent interest in the team in 1985 to Utah luminary, Larry Miller, a businessman and philanthropist. Miller made his first fortune selling cars -- he would eventually own 54 automotive dealerships throughout the western United States. He also owned a variety of other businesses as well. One year later, Miller would buy the rest of the Jazz and become sole owner.

Upon Miller's death in 2009, his son Greg Miller took over as CEO and would run the team until stepping down in 2015. Greg's mother, Gail Miller, remains the owner of the team. The record will show that the New Orleans Jazz have zero championships. If only... Pete Maravich had stayed healthy and become *the* player he was destined to be. If only... they'd not made the Goodrich trade and ended up with Magic Johnson and Moses Malone. If only… Michael Jordan had decided to try his hand at baseball a few years earlier.

NBA Finals Appearances: 2   Wins: 0
Forbes 2017 Valuation: $910 Million

Washington Wizards

Former names: Chicago Packers 1961-1962; Chicago Zephys 1962-1963; Baltimore Bullets 1963-1973; Capitol Bullets 1973-1974; Washington Bullets 1974-1995.

Year	Owner(s)	Purchase Price
1961-1964	Dave Trager	$250,000
1964-2009	Abe Pollin	$1.1 Million
2009-2010	Irene Pollin	Inherited
2010-	Ted Leonsis	$551 Million

In 1938, a pilot flew from Long Beach, California, to New York City, filed his flight plan back to Long Beach, took off on a cloudy day, and ended up landing in Ireland 28 hours later -- and was thereafter known as "Wrong Way Corrigan." And if basketball teams were permitted to have patron saints, he would surely be looking down on the Washington Wizards.

The first expansion team of the modern NBA (in 1961), the Washington Wizards are a perfectly credible franchise: they had one NBA championship (out of four NBA Finals); made the playoffs 12 consecutive years (1968 to 1980); were the only team to appear in four NBA Finals in the 1970s, and since then have been never all that bad and never all that good, comparable to any number of other teams in the NBA. Yet, there is something about the Wizards franchise that has always been a little off-kilter.

In 1961, Chicago sportsman and businessman Dave Trager, president of Associated Life Insurance, headed a small group of six local businessmen and was awarded an NBA expansion team. Because their home arena, the International Amphitheater, was in the meatpacking district and located right next door to the famed Union Stock Yards, Trager chose for his team's name the Chicago Packers. This did not go over too well with Chicago's sports fans, who loved their Cubs, White Sox,

Blackhawks, and especially, their Bears. Realizing a name change was desperately needed, Trager came up with one: the Chicago Zephyrs, which was certainly an improvement except that nobody knew what a Zephyr was. (In a nod to the city's nickname of the "Windy City," zephyr is a light breeze). Rather than trying to come up with a third name, Trager moved his team to Baltimore instead. The Bullets had been an old BAA franchise and were in the NBA for a few seasons in the 1950s before folding. One year later, in 1964, Trager would sell the Baltimore Bullets to local construction contractor and real estate developer Abe Pollin, who owned the team for the next 46 years, becoming the NBA's longest-tenured owner at the time of his death in 2009.

On the court, the team would in two successive years, using two number-two picks in the first round, select Earl Monroe (1967) and then Wes Unseld (1968) to form the nucleus of what would be a truly great team in the 1970s. The five divisional playoff series between the Baltimore Bullets and New York Knickerbockers of those early-mid 1970s are remembered for the great individual match-up battles between Wes Unseld and Willis Reed; Earl Monroe and Walt Frazier; Dave Debusschere and Gus Johnson; Bill Bradley and Jack Marin, and Dick Barnett and Kevin Loughery. All hard-fought and bruising affairs against evenly matched opponents; the Bullets would win only once.

The 1970s represent the good days of the Baltimore Bullets -- four finals appearances, a loss to Abdul-Jabbar and Oscar Robertson's Milwaukee Bucks (1971), a loss to the Golden State Warriors (1975), a title win over the Seattle SuperSonics (1978), and a loss to the Seattle SuperSonics (1979).

But that is now well over 40 years ago and the team that would become the Capital Bullets, then the Washington Bullets, then Washington Wizards playing in the Capital Center in Landover, Maryland, and then in the Verizon Center in downtown Washington (in that city's Chinatown neighborhood), has taken one misstep after another to a point that, if not humorous, is comical.

It would, in 1995, finally occur to Abe Pollin, after spending 31 years in two cities with among the highest violent crime and homicide rates in the country (Baltimore and Washington, D.C.), that maybe Bullets was an indelicate nickname for his team. Curiously, Pollin's ineptitude in picking a team nickname would rival his predecessor's. Both Baltimore and Washington, D.C., cities more southern than northern, with large African-American communities, did not embrace "Wizards" (which is a rank in the Ku Klux Klan) warmly or with much enthusiasm.

And there is the visual of having the tallest player ever (Manute Bol) on the same roster with the shortest player ever (Muggsy Bogues); bringing in a line of high-priced superstars well past their prime and mostly shot (Spencer Haywood, Bernard King, Moses Malone, for example); and sullying the reputation of the greatest basketball player ever -- Pollin would unceremoniously fire Michael Jordan. This one, though, does have extenuating circumstances. While Jordan was a bad general manager, he would, upon divesting himself of his ownership stake and returning as a player at age 38 (thicker, slower and oft-injured), in 2001 average 25 points, five assists, and five rebounds in the first half of the 2001 season before getting hurt and shutting it down ... only to return the following year to play in all 82 games and average 20 points, seven rebounds, four assists, and two steals while averaging 37 minutes per game. Their parting of ways could and should have been handled in a more dignified and graceful manner.

Levity aside, Abe Pollin was one of the most respected and highly regarded owners in the NBA -- not only for the length of his stewardship of his franchise but for building two of the greatest state-of-the-art (at the time) basketball arenas: the Capitol Center and later the Verizon Center. He was known too for owning the Washington Capitals of the NHL, and for his extensive philanthropic endeavors. After he died, his Washington Sports & Entertainment, Limited Partnership passed to his wife, Irene. A year later, she would sell to long-time minority owner Ted Leonsis.

Early in his career, Leonsis owned the Redgate Communications Corporation, which in 1994 was acquired by AOL, where he would become a senior executive before founding Revolution Growth Fund. The CEO of Monumental Sports and Entertainment, Leonsis was now the owner of the former assets of Abe Pollin: the Washington Wizards, the Washington Capitols, and the Verizon Center, among others. Known to be accessible to fans through his website and email, etc., upon taking over Leonsis wrote a manifesto of 101 changes he would be implementing, including changing the team colors back to the red, white, and blue of the vintage Baltimore Bullets uniform (although not reverting to their former name).

Oh yes. Douglas Corrigan was a highly skilled aircraft mechanic who was one of the builders of Charles Lindbergh's "Spirit of St. Louis." Wanting to attempt his own solo, nonstop, trans-Atlantic flight, he repeatedly applied to the Bureau of Air Commerce for permission and was repeatedly denied. Making modifications to his plane for the flight, he would claim "navigational error" for the rest of his life, never recanting and never admitting otherwise. After his flight, when he returned to America, "Wrong Way Corrigan" received a Broadway ticker-tape parade in New York City larger than Charles Lindbergh's a few years before. One can only hope that the Washington Wizards will one day soon accomplish the basketball equivalent.

NBA Finals Appearances: 4   Wins: 1
Forbes 2017 Valuation: $1 Billion

National Football League

Arizona Cardinals

Former names: Chicago Cardinals 1920-59; St. Louis Cardinals 1960-87; Phoenix Cardinals 1988-93; Arizona Cardinals 1994 – present.

Year	Owner(s)	Purchase Price
1920-1928	Chris O'Brien	$100
1929-1932	David Jones	$25,000
1933-1946	Charles Bidwill Sr.	$50,000
1947-1961	Violet Bidwill Wolfner	Inherited
1962-1971	Bill and Charles Bidwill Jr.	Inherited
1962-	Bill Bidwill	$6.5 Million

      The Arizona Cardinals and the Chicago Bears are the only original charter members of the 1920 NFL still in existence. The Cardinals franchise dates way back to 1898 when Chris O'Brien, a painting and building contractor, founded the team as an amateur Chicago-based Athletic Club team, part of the Morgan Athletic Club. He renamed the club the Racine Cardinals because the club was located on Racine Avenue. They weren't named the Cardinals after the bird, rather for the color of the original jerseys, which faded due to overuse from maroon to cardinal red. While the team's first name would change throughout the years, they were always the Cardinals due to those original jerseys.

      In the early 1900s, football hadn't yet gained popularity and finding players let alone opponents was difficult. Football teams were mostly "company" teams designed to promote local businesses. There was little competition in Chicago, which caused O'Brien to halt operations from 1906 to 1913. The team played again in 1917 and won the Chicago City Championship. But, like most teams in 1918, the Cardinals had to shut down operations once again due to World War I.

      In 1920, shortly after the war, several owners of other successful city-league teams out of Ohio and New York decided to come together for a meeting in Canton, Ohio. Two of those owners, George Halas and Ralph Hay, were impressed with the popularity O'Brien cultivated with his Chicago football efforts and invited him to attend. The meeting resulted in the formation of the American Professional Football Association (APFA). Each owner paid a franchise fee of $100. The goal was to keep operating costs down, prevent bidding for players, and to create an organized system of inter-city games to create local competition and increase attendance.

      Some say O'Brien is the great-grandfather of modern day pro football because he was one of the original co-founders of the APFA, which was soon thereafter renamed the National Football League. To eliminate confusion, O'Brien renamed his team the Chicago Cardinals so as not to be confused with another charter NFL team called the Racine Legion from Racine, Wisconsin.

In those early NFL days, the Chicago Cardinals were competing for the same fan dollars as the Chicago Tigers, another Chicago APFA team. O'Brien suggested the two teams have a playoff to see which team would win the right to represent Chicago. The loser would fold operations. Luckily, the Cardinals won the game and became the official city team. However, in 1922, George Halas, owner of the Decatur Staleys, asked the NFL and O'Brien for approval to move his team to Chicago too. Nobody knows exactly why but it was agreed upon. Halas changed his team's name to the Chicago Bears, and one of the earliest NFL rivalries was born.

While the Cardinals are said to have won the 1925 NFL Championship, there is much controversy surrounding that title because some believe the Pottsville Maroons were the more deserving winner. Back then, the Champion title was awarded to the team with the best record. Apparently, the Maroons played an illegal game that year and included that win in their overall record. Their title was stripped away and given to the Cardinals, who were technically in second place. But, even with a championship season, O'Brien worried the trend in football would flatten out. It didn't help that the Chicago Bears were clearly the more popular team.

O'Brien sold his team to Dr. David Jones, a Chicago physician, for a reported $25,000 in July 1929. Jones only owned the team for a few years when he realized pro football ownership was serious business, one in which he was not well versed.

In 1933, Jones attended a dinner party on the yacht of Charles Bidwill, a wealthy lawyer and then vice-president of the Chicago Bears. During dinner conversation, Bidwill's wife casually suggested her husband buy the team from Jones. He listened, and the Cardinals became Bidwill's team for $50,000, $2,000 down and a handshake on the balance. At the time, it was a well-known fact that Bidwill would have preferred to buy into the Bears, but Halas refused. Bidwill sold his stock in the Bears and took over full ownership of the Cardinals in 1933.

Charles Bidwill's family had been involved in Chicago politics and reportedly had ties to organized crime. As a lawyer and successful Chicago businessman who owned racing stables, a printing company, and a luxurious yacht, one wondered if his "political connections" helped him acquire the Cardinals at a time when owning a team was such a financial risk.

Under Bidwill's ownership, the Cardinals were unsuccessful during the '30s and early '40s. Some believe there was a curse put on the team from the 1925 title controversy. In reality, however, the Great Depression, World War II, and the new rival league, the All American Football Conference (AAFC), who placed the Rockets in Chicago, were factors that didn't help matters – curse or no curse. Bidwill was sometimes seen as an ambivalent owner, often rooting for the opponent instead of his own team. Fans began to wonder what was up.

By the mid '40s, Bidwill, becoming more competitive and proud, (and rich), decided to rebuild his Cardinals to make them a winner, if for no other reason than to beat the team he couldn't buy, Papa's Bears. He set out to get the best players he could, and formed what is called "Bidwill's Dream Backfield." Paying more than any other owner at the time, he signed Charley Trippi for a whopping $100,000, which, at the time, was an outlandish amount of money. His investment proved successful. The 1947 team finally brought the Cardinals their first undisputed NFL championship title. Ironically, Bidwill died earlier the same year and did not see his team victorious. Charles Bidwill was inducted into the Pro Football Hall of Fame.

When Bidwill died in April 1947, his wife, Violet Bidwill, took over ownership. She was the first female principal owner of an NFL team. In 1949, Violet married a prominent St. Louis businessman, Walter H. Wolfner. By 1959, it became obvious the Cardinals couldn't compete with the Bears *and* the emergence of the AFL. The NFL saw the benefit of moving the Cardinals, and it made sense for Violet to select St. Louis, the home of her new husband. The twelve NFL owners approved the move and the Cardinal's 62-year life in Chicago was over. From 1960 to 1987 the team played as the St. Louis Cardinals.

When Violet died in January 1962, her adopted sons, Charles and Bill, inherited the team and became co-owners. Before the 1972 season, Bill bought Charles's 50-percent stake for a reported $6.5 million and became the team's sole owner. The Cardinals stayed in St. Louis for 28 years, during which time they couldn't manage to become a winning team. However, during their time in St. Louis, the Cardinals can boast their highest winning percentage of the three cities in which they played.

In 1987, Bidwill realized St. Louis wasn't going to the replace the 21-year-old outdated Busch Memorial Stadium, so he obtained NFL approval to move the team to Phoenix, Arizona. In 1988, the team became the Phoenix Cardinals until 1994 when they were renamed (once and for all) the Arizona Cardinals.

Bill Bidwill has the reputation of being one of the cheapest owners in the NFL. His nickname became "Dollar Bill" because of his reputation for stiffing his players and staff financially. He once offered his staff a mediocre post-game meal, then deducted the cost from the players' paychecks. His frugal ways are ironic because his father was just the opposite. Charlie used his wealth generously and built a successful franchise. "Dollar Bill" is often criticized for standing by and allowing his team to fail because he isn't willing to spend an extra dime. The Arizona Cardinals had one of the lowest payrolls in the NFL. Consequently, the team had only one winning season between 1984 and 2008.

Even when the Cardinals made it to the Super Bowl in 2009, Bidwill was criticized. Fans claimed that Bidwill was only willing to spend *after* the new stadium had been built in 2006, and *after* selling the stadium naming rights to the University of Phoenix, a deal on which he made a quick $7.5 million. Nevertheless, the team did make it to the 2009 Super Bowl -- but lost to the Pittsburgh Steelers in the final seconds, 27-23. In 2012, the Cardinals became the first NFL franchise to lose 700 games since its inception.

Over the past few years, Bidwell has taken a back seat to his two sons who have become president and vice president. Since then, with quarterback Carson Palmer and future Hall of Fame receiver, Larry Fitzgerald, the team has been winning, making the playoffs in 2014 and 2015, but slipped out of the playoffs in 2016.

Among NFL franchises, only the Chicago Bears and New York Giants have been controlled by one family longer than the Cardinals, who have been in the Bidwill family for 85 years. After the death of former Buffalo owner Ralph Wilson in 2014, "Dollar Bill" Bidwill became the longest-tenured owner (55 years) in the NFL.

Super Bowl Appearances: 1   Wins: 0
Forbes 2017 Valuation: $2.15 Billion

Atlanta Falcons

Year	Owner(s)	Purchase Price
1966-1997	Rankin Smith	$8.5 Million
1997-2001	Taylor Smith	Inherited
2002-	Arthur Blank	$545 Million

Rankin Smith Sr., an Atlanta native, founded the Atlanta Falcons in 1965. Smith graduated from the University of Georgia and went to work for his family's insurance business, Life Insurance Company of Georgia, where he ascended to president and chairman of the board in 1970. Being a successful Atlanta businessman, it was only natural when the new AFL wanted to expand to Atlanta that Smith would be considered for the franchise. However, it wasn't that simple. The deal was contingent upon acquiring exclusive stadium rights from the city, which stalled the process, giving the NFL time to step in. It was rumored the NFL might have had a hand in that stall.

The growing rivalry between the AFL and NFL was an exciting game itself, so it came as no surprise when Smith pulled out of the AFL deal upon learning the more prestigious NFL also wanted a team in Atlanta. NFL commissioner Pete Rozelle who got wind of the AFL's deal, pressured the city to choose between the two leagues. In the end, Atlanta went with two old classics – the NFL and Smith, who paid $8.5 million, the highest price paid for an NFL team at the time, and Smith became the first owner of the Falcons. Subsequently, after the AFL lost Atlanta, they chose Miami, where the Dolphins went on to achieve great success.

Aside from winning one division title in 1980, and making it to the playoffs five times, the Falcons' record was not stellar under Smith's ownership. However, one of Smith's greatest contributions was spearheading the development of the Georgia Dome, which opened in 1992 and hosted the Super Bowl in 1994. In January 1917, the Falcons played their last game in the Georgia Dome, defeating the Green Bay Packers in the NFC championship game to make it to their second Super Bowl.

In 1997, Smith died of heart failure, leaving behind his five children and his second wife, Charlotte Topping, the widow of former New York Yankees owner Dan Topping. Rankin Smith's shares were distributed to his children. Prior to his death, Smith had turned control of the team over to his son, Taylor Smith, who had been team president since 1990. Taylor further took over as the Falcons' managing owner, until selling the team in 2002 to Home Depot co-founder Arthur Blank. Under Taylor Smith's ownership, the Falcons made their only Super Bowl appearance, but lost to John Elway's Denver Broncos.

Born in Queens, N.Y., Blank excelled in school, graduating high school in three years. He joined Daylin Corporation and eventually became vice president of finance for the Handy Dan Home Improvement Centers. When power struggles mounted, Blank and CEO Bernard Marcus were unexpectedly fired. This was a fortunate twist of fate as they went on to found Home Depot in 1978, and a few more billionaires were born. It only seemed natural that Blank would start looking for a new endeavor upon retiring as co-chairman in 2001.

A longtime fan of the Falcons, Blank (like so many other fans) was frustrated watching a team mired in mediocrity. In 42 years, the Falcons never had back-to-back winning seasons. Being a competitive businessman and passionate football fan, Blank made a bid for the Falcons. In 2002, he paid the Smiths $545 million for the team.

It hasn't been all peaches and cream in the "Peachtree" city, as controversy is no stranger to Blank's Falcons. In 2007, star quarterback Michael Vick was charged and found guilty in a dogfighting and gambling ring. After being suspended by the NFL indefinitely, Blank spoke out at a press conference, saying the Falcons were seeking to be reimbursed $20 million out of Vick's $37 million signing bonus because he was knowingly involved in the illegal activity when he signed and accepted the bonus in

2004. The case went to arbitration, where Vick was required to pay the Falcons $19.97 million.

In 2015, the NFL fined the Falcons $350,000 and a future fifth-round draft pick for pumping artificial crowd noise into the Georgia Dome. Blank, on behalf of his management, made few excuses. In an interview with ESPN, he admitted to his organization's wrongdoing, saying, "I think what we've done in 2013 and 2014 was wrong. Anything that affects the competitive balance and fairness on the field, we're opposed to, as a league, as a club and as an owner. It's obviously embarrassing but beyond embarrassing it doesn't represent our culture and what we're about."

In addition to owning the Falcons, Blank founded Atlanta United, a Major League Soccer team, for the $70 million franchise fee. Both teams will play in the new Mercedes-Benz Stadium in which Blank, in 2014, invested $1.4 billion to develop. It is planned to open in late 2017. Blank has already proclaimed that the new stadium will have the lowest concession prices in the country. The new Mercedes-Benz Stadium will host the Super Bowl in 2019, the NCAA College Football Title Game in 2018, and the NCAA Final Four in 2020.

Blank, who recently won a bout with prostate cancer, continues to give generously to the Atlanta community through the Blank Family Foundation.

On Februrary 5, 2017, Arthur Blank stood on the sideline, hand-in-hand with his wife, and watched his Falcons suffer the most humiliating defeat in Super Bowl history, blowing a 25-point lead and losing to the Patriots in the first overtime game in NFL history. It was a crushing blow for the proud city.

Super Bowl Appearances: 2   Wins: 0
Forbes 2017 Valuation: $2.475 Billion

Baltimore Ravens

Year	Owner(s)	Purchase Price
1996-2003	Art Modell	NA
2004-	Steven Bisciotti	$600 Million

In "The Raven," Edgar Allen Poe's classic poem, the Raven utters only one word: "Nevermore." Poe's forlorn narrator seeks an answer for his lost lover, Lenore, so he pleads with the Raven perched at the front door. The Raven utters, "Nevermore."

Perhaps the fans in Baltimore remembered that omen when they finally reincarnated their "lost" Baltimore Colts into the Baltimore Ravens in 1996, "nevermore" to lose them again as they had twice before. Edgar Allen Poe lived his early years in Baltimore, where he was buried in 1849.

For 12 years, the City of Baltimore and its football fans were ravenous to get an NFL franchise back to their town. They thought they had it in their bag when the NFL announced expansion plans in the early '90s. But the NFL, aware that Jack Kent Cooke was angling to relocate his Redskins to Baltimore, convinced the NFL owners to pass on Baltimore and award their expansion franchises to the smaller-market cities of Charlotte, North Carolina, and Jacksonville, Florida.

When Cooke's plan to relocate the "Skins" to Baltimore failed, the city was left holding an empty bag. Baltimore was pissed ... again. Not only had they lost their Colts to Indianapolis in 1983, when Robert Irsay stole them away in the dead of night, they lost their "sure-thing" expansion team to two less-deserving cities. Their only option at this juncture was to look for an existing franchise that might want to relocate to their already planned state-of-the-art new stadium.

Baltimore was aware of the financial problems Art Modell was having in Cleveland and discreetly started courting Modell to move the Browns to Baltimore. Art Modell made a name for himself in NFL circles as the controversial owner of the Cleveland Browns for 35 years, until he got caught with his hand in the Browns' cookie jar and was more or less humiliated into finding another city for his franchise.

Modell was hot to trot. His courtship with Baltimore became marriage when Modell announced his move in 1995. Now Cleveland was pissed. Not only had Modell lost his personal luster in Cleveland, he was now a liar and traitor. During the Browns' final game in Cleveland under Modell's ownership, the angry fans tore up parts of the stadium and threw seats, bottles, and trash onto the field.

Modell's plan was to name the team the Baltimore Browns. The jilted City of Cleveland sued Modell. The NFL stepped in and negotiated a settlement: Modell was granted the right to move his players and personnel but was forced to give up the Browns' namesake and history. He also had to pay the City of Cleveland, which would be without a team for three years, $11.5 million for lost revenues and legal fees. Hence, Modell's Baltimore Ravens became an expansion franchise.

The Ravens played their first two years in Memorial Stadium while the new stadium was being built. Completed in time for the 1998 season, the M&T Bank Stadium was, at the time, considered one of the better stadiums in the league. It is located next to Camden Yards, where the baseball Orioles play. PSI-Net bought the naming rights in 1999 but went bankrupt in 2002 and the name reverted to Ravens Stadium. Modell's team lived up to its name using a ravenous defense, led by the great linebacker

Ray Lewis, to win the Super Bowl in 2000, a remarkable feat for a five-year-old expansion team that wasn't truly an expansion team.

This would mark the zenith of Modell's reign as an owner. The NFL, aware of Modell's continuing financial woes, ordered him to sell the team. Strapped, Modell sold 49 percent of the team to Steve Bisciotti for $275 million in 2000. Bisciotti, who negotiated an option to purchase the other 51 percent for $325 million, exercised it in 2004 and remains the principal owner today.

Bisciotti, born in 1960, grew up a Baltimore sports fan, attending Orioles and Colts games with his father. He attended both high school and college in Maryland, planting his roots there ever since. In 1983, he and his cousin Jim Davis (who is also a billionaire) co-founded a staffing agency focused on filling aeronautics, engineering, and light industrial jobs. Today, Allegis Group has revenues over $10 billion.

In 2012, led by quarterback Joe Flacco on offense and an aging Ray Lewis still on defense, Bisciotti's Ravens won the Super Bowl. The Ravens are the only NFL team to play in multiple Super Bowls and remain undefeated. The Jets, Bucs, and Saints are also undefeated but each only played in one Super Bowl. There are only eight teams that have never won a Super Bowl, and half of them (Browns. Lions, Jaguars, and Texans) never even made it to the big dance. The Jags and Texans can be excused because they are relatively newer franchises, but the Browns and Lions have no such excuse.

Super Bowl Appearances: 2   Wins: 2
Forbes 2017 Valuation: $2.5 Billion

Buffalo Bills

Year	Owner(s)	Purchase Price
1960-2014	Ralph Wilson	$25,000
2014-	Terry and Kim Pegula	$1.4 Billion

Pro football had been played in Buffalo since the turn of the 20th century. The Buffalo All-Americans joined the NFL in 1920. They competed off and on during the Roaring Twenties under different names, but folded for good in 1929. In 1938, Buffalo began hosting NFL games, which kept the sport in front of the fans.

When the AAFC formed after World War II, Buffalo was invited to join the league and did so as the Buffalo Bills, a named derived from a barbershop quartet. When the AAFC merged with the NFL in 1949, those Bills were merged into the Cleveland Browns. That team had no financial or historical relation to the Buffalo Bills franchise of today.

Ralph Wilson was the original founder and owner of the Buffalo Bills for 54 years, from 1960 until his death in 2014. Born in Detroit, Michigan, Wilson attended the University of Virginia followed by the University of Michigan Law School, and served in the U.S. Navy during World War II. After the war, Wilson returned to take over his father's insurance business. He began building his fortune with investments in local Michigan-area mines and factories, and eventually formed Ralph Wilson Industries, which included manufacturing, construction, radio and television stations, and insurance.

When Lamar Hunt spearheaded the formation of the AFL, Buffalo was one of his target cities. Harry Wismer, who was to get the New York franchise, suggested Ralph Wilson. At that time, Wilson was a minority owner of the Detroit Lions, and Wismer owned a small slice of the Redskins. Hunt gave Wilson the choice of several cities including Atlanta, Miami, Louisville, and Buffalo. Wilson enthusiastically said he was all-in and agreed with Hunt to put his team in Buffalo. He chose Buffalo because of its demographic similarities to Detroit. It was another Rust Belt city that had proven good attendance when the former Bills played in the AAFC from 1946 to 1949. The region had gone without football for 10 years and the city was eager to bring it back.

Thus, Wilson, Hunt, and six other wealthy businessmen were in serious cahoots and financially committed to form the new league. It was 1959, a time when baseball was the most popular American sport and considered *the* national pastime. But Wilson and the other founding members of the AFL (often referred to as "The Foolish Club," for seeming so foolish as to try to take on the established NFL) saw football's popularity on the rise and were ready to invest. Wilson paid the $25,000 franchise fee to take on one of the original eight teams to make up the AFL.

The Bills had their ups and downs. In the '70s, they had the services of perhaps the greatest running back of all-time, now a disgraced criminal, "The Juice," O.J. Simpson, who had set the single-season rushing record of just over 2,000 yards. In the late '80s and '90s, the Bills were led by the ever-popular Hall of Fame quarterback, Jim Kelly, who led the Bills to four straight Super Bowls, but lost them all. (The Vikings are also 0-4 in Super Bowls).

In addition to his many contributions to the sport, it was Wilson's dedication to Buffalo that helped garner him induction into the NFL Hall of Fame. Until his health began to deteriorate in 2012, Wilson never missed a game during his 50-year reign. Wilson died in 2014 at the age of 95. He was the oldest owner in the NFL, and the third-longest tenured owner in NFL history.

The franchise was held in trust until it was sold to Terrence and Kim Pegula, husband and wife co-owners of the NHL Buffalo Sabres. The Pegulas were the favorite choice among fans and local government to purchase the Bills because of their dedication to western New York, coupled with their personal story of passion and perseverance. It is reported the Pegulas' $1.4 billion cash bid beat out a bid by Donald Trump and Jon Bon Jovi. The NFL approved the Pegulas' purchase in October 2014. Of all professional sports team owners, the Pegulas' story is unique because it's a Cinderella story at its best.

Kim Pegula was born in Seoul, South Korea. When she was five, her parents, knowing the authorities would place her in a better home, gave her up for adoption. That new and better home would be with a loving family in upstate New York. The Kerrs adopted Kim in 1974 and brought her up with all things Americana, including football. Following college, Kim concocted a plan with her best friend to travel to Alaska to work in a fish camp where she heard they could make big money. However, a happenstance meeting with Terry Pegula changed those plans. Pegula took a shine to Kim and was impressed by her ambition and energy, not to mention her personality. In short time, Kim began working for Terry's East Resources natural gas drilling company, the business he founded in 1983 with $7,500 raised from friends and family.

Terry Pegula is a self-made billionaire who came from humble beginnings in a small town near Scranton, Pennsylvania. A 1973 graduate of Penn State University, Terry learned the ropes in the oil and natural gas business with Getty Oil in Texas. He struck it rich when his company tapped into the gas-rich Marcellus Shale, which stretches from New York to West Virginia. He joined the fracking frenzy across the Rust Belt and, to the dismay of the anti-frackers, made a fortune. While Terry was an expert in oil drilling and discovering natural gas, he realized he needed a visionary, someone who was brilliant with communication and investor relations. Kim was his perfect match, just the kind of spark he needed personally and professionally. They married in 1993 and have five children, two being from Terry's previous marriage.

In 2010, Pegula sold a majority stake in East Resources to Royal Dutch Shell for $4.7 billion, of which he reportedly netted $3.3 billion. In 2011, he purchased the Buffalo Sabres for $189 million. In 2014, he paid $1.4 billion to buy the Bills, with a vow to keep them in Buffalo.

Turning to philanthropy, the Pegulas donated $88 million to Penn State University to build a Division 1 hockey program. They also developed the Harbor Center project, a hotel and ice rink complex aimed at turning the area around Buffalo's First Niagara Center into a venue for youth and amateur hockey events.

Terry and Kim co-own the Bills. Kim acts as president and CEO of Pegula Sports and Entertainment, the umbrella company they created to house their holdings. The Pegulas are known as Buffalo's first family because they saved Buffalo's most prized possession, the Bills, from the grips of other greedy and ill-intentioned bidders who might have wanted to relocate the franchise. To unite the city, the Pegulas created an umbrella slogan to tie the Sabres and Bills fans together: "One Team; One Goal; One Community; One Family; One Buffalo."

Super Bowl Appearances: 4   Wins: 0
Forbes 2017 Valuation: $1.6 Billion

Carolina Panthers

Year	Owner(s)	Purchase Price
1993	Jerry Richardson	$206 Million

For many decades, the idea of an NFL franchise in Charlotte, North Carolina, was considered improbable at best, impossible at worst. In fact, the viability of *any* professional sports team in North Carolina was a long shot. Geographically, more than any other region in the United States, North Carolina was synonymous with college basketball. The great "tobacco road" triumvirate of Duke, the University of North Carolina, and North Carolina State (and throw in Wake Forest and Davidson) monopolized the relatively small but passionate local fan base.

However, by the time Jerry Richardson determined to bring an NFL franchise to the area, timing and circumstances had aligned perfectly with his singular focus. Starting in the 1980s, Charlotte and Raleigh-Durham were transforming into very desirable locales for the tech industry, and financial services as well. This in turn stimulated economic growth and attracted a significant influx of young professional people. In addition to employment opportunities, the real estate market and cost of living across the board was attractive and welcoming to young families just starting out.

Richardson, a native of Spring Hope, North Carolina, who went on to be a star football player at Wofford College in Spartanburg, South Carolina, and later played two seasons in the NFL, returned to the area after his pro career ended in 1959. With his former Wofford College teammate, Charles Bradshaw, Richardson opened the first Hardee's restaurant franchise in Spartanburg in 1961. Richardson and Bradshaw would go on to form Spartan Food Systems, Inc., which would have 220 Hardee's restaurants by the time they sold their company in 1979.

Richardson announced his bid for an NFL expansion team in 1987 and the Carolina Panthers were accepted into the league in 1993. As an owner, Richardson is rather unusual in several regards: he is a former NFL player; other than Bob McNair (Houston Texans), he is the only individual in NFL history to be his team's sole owner from inception; he is one of only a handful of NFL owners who owns his team's stadium outright; and, finally, his Carolina Panthers are the only expansion team to have experienced significant success right from the beginning.

The Panthers' first season record was a more than respectable 7-9 and in only their second season, they won their division with a 12-4 record, earned a first-round bye, defeated the Dallas Cowboys in the divisional round, and lost to the Green Bay Packers (the eventual Super Bowl winner) in the NFC Championship Game. In 2004, Jerry's Panthers made it to the Super Bowl but lost. In 2016, the Carolina Panthers, led by Cam Newton, appeared in the Super Bowl, losing to the Denver Broncos.

Richardson's publicly stated desire was to have one of his two sons take over the franchise one day. With the death of one son, and the other stepping away, he has said he intends the team be sold upon his death. The Carolina Panthers in a very short time have firmly established themselves in the NFL and in fact are immensely popular not only in North Carolina but in South Carolina as well. Perhaps, with a wink and a nod, the shade of blue of their team uniform is called "process blue," a shade lighter than Duke yet a shade darker than North Carolina.

Super Bowl Appearances: 2   Wins: 0
Forbes 2017 Valuation: $2.3 Billion

Chicago Bears

Former names: Decatur Staleys 1920; Chicago Staleys 1921

Year	Owner(s)	Purchase Price
1920	A.E. Staley	
1921-1983	George Halas	$100
1983-	Virginia Halas McCaskey	Inherited

Augustus Eugene Staley (A.E. Staley) was born in 1867 to a red clay farmer in North Carolina. Growing up as a farmer's son, Staley soon realized he was more interested in selling the produce than working in the fields. When Staley was a young boy, he attended a church conference with his father and met a missionary who had returned from China with a new crop, the soybean. The missionary gave them a handful of the beans to take home. While Staley's father wasn't interested in a new crop, Staley was mesmerized by the bean's eastern heritage and its promise of being a great source of food and of other commercial value. He planted the discarded beans and saved the seeds for the following year. If nothing else, he believed they would be good for the soil.

By the age of 16, he left the farm to become a traveling salesman pushing produce and starch for other companies. Successful at selling, he decided to open his own company in 1898, the A.E. Staley Company. He soon realized that by cutting out the middleman, he could produce his own proprietary cornstarch, and opened his first manufacturing plant in Decatur, Illinois, in 1909.

The plant nearly went bankrupt during its first few years. The Midwest had been over-corned, because proper crop rotation was lacking. Being a visionary, Staley drew out his secret weapon, those soybean seeds from years ago.

He was determined to sell the seeds to local farmers and, because the soybean had not yet trended in the Midwest, he quickly became a missionary for the bean. From 1916 to 1922, he sent a fleet of employees to many of the farms in Illinois to proclaim that the soybean was an excellent source for oil, meal, and flour. He managed to generate enough supply and demand for the bean to warrant the diversification of his corn processing plant to include soybean processing too. He is said to be the "father of the soybean: because he not only introduced the bean to the Midwest, but he discovered that its oil byproducts could also be used in foods like margarine.

Cha-ching! As operator of the only soybean processing plant in the region, he would buy all the beans the farmers could produce and, *voila!* A. E. Staley Manufacturing grew into one of the largest corn and soybean refineries in America.

Being a marketer as well as a salesman, he decided to participate in another sweeping trend: sports teams. In 1919, Staley founded the Decatur Staleys as a means of promoting his company. He put the players on his company payroll and hired George Halas and Edward "Dutch" Sternaman to run the team. The team was a charter member of what became the National Football League in 1920. The team was very successful and before too long Staley realized the small, 1,500-capacity Decatur stadium wasn't big enough. He knew the team's rising popularity and stellar record needed a larger home.

According to the agreement Staley reached with Halas and Sternaman, Halas would purchase the rights to the club from Staley for $100. The 19 players would remain on the Staley payroll for that first season, and Staley agreed to pay Halas a $5,000 bonus to keep the Staley name (Chicago Staleys) for one year. In 1922, Halas renamed the team the Chicago Bears, relating to baseball's Chicago Cubs, with whom they would share Wrigley Field.

Halas was a Chicago native and terrific athlete. He played football for the University of Illinois, helping them win the 1918 Big Ten Conference. He was named MVP of the 1919 Rose Bowl, and he played 12 games as an outfielder for the New York Yankees that same year. After that brief baseball stint, he moved to Decatur, Illinois, to take a job with none other than A.E. Staley Company. He acted as a company sales representative, an outfielder on the company-sponsored baseball team, and the player-coach of the company-sponsored football team.

Halas played and coached the team for nearly a decade. He was also responsible for ticket sales and the business side of running a club. In 1930, he stepped down as a player and handed coaching duties over to Ralph Jones of Lake Forest Academy. Halas became the sole owner of the team by 1932. When the Great Depression kicked in, he stepped back in as coach to save money.

When World War II broke out in 1942, Halas joined the navy and spent 20 months overseas, away from his beloved Bears. He returned to the field in 1946 and spent another 20 years coaching the team. In his 40 years as coach, he endured only six losing seasons. George Halas was one of the most prominent figures in American football. Often referred to as "Papa Bear" because he was at the helm of the Bears from their inception, Halas was a player, coach and one of the original co-founders of the NFL. He died of cancer in 1983.

His eldest daughter, Virginia Halas McCaskey, has been the principal owner of the team since his death. Virginia McCaskey, who remains one of only three women owners in the NFL, inherited an incredible nucleus of a team and was the owner when the Bears, coached by Mike Ditka, won the 1986 Super Bowl, demolishing the Patriots 46-10. Her son, Michael McCaskey, was team president from 1983 to 1999, and chairman of the board until May 6, 2011, when his brother George McCaskey assumed the position. Virginia Halas's husband, Ed McCaskey, was previously the chairman and treasurer of the Bears. Although Ed McCaskey never had any official share of ownership, he acted as co-owner alongside his wife. He died in 2003.

Virginia's Bears won the NFC Championship in 2007, but lost the Super Bowl to Peyton Manning's Colts 29-17. The NFC Championship Trophy bears the name of legendary NFL co-founder, George Halas.

Super Bowl Appearances: 2   Wins: 1
Forbes 2107 Valuation: $2.85 Billion

Cincinnati Bengals

Year	Owner(s)	Purchase Price
1968-1990	Paul Brown	$10 Million
1991-	Mike Brown	Inherited

A seminal figure, Paul Brown is simply one of the most important and influential owners in the history of the NFL. Consider that Brown was elected to the pro football Hall of Fame one year before he led a group in 1968 that purchased the expansion Cincinnati Bengals for $10 million. It is not without a touch of irony that Brown's resume is far more lustrous than that of the franchise, which bears his imprint -- the Cincinnati Bengals being one of 13 teams that have never won a Super Bowl.

A native of Massillon, Ohio, Brown's association with football in that state (high school, college, and professional) is unequaled and preeminent. In 1968, five years after being unceremoniously dismissed as head coach of the Cleveland Browns by team owner Art Modell, Brown was looking to get back into the league as an owner, as well as a coach. The state of Ohio was his only area of interest and he was scouting Columbus and Cincinnati as potential homes for his franchise. Brown would ultimately choose Cincinnati for two reasons: first, the Cincinnati Reds baseball team desperately needed a new ballpark to replace the dilapidated Crosley Field, and second, Cincinnati was geographically and demographically well suited to support a new football team -- within a 110-mile radius of Louisville and Lexington, Kentucky; Columbus, Dayton, and Springfield, Ohio; and Indianapolis, Indiana.

Once a favorable deal was struck between Cincinnati, Hamilton County, and the Reds for a multi-purpose stadium to be constructed, Riverfront Stadium, Brown's decision became an easy one. Knowing full well the NFL needed to add one more expansion team in preparation for the 1970 merger (so the NFL would boast 26 teams in total), Brown negotiated and accepted a reduced NFL fee of $10 million, as opposed to the $25 million fee the other expansion teams had paid.

Paul Brown's legendary status in Ohio football has deep lifelong roots. After playing and starring at Massillon High School, Brown first enrolled at Ohio State University, where, being undersized, he failed to make the varsity. He then transferred to Miami University in Oxford, Ohio, where he played quarterback, succeeding that team's prior star quarterback, Weeb Ewbank. He would soon return, at age 24, to coach his high school team, leading them to a nine-year record of 80-8-2. In 1941, at age 33, Brown was hired to be the head coach of Ohio State University. One year later, under Coach Brown, Ohio State won its first national title in 1942.

During 1944, Brown was stationed at the Great Lakes Naval Training Station where he coached the Great Lakes Bluejackets, who competed against other service teams as well as colleges. Also in 1944, a new eight-team league, the All-America Football Conference, or AAFC, was created to compete against the NFL after the war was over. In 1945, Brown was named head coach of the new AAFC Cleveland franchise. Despite his objections, the team was named the Cleveland Browns in his honor. Paul Brown led this team to four consecutive championships (1946-'49).

In 1950, three teams from the AAFC merged into the NFL: the San Francisco 49ers, Baltimore Colts, and Cleveland Browns. Paul Brown led his team to the 1950 championship, defeating the Los Angeles Rams, and became the first coach to win both the college and pro championships. Under Coach Brown, the Cleveland Browns would appear in five more consecutive championship games, losing in '51 to the Los Angeles Rams, losing in '52 and '53 to the Detroit Lions, beating the Detroit Lions in '54, and beating the Los Angeles Rams in '55. Brown's remaining tenure in Cleveland, 1956 to '63, would not see any more championships. Within the football world, Brown, while universally respected for his systemic approach, was a difficult man and not well liked by all. A fervent disciplinarian and taskmaster, he demanded of his co-owners complete and total autonomy in all aspects of running his teams and was likewise unrelenting with his players. By 1963, Art Modell, who had purchased the team in 1961, went back on his word and fired Brown.

In 1968, when Paul Brown reemerged in the NFL with the Cincinnati Bengals, it was with a franchise over which he had complete and total control, as both owner and head coach. He named the team and chose the team colors, a different scheme of the Cleveland Browns colors. They were white, black and orange; his would be orange, black, and white. The Browns helmet was orange with a white stripe; his would be solid orange.

Coaching the Cincinnati Bengals for their first eight years, Brown and his staff are credited with innovations that revolutionized pro football. The most well-known were the "no-huddle offense," the "west-coast offense," and the "zone blitz defense," the latter two credited to assistants on his staff, Bill Walsh and Dick LeBeau, respectively.

Paul Brown died in Cincinnati in 1991, leaving his estate to his son, Mike. The Cincinnati Bengals moved into Paul Brown Stadium in 2000. In 2011, Mike Brown purchased shares from original co-owner Austin Knowlton and is now the majority owner.

Paul Brown's contributions to football cannot be overstated. A partial list of innovations attributed to him are the invention(s) of the "draw play," the modern facemask, studying game film, the hiring of full-time assistants, the "playbook," hand signals to send in plays from the sideline, structured, regimented, and highly organized practices, the "taxi-squad," and the integration of football.

From his earliest days coaching high school and college through his professional tenure, Paul Brown was a pioneer in bringing African-American players onto his teams. Finally, Paul Brown's "coaching tree" is at least the equal of the mid-1950s New York Giants staff of head coach Jim Lee Howell, which featured coordinators Vince Lombardi and Tom Landry. The coaches who worked directly under Paul Brown were Don Shula, Weeb Ewbank, Bill Walsh, and Chuck Noll. In a word, today's NFL and the game of pro football would be unrecognizable absent the legacy of Paul Brown.

Super Bowl Appearances: 2   Wins: 0
Forbes 2017 Valuation: $1.8 Billion

Cleveland Browns

Year	Owner(s)	Purchase Price
1946-1952	Arthur "Mickey" McBride	$300,000
1953-1960	David Jones & partners	$600,000
1961-1996	Art Modell & partners	$3.95 Million
1999-2002	Al Lerner	$530 Million
2002-2012	Randy Lerner	Inherited
2012-	Jimmy Haslam	$1 Billion

The Cleveland Browns have a complicated and convoluted past. If ever there was a team whose performance on the field reflected the ownership's trials and tribulations, it was the Cleveland Browns, who remain one of the four NFL teams that have never appeared in the Super Bowl. Yes, they did have some great years in the pre-Super Bowl days of Otto Graham and Jimmy Brown, but over the last several decades, which included three years with no team at all thanks to Art Modell, their record has been mediocre at best, sometimes laughable.

Arthur "Mickey" McBride founded the Cleveland Browns in 1944. He was born in Chicago in 1888 and started working as a newspaper boy at age six. As he grew older, he learned how to control the best street corners and newsstands so *his* papers could sell out first. He landed his first job working for William Randolph Hearst and settled in Cleveland in 1913. He employed the same hustle he learned as a kid and made good money, enough to buy a series of taxicab companies. Proving successful once again, McBride expanded and began one of the first wire services that supplied bookies the results from horse races.

This put him in touch with organized crime members whose gambling interests relied on such wires. Two mobsters owned publications and McBride invested in both. He was never arrested or convicted for his involvement, but in 1940 a federal grand jury indicted 18 people, including McBride, for involvement in the passing of information used in organized crime.

In 1944, his friend, Arch Ward, sports editor of the Chicago Tribune, gave him a heads-up that the All-America Football Conference (AAFC) was forming. McBride jumped on the opportunity. In 1946, he paid $300,000 to become founder and owner of the Cleveland Browns.

His first order of business was to hire Paul Brown, the Browns' first coach and namesake. Under Brown's leadership, the team won every AAFC championship between 1946 and 1949. Fans admired McBride for letting Brown do what he did best, coach. When the league dissolved in 1949, the Browns were incorporated into the NFL where they had one of the best records from 1950 to 1955.

However, in 1951, the heat from the nationally televised hearings in the federal case against McBride got to him. While his ties to the Mafia were never confirmed, it is speculated the public airing of the nitty-gritty, and the notoriety, persuaded him to sell the team and get the hell out of "Dodge." He sold the Browns to a group of prominent Cleveland businessmen led by David Jones. They paid $600,000 – more than twice the largest sum ever paid for a pro football team at the time.

The next owner of the Browns was one of the more controversial owners because he seemed to have a knack for going against his promises. Art Modell, an ad executive from New York City, bought the team from David Jones in 1961 for $3.95 million. He put in $250,000 of his own money, and found partners to cover the rest. One of those partners, Bob Gries, whose family had been shareholders since the team was founded, ponied up for a total of 43 percent minority ownership. I mention this because it's a name that would come back to haunt Modell some 30 years later.

One of the first things Modell announced was that he had no plans of firing head coach Brown, and he extended Brown's contract for another eight years. Then in 1963, Modell went back on his word, firing Brown because they were unable to see eye to eye on the management of the team. Adding insult to injury, not only had Modell gone against his word, but he didn't consult anyone else, including fellow management and other minority owners. The news came as a shock to the city and the dedicated fans. They couldn't fathom how the great Paul Brown could be let go after leading the Browns for 17 years.

Modell may have confronted some challenging financial issues during the 45 years he was an NFL owner, but he was a great marketer and promoter. For 31 years, from 1962 to 1993, he represented the NFL owners in negotiating lucrative television contracts that generated billions for the league and gave the fans Monday Night Football. He served as the NFL's first and only president from '67 to '69.

But the deal Modell made in 1973 with the City of Cleveland would resurface to be the beginning of the end. Modell created a new entity, Stadium Corp., which agreed to rent Cleveland Municipal Stadium from the city over a 25-year period for $1 per year and assume all operating costs. Everything was fine and dandy for a while, but soon Modell's financial troubles caught up to him: Modell had Stadium Corp. buy land he had previously acquired as the potential site for a future new stadium. Modell originally paid $625,000 for the land, but sold it to Stadium Corp. for more than $3 million. Later, in 1981, he sold Stadium Corp. to the Browns for $6 million. This led to a fight with Bob Gries, whose complaint was that Modell treated the Browns and Stadium Corp. as his own kingdom, rarely consulting him about the team's business. The sale of Stadium Corp. to the Browns, he argued, enriched Modell at the team's expense. He sued Modell.

Gries's case went to the Ohio Supreme Court, where he won. In 1986, Modell had to reverse the Browns' purchase of Stadium Corp. and pay $1 million in Gries's legal fees. This left Modell in need of financial help, which came from Al Lerner, a banking and real estate executive who bought half of Stadium Corp. and five percent of the Browns.

Modell's reputation in Cleveland was busted. The city, the fans, and perhaps even the team had been duped again. But little did they know Modell was acting like "a dog with his tail between his legs" as he began private conversations with the City of Baltimore about moving his franchise there. Modell couldn't take the financial, legal and social pressure and wanted out. Where he had once been the most loved citizen, he was now a traitor.

Modell balked at how he had lost $21 million in the previous two seasons. The city, dedicated to its rich pro football history, was determined to do whatever it took to keep its team in town. Voters passed a $175 million proposal for stadium renovations. Nevertheless, it wasn't enough to change Modell's mind, and in 1995, Modell announced his move to Baltimore -- another promise broken.

If Modell thought Cleveland didn't like him before, he had another think coming after the announcement. There was a target on his back. In the last game of the Browns' final season in Cleveland, riots broke out in the stadium. Fans threw bottles and trash on the field and even ripped out sections of bleachers and threw those on the field. Outraged and betrayed, the city sued Modell in 1998 for breach of contract.

The NFL stepped in to help settle the dispute and eventually reached a compromise: Modell would be allowed to take his players and personnel to Baltimore, but had to pay the City of Cleveland $9.3 million for lost revenues and $2.25 million for their legal fees. The city got to keep the Cleveland Browns identity, team history, and heritage for a new team that had to be built from scratch, unless another NFL franchise chose to relocate to Cleveland. Play was suspended for three years. The $175 million the city raised for stadium improvements, plus $48 million in financing from the NFL, was to be used instead to build a new stadium. As a result, the settlement meant that Modell's new team would be an expansion franchise, the Baltimore Ravens. Modell supposedly never showed his face in Cleveland again.

In 1998, it was announced that Al Lerner, chairman of the credit card company MBNA, would be the new owner of the reinstated Cleveland Browns. He purchased the rights to the franchise for $530 million and the team was reactivated in 1999. Lerner and Modell had a bit of a history. Lerner had owned a 5 percent stake in the Browns, so he had a vested interest in the move to Baltimore and used some of his banking relationships to help Modell negotiate his deal with the city. Knowing Cleveland might chop Lerner's head off if he continued associating with Modell, he and Modell reportedly never spoke or appeared in public again. Lerner died of brain cancer in the middle of the 2002 season, and the reins were given to his son Randy.

The Lerner family owned the Browns from 1999 to 2012, when they sold the team to Jimmy Haslam for $1 billion. Haslam was born in 1954 and joined his father's business, Pilot Corporation, a successful chain of retail gas stations and truck stops. After working his way up the steps of the family corporate ladder, Haslam became CEO of Pilot Flying J Truck Stops. Consistent with controversy involving the Cleveland Browns owners' histories, Pilot and Haslam were accused of fraud by the Justice Department for their pricing policies and settled for a fine of $92 million.

The Cleveland Browns, once a major force in the NFL, currently have the worst record in the entire league. That gives them first pick in the next draft. Let's hope they can get it right this time and draft a star around whom they can begin to build a respectable team and hold their heads high like their successful cousins, the Cleveland Indians (2016 World Series) and the Cleveland Cavaliers (2016 NBA champions).

Super Bowl Appearances: 0
Forbes 2017 Valuation: $1.95 Billion

Dallas Cowboys

Year	Owner(s)	Purchase Price
1960-1983	Clint Murchison, Jr.	$1 Million
1984-1988	H. R. "Bum" Bright	$80 Million

Clinton William Murchison, Jr. was the Dallas Cowboys' founding owner. He was born in 1923 in Dallas, Texas, to the rich and famous oil baron Clint Murchison Sr., who made his fortune during the oil boom of the 1920s. Murchison Jr. and his brother, John, were given a thriving business portfolio and let loose to find their own way, albeit on a path paved in gold. They began doing business together as the Murchison Brothers in the late 1940s. But Murchison Jr. fashioned himself more as a wheeling and dealing playboy, and wasn't interested in taking over hand-me-down business opportunities from his rich father. He craved instead to own a professional football team.

Texas was, and still is, a hotbed for college football, but Murchison Jr. felt Dallas was *the* prime spot for a pro team, as did everyone else. In 1960, Lamar Hunt formed his AFL franchise in Dallas, known as the Texans (later to become the Kansas City Chiefs), after previously being denied an NFL expansion license. As the rivalry between the AFL and NFL mounted, the NFL was anxious to have a team in Dallas. And Clint was dead set on owning that team.

In 1958, Clint got wind that George Preston Marshall might want to sell the Washington Redskins because the team was doing poorly and needed money. Clint was hot on his heels to buy, but just as the deal was about to be approved, Marshall demanded a change in terms. Murchison was fed up with Marshall's shenanigans and cancelled the deal out of spite. If he couldn't buy a team he would start his own, and he applied to the NFL for an expansion team in Dallas.

For an expansion team to be approved, the NFL owners had to agree unanimously. And they did ... all except for one, George Preston Marshall, who was determined to keep Clint out of Dallas. At that time, Marshall's Redskins were the only pro team in the South and he wanted to keep it that way. But maverick Murchison wasn't about to let his dream die and, for revenge, he paid $2,500 to acquire the rights to the Redskin's fight song, "Hail to the Redskins." Just before the next NFL owners vote, Clint delighted in telling Marshall he could no longer play his fight song at Redskin games unless he voted in favor. Clint's spiteful little trick worked and, in January 1960, Murchison Jr. and the City of Dallas were granted an NFL franchise for a fee of $1 million. The owners were Clint Murchison Jr., John Murchison, and Bedford Wynne.

Clint was majority owner of "America's Team" for 23 years. Under his reign, the Cowboys appeared in five Super Bowls, winning in '72 and '78. Clint, having other more pleasurable things on his mind, was smart enough to hire expert management. He brought in Tex Schramm as general manager and Gil Brant as director of player personnel, and hired legendary head coach Tom Landry. He also spearheaded the development of Texas Stadium with the domed roof that allowed God to watch the Cowboys' games.

But, as hands-off as Clint was in certain regards, he wasn't in others and became embroiled in messy personal dramas. For example, in the mid-'70s, he struck up an affair with Gil Brant's wife, Anne, who would become Clint's second wife. It was this type of behavior that eventually led to his downfall. It is reported that the playboy became addicted to the thrill of the chase and that he struggled with alcohol and drug abuse. He made a series of risky investments in oil and real estate, turning his inherited fortune into a mountain of debt.

In 1983, he fell ill with an ALS-like disease. Because he had burned through his fortune, he was forced by his creditors to sell the team to H.R. "Bum" Bright and a group of Dallas businessmen for $80 million. Clint filed for personal bankruptcy in 1985 and died in 1987. A few years later, Bright, in financial trouble, sold the Cowboys and Texas Stadium to Jerry Jones for $140 million.

Jerry Jones has owned the Dallas Cowboys since 1989. He is the only NFL owner to see his team win three Super Bowls within his first seven years: '93, '94 and '96. They drew the three largest television audiences in broadcast history. They also set an NFL record with 160 consecutive sold-out stadiums, both home and away. Today, the Cowboys are the most valuable team in America.

Jerry wasn't always successful. His early business attempts were failures. He reportedly borrowed $1 million from Jimmy Hoffa's Teamsters Union to open a chain of Shakey's Pizza Parlor restaurants in Missouri. They went under. He also asked the Teamsters Union for a loan to purchase the AFL's San Diego Chargers in 1967 but his father talked him out of it because the AFL was losing money hand over fist. Jerry persevered until he struck it rich in oil and gas exploration in the southwest.

While he may not be liked by some for his over-the-top involvement with the team, Jones is responsible for building one of the most successful sports brands of all time. The saying, "everything's bigger in Texas" isn't an understatement when it comes to Jones's ways. The stadium he built (AT&T) for a cool $1.15 billion in 2009 is often referred to as "Jerry's World."

Regardless of the brand's success, the Cowboys' record for the last 20 years, under Jerry's leadership, has been disappointing at best. Hold the press! In 2016, with rookie quarterback Zak Prescott filling in for injured Tony Romo, the "Boys" had the best record in the NFL, but Jerry's Cowboys lost to the Green Bay Packers in a January 2017 nail-biter, leaving his team still without a playoff win in the last 21 years.

Super Bowl Appearances: 8   Wins: 5
Forbes 2017 Valuation: $4.8 Billion

Denver Broncos

Year	Owner(s)	Purchase Price
1960	Bob Howsam	$25,000
1961-1964	Cal Kunz, Gerald Phipps, Allan Phipps	NA
1965-1980	Gerald Phipps and Allan Phipps	$1.5 Million
1981-1983	Edgar Kaiser, Jr.	$30 Million
1984-2014	Pat Bowlen	$70 Million
2014-	Pat Bowlen Trust	

In Denver, Colorado, in the late 1950s, Bob Howsam led his family-owned minor-league baseball team, the Denver Bears. At the time, the Bears were the Triple-A affiliate of the New York Yankees. In 1959, Howsam spent a lot of money expanding Bears Stadium to hold 34,000 people because Denver had been named a charter member of the new Continental League.

When MLB chose expansion rather than competing against the new league, Howsam was suddenly left standing when the music stopped playing. There would be no new baseball league and the debt burden of his newly renovated Bears Stadium was onerous. In 1960, with an obvious need to utilize his stadium, Howsam looked to the NFL and requested a franchise for Denver.

Led by the most vocal opposition of George Halas, the NFL denied his request. In response to this setback, Howsam helped create the American Football League, with his brand-new Denver Broncos as a charter member. A baseball man at heart, Howsam sold the Broncos just one year later to Cal Kunz and Gerald and Allan Phipps. Howsam would go on to become a principal architect of the Cincinnati Reds' "Big Red Machine," as the team's general manager and president.

The Phipps brothers, whose family fortune was made in construction, bought out their partner Kunz in 1964. The Phippses would in turn sell the team to shipbuilder and industrialist Edgar Kaiser, Jr. in 1981 for $30 million. He would sell it three years later to Pat Bowlen for $70 million. Bowlen, whose father had struck it rich as an oil field wildcatter, would make his own fortune as a highly successful lawyer in Oklahoma, with additional successes in the mining and real estate industries.

In 1988, upon learning of Bowlen's offer to sell John Elway a 10 percent stake of the team, Kaiser sued Bowlen. It was Kaiser's contention that he'd retained right of first refusal for the purchase of any shares of the team, as per the terms of the original sale agreement of 1984. In 2004, a federal judge ruled in Kaiser's favor, finding that he was entitled to buy back 10 percent of the Broncos under the identical terms offered to Elway by Bowlen. In 2006, this decision was reversed upon appeal by a three-judge panel finding in Bowlen's favor.

In 2014, announcing that he was afflicted with Alzheimer's disease, Bowlen transferred ownership of the team to his family and relinquished day-to-day operations to president, chairman, and CEO Joe Ellis and executive vice president of football operations and general manager, John Elway. The Pat Bowlen Trust retains sole ownership of the Denver Broncos.

The Denver Broncos have always been well managed and have achieved an enviable record making it to eight Super Bowls. Only four teams have made it to eight Super Bowls: the Steelers, Cowboys, and Patriots being the other three.

Super Bowl: Appearances 8   Wins 3
Forbes 2017 Valuation: $2.6 Billion

Detroit Lions

Former name: Portsmouth Spartans 1930-33

Year	Owner(s)	Purchase Price
1930-1931	Harry Snyder	Unknown
1932-1933	Homer Selby	Unknown
1934-1939	George Richards	$7,952
1940-1947	Fred Mandel	$225,000
1948-1949	Lyle Fife	$165,000
1949-1960	Edwin Anderson	
1961-2014	William Clay Ford	$6 Million
2014-	Martha Ford	Inherited

Before the franchise became the Detroit Lions, the team was the Portsmouth Spartans, the name it was founded under by Harry Snyder, the team's president when it joined the NFL in 1930.

Homer Selby took over as the Spartans' president in 1932 after leading an investment drive that saved the team. It was also in 1932 that the Spartans tied for first place with the Chicago Bears, prompting what would later be called the first NFL playoff game. It marked the beginning of the Eastern and Western Conferences and an annual championship game. In 1934, George Richards, owner of powerful Detroit radio station WJR, and a group of Detroit businessmen bought a majority stake in the Portsmouth Spartans for $7,952. The club was soon moved to the Motor City and renamed the Detroit Lions.

Even though the Lions had been successful on the field that first year, they were the new kids on the block, drawing weak crowds, no greater than 15,000 that season. To boost their audience, Richards leveraged his radio connections and struck a deal with NBC radio where the Lions' Thanksgiving Day game (and the Western Division Playoffs), would be broadcast nationally across 94 stations. This created quite the buzz and a record-breaking 26,000 fans watched the game while thousands more were turned away, for the first time, from the University of Detroit Stadium. The Lions did not win the game but one of the oldest and strongest NFL traditions was born, the Lions Thanksgiving Day game. This tradition is older than 24 current NFL franchises.

In 1940, the Lions were sold to Chicago department store executive Fred Mandel and two other Detroit businessmen for $225,000, with Mandel as the team's majority owner. In 1948, Mandel sold his shares to a group of seven Detroit businessmen for $165,000. Lyle Fife was named the team's president until power struggles with Edwin Anderson, head of the Detroit business syndicate that owned the Lions, escalated to a breaking point.

Anderson took over in 1949 and then sold the team in 1963 to William Clay Ford for a reported $6 million. At the time, this was the largest cash price paid for a sports team. Ironically, Ford's NFL deal was approved on the morning of November 22, 1963, the day President John F. Kennedy was assassinated. Despite animosity within the franchise before Ford took over, the 1950s marked the Lions' "Glory Years" with three NFL championships.

William Clay Ford was the last surviving grandchild of Henry Ford, founder of the Ford Motor Company. He owned the Lions for 50 years, during which time he moved them back to downtown Detroit and into their new Ford Stadium. The cost to build the new $430 million stadium was financed through private and public money, and the sale of naming rights to Ford Motor Company for $40 million payable over 20 years.

In 2006, Super Bowl XL was held in Detroit, bringing with it $260 million to the local economy, and putting Ford Field on the national stage. Ford was dedicated to the Lions and to the city of Detroit, giving back to the community through numerous Detroit Lions charity efforts that continue to this day. In 1947, Ford was married (in the society wedding of the decade) to Martha Parke Firestone, granddaughter of the tire magnate Harvey Firestone, uniting two of America's industrial dynasties. Following Ford's death in 2014, his wife Martha took control of the team.

Martha Ford is among a small group of female NFL owners. The others are Virginia Halas McCaskey, owner of the Chicago Bears, Kim Pegula, co-owner of the Buffalo Bills, and Carol Davis, co-owner of the

Oakland Raiders. When Lions ownership was awarded to Ford's widow, skeptics were concerned that it was too big a job for this soon to be 90-year-old. But Martha proved them wrong by taking the reins and making tough decisions, like the 2015 dismissal of team president Tom Lewand and general manager Martin Mayhew. Where her husband had been dubbed a "too patient" owner, Martha is "too impatient" to bring Detroit a championship.

Among her recent decisions to do whatever it takes for the Lions to win again was to elevate her three daughters to hold equal executive positions as their brother Bill, Jr., who had been involved with the Lions for years while his father was in charge. If nothing else, the fact that she demoted her son (or promoted her daughters), showed players and fans that she is in the driver's seat, ready to take the team to victory, and to erase the embarrassing stain of being the oldest of only four NFL teams never to have appeared in a Super Bowl.

Super Bowl Appearances: 0
Forbes 2017 Valuation: $1.7 Billion

Green Bay Packers

Year	Owner(s)	Purchase Price
1919-1921	Earl "Curly" Lambeau	N/A
1921-1922	J.E. Clair	Unknown
1923	Andrew Turnbull, Gerald Clifford, Dr. Webber Kelly, Curly Lambeau	$5,000 (Public Sale)
1923-	Green Bay Packers, Inc.	N/A

In each sport, in each league, there are a few teams that are the crème de la crème (the winningest, the richest, the most popular, the most historic, etc.) but there is only one team that can fairly and accurately be called unique: the Green Bay Packers of the NFL.

Interestingly, what makes the Green Bay Packers unique is not a pioneering owner (Curly Lambeau) on equal footing with the greatest-ever patriarchs of the NFL such as Halas, Mara, Brown, and Rooney; a head coach (Vince Lombardi) considered the gold standard against which all other coaches are measured; a dynastic period of five championships in seven years (including the first two Super Bowls); or a generational fan base that is as loyal as any in the NFL, having sold out every game (pre-season, regular season, post-season) since 1960.

What separates the Green Bay Packers from the New York Yankees, Boston Celtics, and Pittsburgh Steelers of the world is that they have not had an individual or group ownership entity since 1923 (they are a nonprofit, publicly held company with thousands of stockholders), and that Green Bay, Wisconsin, is the smallest city in North American professional team sports, with the smallest television market, playing outdoors in the coldest climate.

Lambeau was a native of Green Bay. A gifted high school athlete, after graduating from Green Bay East High School he matriculated at the University of Wisconsin. After freshman football was cancelled there, he left to attend Notre Dame, where he played for head coach Knute Rockne, but left school after his freshman year due to an acute case of tonsillitis.

Returning home to Green Bay, Lambeau would go to work for the Indian Packing Company. In 1919, Lambeau, along with his former high school football rival, George Whitney Calhoun, solicited $500 from the company's owner, Frank Peck, for uniforms and equipment in exchange for naming rights, and founded a semi-pro football team, which would compete against other semi-pro football teams in Wisconsin and the Upper Peninsula of Michigan.

Within a matter of months, the Indian Packing Company would be taken over by the Acme Packing Company, but Lambeau would continue to own, play, and coach the now Acme Packers despite severe financial struggles. Choosing blue and gold as his team's colors (in honor of Notre Dame), Lambeau's Packers were nicknamed the "Blues."

In 1921, Lambeau would lose the franchise because of dire financial stress. A principal of the Acme Packing Company, J.E. Clair, would retain the title to the team and be granted admittance into the brand new American Professional Football Association.

That same season, there were three players on the roster using assumed names, because they had played at Notre Dame, and the Acme Packers were kicked out of the APFA, which the next year would become the National Football League. Thus, in 1922, having financial struggles of his own, despite his team being readmitted into the new NFL with Green Bay granted a franchise as a charter member, J.E. Clair turned the team back to the NFL. It was a timely turn of events for Curly Lambeau, who desperately wanted to reacquire the team he'd founded for $500 three years earlier. Lambeau would regain ownership of the team by enlisting four local Green Bay investors to join him: attorney Andrew Turnbull, attorney Gerald Clifford, Dr. Webber Kelly, and Leland Joannes, a wholesale grocery magnate.

Along with Lambeau, these men came to be known as the "Hungry Five," so-called because they always seemed to have their hand(s) out looking for money. They would go on to make the Green Bay Packers a nonprofit, public company in 1923. Each man would serve on the board of directors, with only Lambeau receiving a salary. Turnbull, who also published the Green Bay Press-Gazette, was the team's first president while Kelly, who would also serve one year as president, was the team's physician.

Remarkably astute and forward thinking, the decision to form the company as a not-for-profit would effectively remove any reasons for the franchise to leave Green Bay for a bigger and more lucrative market. The Green Bay Packers, the third oldest NFL team, have been playing in their original city longer than any other NFL franchise.

The Green Bay Packers' ownership structure is in direct violation of the NFL's current league rules regarding team ownership that stipulates there can be no more than 32 owners per team and further that there be one entity holding at least a 30 percent stake in each team. However, these rules, formed by the owners in the 1980s, are not applicable to the Packers, whose ownership model was grandfathered into the NFL decades earlier.

Including the original stock sale of 1923, wherein 1,000 shares were sold at $5 apiece, there have been five stock sales in the team's history, the most recent in 2011-2012, which generated $143 million (269,000 shares sold at $250 per) to fund renovations to Lambeau Field. Based on the original 1923 Articles of Incorporation, no individual is permitted to hold more than 200,000 shares (approximately four percent of the team); and shares do not include equity interest nor pay dividends, cannot be traded, have no securities-law protection, bring no season ticket purchase privileges, and cannot be resold except back to the team for a fraction of the original price. Lastly, transfer of ownership is only allowed between immediate family members. What then, would $250 buy one if they were lucky enough to become a shareholder of the Green Bay Packers? The ability to buy shareholder-only merchandise, voting rights, and an invitation to the corporation's annual shareholder meeting -- but still in all, for a "Cheesehead" to be able to own a piece of their franchise is a cool perk. At present, there are a total of 5,011,557 shares of the Green Bay Packers, Inc., owned by 360,584 stockholders, and the team is operated by a seven-member executive council elected from a 45-member board of directors.

Under Curly Lambeau, the Green Bay Packers would win the first three of their (all-time league-best record) 13 NFC championships, consecutively in 1929, '30, and '31. After a brief respite, the Packers would reel off three more championships in 1936, 1939, and 1944.

Lambeau would retire after the 1949 season and the team would fall on hard times for the next decade, although 1950 would be significant for another reason: green would replace blue, and while losing their nickname, the Green Bay Packers' new colors (green and gold) would become as classic and iconic as any. This relatively short-lived lull would end abruptly with the hiring in 1959 of head coach Vince Lombardi, whose imprint on not only the Green Bay Packers, but on the National Football League, is incalculable.

A native of Brooklyn, New York, Lombardi attended Cathedral Preparatory Seminary in Queens and studied to be a Catholic priest, but would ultimately decide not to be a priest and transfer to St. Francis Prep High School from which he graduated. At Fordham University, Lombardi would in his senior year be one of the famous "seven blocks of granite" offensive linemen.

After coaching for several years at St. Cecilia High School in Englewood, New Jersey, Lombardi would become an assistant coach at Fordham and then at the U.S. Military Academy at West Point before becoming an assistant coach on Jim Lee Howell's New York Giants staff, where one of the assistant coaches was Tom Landry.

The Lombardi teams of the 1960s, with names like Bart Starr, Jim Taylor, Paul Hornung, Forrest Gregg, and Jerry Kramer on offense; and Willie Davis, Willie Wood, Ray Nitschke, and Herb Adderly on defense, set a standard of excellence to which all future great teams would aspire. They would win the first Super Bowl in 1966 by defeating the Kansas City Chiefs of the AFL. In 1967, a watershed year for the Green Bay Packers, they would take part in one of the most iconic games of all time, the so-called "Ice Bowl" championship game in Lambeau Field against the Dallas Cowboys (coached by Tom Landry). To this day, it was the coldest game ever played, memorialized by Bart Starr's last-second quarterback sneak from the two-foot line behind right guard Jerry Kramer's block.

The Packers would then defeat the Oakland Raiders in the second Super Bowl, completing Lombardi's epic stint as head coach. He stepped down to become general manager in 1968, before departing Green Bay to become head coach and general manager of the Washington Redskins in 1969.

The Packers would have little success for the next two decades, 1968 to 1991 to be exact, but that would change with the arrival of Ron Wolf, a highly regarded football executive who'd come out of the Oakland Raiders' scouting department. In 1992, in quick succession, Wolf would hire Mike Holmgren as his head coach, acquire Brett Favre from the Atlanta Falcons for a first-round draft pick, and, the following year, sign the most coveted free agent of 1993, Reggie White. With those three foundational pieces in place, the Packers would steadily develop back into a playoff team, first experiencing several disheartening post-season losses to the Dallas Cowboys before winning another Super Bowl in 1997, defeating the New England Patriots and then losing the Super Bowl the following year to John Elway's Denver Broncos.

And, after fashioning a Hall of Fame career there, Brett Favre would contentiously move on from the Green Bay Packers, giving way to quarterback Aaron Rogers who would lead the team to its most recent Super Bowl victory in 2011.

Today, with Rogers considered an elite quarterback, and by many the best in the game, the Packers are a highly competitive team, year in and year out, always vying for another Super Bowl appearance. And, as fans of other NFC teams will tell you, that the road to the Super Bowl runs through venerable Lambeau Field is far from a comforting thought.

The oldest (as well as coldest) continuously operating stadium in the NFL, Lambeau Field, first opened in 1957 as the (new) City Stadium, which had replaced the original City Stadium, which had been the Packers' home since 1925. It was renamed for Curly Lambeau in 1965. In all American professional sport, only Fenway Park and Wrigley Field have been homes to their respective teams longer.

Super Bowl Appearances: 5   Wins: 4
Forbes 2017 Valuation: $2.55 Billion

Houston Texans

Year	Owner(s)	Purchase Price
2002-	Robert McNair	$700 Million

Robert McNair was born in a small North Carolina town in 1937. He graduated from the University of South Carolina with a Bachelor of Science degree in 1958. He and his wife, Janice, who he married in college, moved to Houston in 1960 and have lived there ever since.

Before bringing the city of Houston a new NFL expansion franchise in 1999, McNair was best known as the founder of Cogen Technologies, a recyclable energy company. In 1984, McNair, who was close to declaring bankruptcy when his auto and truck leasing company ran out of capital, saw an opportunity. After decades of dealing with Texas refineries and chemical plants through his trucking business, he learned that corporate owners were tired of paying exorbitant public utility bills. Having studied science in college and being a die-hard entrepreneur, McNair stepped out on a limb to test his theory that a private utility company could provide cheaper energy than a public utility. He was right-on.

McNair entered into a 20-year contract to sell power to Jersey Central Power and Light, and Cogen Technologies, the first privately owned co-generation plant, was born. The company grew to be the largest of its kind, and was sold to Enron in 1999 for $1.4 billion. Two years later, Enron went bust.

After the Houston Oilers moved to Tennessee and became the Titans in 1996, McNair became dead set on bringing an NFL franchise back to Houston. To make his NFL bid more appealing, McNair and a partner, Steve Patterson, decided they had to build a new state-of-the-art domed stadium, believing that "if we build it, they will come."

In 1997, they teamed up with the Houston Livestock Show & Rodeo, the biggest game in town, and raised $352 million, and Reliant Stadium, now called NRG Stadium, became a reality.

McNair's strategy worked! In 1999, he paid a $700 million expansion fee and founded the Houston Texans. The Texans played their first season in 2002 and have been trying to prove themselves ever since. Houston hosted the Super Bowl in 2004 and again in 2017.

McNair is a popular team owner and is recognized in Houston for his philanthropy. McNair is a fighter too. Not only did he survive near financial bankruptcy, he is a two-time cancer survivor, beating CLL (chronic lymphocytic leukemia) and squamous cell carcinoma. Now with his clean bill of health, he is determined to be on the sidelines for every game. His Texans remain one of the four NFL teams who haven't made it to the Super Bowl.

Super Bowl Appearances: 0
Forbes 2017 Valuation: $2.8 Billion

Indianapolis Colts

Former name: Baltimore Colts 1953-83

Year	Owner(s)	Purchase Price
1953-1971	Carroll Rosenbloom	$13,000
1972-1996	Robert Irsay	Trade
1997-	Jim Irsay	Inherited

The Indianapolis Colts used to be the Baltimore Colts. The original Baltimore Colts played from 1947 to 1949 in the AAFC until that league merged with the NFL in 1950. The merger brought those original Baltimore Colts, the San Francisco 49ers, and the Cleveland Browns into the NFL. The 1951 Colts, with a record of 1-11, played only one year before the NFL canceled the franchise due to financial problems. In 1953, Bert Bell, NFL commissioner at the time, was looking for someone to buy and relocate the failed Dallas Texans franchise to Baltimore.

Bell knew Carroll Rosenbloom from their college days at Penn, when Rosenbloom played halfback and Bell was backfield coach. Bell felt Rosenbloom would be an excellent owner so he pitched the idea to him. Rosenbloom was keen. Bell challenged the City of Baltimore to sell 15,000 season tickets in six weeks to qualify for the franchise. They sold the tickets and the NFL sold the Dallas Texans franchise to Baltimore under the majority ownership of Rosenbloom, a controversial character whose group paid the $13,000 expansion fee. Rosenbloom reinstated the Baltimore Colts name. It is this second version of the Baltimore Colts that became the Indianapolis Colts we know today.

Carroll Rosenbloom was born and raised in Baltimore in a large Jewish immigrant family. He was the eighth child out of nine. After college, Rosenbloom returned to Baltimore to work for his father's clothing company. One of his first assignments was to go to Roanoke, Virginia, to liquidate the Blue Ridge Overall Company, a small factory his father had acquired. The factory hadn't been able to survive the Depression, but when Rosenbloom arrived, he saw an opportunity for growth. In 1933, as part of the New Deal, the U.S. Civilian Conservation Corps was authorized to provide relief for needy unemployed men. Carroll knew they were going to need something to wear. He pitched Blue Ridge, scored the factory's largest order, and began selling denim work clothes. By 1940, Blue Ridge was supplying clothes to national chains like Sears, Roebuck and J.C. Penney. Carroll claimed he made enough money to retire at age 34. He moved to Maryland's Eastern Shore, got married, and became a gentleman farmer.

It was a shortlived retirement. His father died in 1942 and Rosenbloom, being named the executor of his father's estate, decided to return to business. He continued to grow the Blue Ridge factory to new heights and was even nicknamed, "The Overalls King."

In 1959, he sold the company to P & R for $7 million cash and $20 million in stock. He and his group of investors went on to acquire control of Universal Products company and American Totalizator (Am Tote), a company specializing in equipment used to control pari-mutuel betting at horse racing, greyhound racing, and jai-alai facilities. He also became the largest shareholder in Seven Arts Productions, which backed the Broadway musical "Funny Girl," and the films "Lolita," "Whatever Happened to Baby Jane?" and "Night of the Iguana."

Carroll Rosenbloom was a tough competitor both in business and on the playing field. In 1954, he hired Wilbur Charles "Weeb" Ewbank as head coach and in 1956 he signed future Hall of Fame quarterback Johnny Unitas. Under Rosenbloom's ownership, the Colts became one of the more successful teams in the league, making two of the first five Super Bowls and winning one.

In 1958, after five years of ownership, Rosenbloom's Colts defeated the N.Y. Giants in the nationally televised NFL Championship game that was called "The Greatest Game Ever Played." That game has been credited with launching the NFL into what it has become today, the most valuable league in the world. Following the "glory days" of the '50s, the team began to falter in the early '60s. After nine years as coach, Weeb Ewbank was replaced by Don Shula, at that time the youngest coach in the league.

Rosenbloom's ownership of the Colts ended in 1972 when there were struggles with city officials over issues regarding the decay of Baltimore Memorial Stadium. He *said* he just wanted out. Instead of selling or moving the Colts, he did, in typical Rosenbloom style, a tax-free swap with his buddy, Robert Irsay, for the Los Angeles Rams. The swap apparently saved Rosenbloom several million in capital gains taxes. Now Irsay owned control of the Baltimore Colts and Carroll Rosenbloom had control of the L. A. Rams.

Carroll Rosenbloom might rank as the most famous and notorious of all NFL owners. Rumors and reports abound about his reputation as a gambler, one who even bet on his own team. Carroll drowned in 1979 while swimming in the ocean near his rented home near Miami. It has been rumored, but never verified, that he had ties to the mob and was murdered because of huge unpaid gambling debts. The coroner concluded he died of heart failure.

In 1966, he had married Georgia Frontieri, an attractive former Las Vegas singer-entertainer who was 20 years younger and had been married seven times before Carroll. They had met at the Palm Beach home of his golfing friend, Kennedy family patriarch Joseph Kennedy, in 1957. (Following Rosenbloom's accidental death, Georgia inherited a 70 percent controlling interest in the Rams and became the first female NFL owner). However, it was also reported that Carroll intended to leave control of the team to his son, Steve, (Georgia's stepson), who helped manage the Rams as vice president, but Carroll drowned before any document was signed. The original signed will, meant to take advantage of estate tax deductions for widows, left the controlling interest to Georgia. She fired Steve and took over control of the team.

In 1960, Rosenbloom helped tap 33-tear-old Pete Rozelle to succeed Bert Bell as NFL commissioner. That same year, the City of Baltimore named Rosenbloom "Man of the Year." During his ownership of both the Colts and Rams, Rosenbloom had earned the best winning percentage (.660) in league history. He was also influential in the NFL/AFL merger and played a major role within the NFL's inner circle (along with Art Modell) in negotiating the NFL's television contracts.

Rosenbloom became a hands-on owner but did not interfere with the running of the team. Instead, like the shrewd businessman he was, he hired the best executives he could find and expected them to perform. His appearance and stature was said to exude confidence and power. He was a one-of-a-kind character who was loved and admired by most of his staff and players, not to mention the fans. That is not to say that he was loved by all.

During his stint in L.A., Carroll and Georgia came to mingle with Hollywood celebrities, many of whom were among the 900 people who attended his funeral. Cary Grant, Warren Beatty, Kirk Douglas, Jimmy Stewart and Henry Mancini were just some of them.

Robert Irsay owned the Colts from 1972 until his death in 1997. During his first 10 years of ownership, the team spiraled downward. To make matters worse, Irsay's temper on and off the field left players and employees even less motivated. Irsay became irate when the City of Baltimore refused to provide funds for stadium renovations. The argument between the two parties escalated to such a heated degree that the Maryland State Legislature stepped in and passed a law whereby Baltimore could seize the team from Irsay under eminent domain. The eminent domain action just needed to be signed.

Meanwhile, Indianapolis had been courting Irsay privately to bring his Colts to their city, boasting about the 1982 construction of the new Hoosier Dome. In March 1984, Indianapolis Mayor William Hudnut offered Irsay a $12.5 million loan, a $4 million training complex, and the use of the brand new $77.5 million Hoosier Dome. There was just one small problem: Baltimore.

Mayor Hudnut and his city were not going to be denied. He knew the scoop and helped Irsay pull a fast one. He called his friend and neighbor, the CEO of Mayflower Transit, who deployed 15 moving trucks to go to Baltimore, pack up the Colts, and speed away in the dead of night. Off they went, each truck in a different direction so as to confuse the Maryland State Police in case they got wind of the late-night escape. And, thank goodness Irsay acted swiftly. The Maryland Senate signed the eminent domain bill the following morning, March 29th. But it was too late, the Colts were already safe and sound in Indianapolis.

With no public announcement and the team fleeing town in the middle of the night, Baltimore fans were in shock. Their beloved team was gone. It took 12 years for an NFL team to return to Baltimore.

Robert Irsay died in 1997 and his son Jim Irsay, who had been managing the team's day-to-day operations, took over ownership. Jim must have inherited his father's genes. He engaged in a legal battle with his stepmother over ownership of the team. He prevailed and, at age 37, became the youngest NFL team owner at that time.

Under Jim Irsay's ownership, the team has had considerable success through draft picks like Peyton Manning in 1998 and Andrew Luck in 2012. But, as life on the field was picking up, Irsay's personal life was about to crumble. After a D.U.I. scandal involving drugs and alcohol, where Irsay's mistress wound up dead from a drug overdose, the authorities stepped in. Irsay, whose wife divorced him in 2013, was sentenced to one year's probation and was suspended by the NFL for six games and fined

$500,000. His daughter, Carlie, took over day-to-day operations while her father went to rehab.

Super Bowl Appearances: 4   Wins: 2
Forbes 2017 Valuation: $2.375 Billion

Jacksonville Jaguars

Year	Owner(s)	Purchase Price
1995 - 2011	Wayne Weaver	$140 Million
2012 -	Shahid Khan	$770 Million

      Jacksonville has two distinctive features of which most Americans are unaware. First, it is the largest city in the United States in landmass. Second, the St. Johns River, which runs through the middle of Jacksonville, under I-95, is one of only two rivers in the world that flow south to north, the other being the Nile in Egypt. A beautiful locale, it spans twenty miles from city center to its gloriously pristine beaches. Its landscape is dotted with golf courses. St. Augustine, America's oldest city, is only a half an hour south on I-95. Historically (and to this day), Jacksonville's most important social event is the annual college football rivalry game between Georgia and Florida, aka "The World's Largest Outdoor Cocktail Party."

      There has always been a provincial and somewhat paradoxical nature to the city of Jacksonville. Situated in close proximity to Georgia, Jacksonville feels more generically southern than specifically Floridian, as do, say, Tampa or Miami.

      As such, when the latest NFL expansion occurred in 1995, Jacksonville, the corporate headquarters of both professional golf (PGA) and professional tennis (ATP), was not considered a particularly compelling candidate, either economically or culturally. After all, other than the college football game, Jacksonville's biggest sports attraction was the famous 17th hole at the Tournament Player's Club at Sawgrass (TPC), professional golf's so-called "Fifth Major." Another minus the NFL had to consider: Its television market ranked 54th in the country.

      But then, the city of Jacksonville had yet to meet J. Wayne Weaver, owner of two shoe companies, Nine West and Carnival Shoes. Weaver, a hard-nosed, self-made businessman (worth an estimated $300 million), from Columbus, Georgia, grew up digging ditches and delivering mail, with no time for college, before becoming a shoe salesman.

Weaver put together a group including future Florida governor Jeb Bush, calling it Touchdown Jacksonville! In short order, Weaver declared that he wouldn't make a bid until local businesses purchased 10,000 season tickets at $1,500 apiece. He also promised every visiting team to the 80,000-seat Gator Stadium $1.1 million instead of $600,000, the standard NFL fee at the time of 40 percent of the gate. And when the city of Jacksonville refused to finance any cost overruns for the Gator Stadium renovation, the 58-year-old Weaver, who trained to climb Mt. Kilimanjaro by climbing stairs at the Nine West headquarters in Stamford, Conn., and by running the Boston Marathon despite never having run more than five miles at a time in his life, simply walked away from the deal. When the city council finally acquiesced, Weaver renewed his bid.

Weaver would own the Jaguars for 16 years and at the end of the 2011 season sell the franchise to Shahid "Shad" Kahn, the Pakistani-born American business tycoon whose net worth is over $6.5 billion. Mr. Kahn is one of only two foreign-born owners of a "big three" franchise, the other being Mikhail Prokhorov, owner of the Brooklyn Nets in the NBA.

Shad's first job while attending college at the University of Illinois was washing dishes for $1.20 an hour. He came from a middle-class family in Pakistan and came to the States in 1967 to study engineering, in which he excelled. After college, he worked in the automotive manufacturing business for Flex-N- Gate, which made parts for the Big Three automakers. He eventually became chief engineer. In 1977, he formed Bumper Works, with the help of a $50,000 Small Business Administration loan, and soon purchased Flex-N-Gate and merged it with Bumper Works. By 1989, Flex-N-Gate was making all the bumpers for Toyota's American cars. In 2015, revenues were close to $5 billion with 18,500 employees in 62 manufacturing plants around the world.

In 2013, Shahid (Shad) Kahn, a Muslim, bought the English Premier League's Fulham football/soccer team from the Egyptian billionaire Mohamed Al Fayed, former owner of Harrod's Department Store and father of Dodi Fayed, who died in the fatal crash with Princess Diana. Khan has served on various NFL Boards and has been instrumental in bringing the NFL to London.

Alas, the Jags have not had a winning season since Khan bought the team.

Super Bowl Appearances: 0
Forbes 2017 Valuation: $2.075 Billion

Kansas City Chiefs

Former name: Dallas Texans 1960-62

Year	Owner(s)	Purchase Price
1960-2006	Lamar Hunt	$25,000
2006-	Clark Hunt	Inherited

Lamar Hunt was one of the most influential people in American sports history. He was born to the great oil tycoon, H. L. Hunt. He graduated from Southern Methodist University in 1956 and dreamed of owning his own NFL franchise in his alma mater city of Dallas. With inheritance in hand, his first order of business was to apply for an NFL expansion franchise. He was turned down. Having deep pockets, he simply moved on to an even better idea.

In 1960, Hunt, who was dubbed "The Quiet Texan" for his mild and humble demeanor, rounded up a group of seven fellow businessmen and formed a new league, the AFL, the American Football League. The franchise fee was $25,000. Hunt owned the Dallas Texans (now the Kansas City Chiefs). The Houston Oilers (now the Tennessee Titans) were owned by his good friend Bud Adams. The other six members of the "Original Eight" were Harry Wismer (New York Titans, now the New York Jets); Bob Howsam (Denver Broncos); Barron Hilton (Los Angeles Chargers, now the San Diego Chargers); Ralph Wilson, Jr. (Buffalo Bills); Billy Sullivan (Boston Patriots, now the New England Patriots); and a group of eight investors led by F. Wayne Valley (Oakland Raiders, who replaced the Vikings). They were called the "Foolish Club" because of their seemingly foolhardy venture in taking on the established NFL.

In reaction to Hunt forming the first pro football team in the coveted Dallas market, the NFL retaliated by awarding Clint Murchison Jr. the first NFL expansion franchise, the Dallas Cowboys. While Hunt's Texans were one of the better AFL teams, tickets sales weren't great. To avoid competing for fans, Hunt decided to move his team to another city.

Kansas City was so anxious to have a pro football team, any pro football team, that Mayor H. Roe Bartle guaranteed Hunt minimum home attendance of 25,000 per game. The city, in fact, sold tickets to the public to see a team whose identity was not yet known. Once the guaranteed seats were sold, the city held a "Name the Team" contest and the Texans became the Chiefs in 1963.

Just four years later, the Chiefs appeared in the first Super Bowl, a name Hunt coined after watching his children play with their favorite toy, a "super-ball." Even though the Chiefs lost to the Packers 35-10, they remained successful through the '60s. In 1970, the AFC's Chiefs won the Super Bowl, beating the Vikings 23-7. It was the last Super Bowl played before the official NFL/AFL merger later that year. The two leagues agreed to the merger in 1966 but it did not become official until 1970. The AFL was the only league to ever merge with an existing league without losing any franchises.

In 1972, Hunt became the first AFL owner inducted into the Pro Football Hall of Fame. The Lamar Hunt Trophy is presented to the AFC Champion each year.

While the KC Chiefs were Hunt's favorite team, he was also involved with six different professional sports leagues and seven sports franchises. He has 13 championship rings from five different professional sports groups: AFL & NFL, NBA, MLS, NASL and the U.S. Soccer Open Cup. He was also one of the founding investors in the Chicago Bulls who, with Michael Jordan, won six NBA championships.

Lamar Hunt died in 2006. Following his death, his son Clark and his three siblings inherited ownership of the Chiefs. Clark, who was named chairman of the board in 2005, continues to serve as CEO. On the field, the Chiefs always seem to be in the "hunt," making the playoffs again in 2017 only to lose to the Steelers' record-setting six field goals.

Super Bowl Appearances: 2   Wins: 1
Forbes 2017 Valuation: $2.1 Billion

Los Angeles Rams

Former names: Cleveland Rams 1937-45; Los Angeles Rams 1946-94; St. Louis Rams 1947-2016

Year	Owner(s)	Purchase Price
1937-1941	Homer Marshman	$10,000
1941-1962	Dan Reeves	$135,000
1971-1972	Mary Reeves	Inherited
1972	Robert Irsay	$19 Million
1972-1979	Carroll Rosenbloom	Swap
1979-2010	Georgia Frontiere	Inherited
2010	Stan Kroenke	$750 Million

The Rams move around a lot: from Cleveland to Los Angeles to St. Louis and then back to Los Angeles. Moving so much is always a mixed bag: one fan base is left feeling betrayed and abandoned while the other opens its arms in a warm and welcoming embrace. But on the other hand, you get to be the only franchise in NFL history to have won championships for three different home cities. And it's not like the Rams are nomadic, they've spent considerable chunks of time in their various cities: 10 seasons in Cleveland, 48 in L.A., and 20 in St. Louis.

Originally an AAFL franchise, the Cleveland Rams franchise was founded in 1936 by Cleveland attorney Homer Marshman and player-coach Damon Wetzel. The Rams would join the NFL one year later in 1937.

Fordham University throughout the 1920s and 1930s had a powerhouse team renowned for its bruising and hard-nosed style of play -- their team nickname, the Fordham Rams. And that is how the Cleveland Rams came to be the only team in NFL history named after a college team. Cleveland had already had its share of professional football teams (the Tigers, Bulldogs, and Indians) but the first to take hold, gain traction, and become a viable, ongoing franchise would be the Cleveland Rams.

In 1941, the Rams would be purchased by Dan Reeves, whose family fortune came from the retail grocery business (they would be bought out by Safeway). Reeves led a small ownership group that included Cleveland native and entertainment titan Bob Hope (who'd briefly boxed professionally under the name Packy East).

The Cleveland Rams would win their first NFL championship in 1945. Right after that, Reeves applied to the NFL to relocate his team to Los Angeles and the request was denied. Upon Reeves's threat to sell the team and get out of sports altogether, the NFL approved the relocation.

The NFL had been without a black player since 1933, and when the Los Angeles Memorial Coliseum had made Reeves's lease conditional upon acquiring a black player, Reeves was only too happy to comply, first signing Kenny Washington and then Woody Strode before the 1946 season.

One of the perks of playing in Hollywood, Strode would be the first of many Los Angeles Rams to transition into a successful acting career after his playing days (later would come the likes of Fred Dryer, Roman Gabriel, Merlin Olsen, Rosey Greer, etc.). While there were certainly other professional sports teams in Southern California (including the L.A. Dons of the AAFL), the Los Angeles Rams were the first *major* sports team in Los Angeles and were for close to two decades synonymous with professional sports in Los Angeles ... until the Dodgers and Lakers arrived.

The Rams of this vintage (1949-1955) were an elite team in the league with the top offense in the sport. They featured a cadre of future Hall of Famers: quarterback Bob Waterfield, who'd won the first championship in Cleveland and was a Southern California product -- he'd gone to UCLA and married his Van Nuys high school sweetheart, the movie star, Jane Russell -- and two splendid wide receivers, Elroy "Crazy Legs" Hirsch, and Tom Fears. The Los Angeles Rams would appear in four NFL championships, winning one in 1951. By that time, Waterfield would be splitting quarterback duties with Norm "The Dutchman" Van Brocklin, who would succeed him.

Another player on those mid-1940s teams would make it into the Hall of Fame, but not for his talent as a player. Fred Gehrke, an excellent halfback (he'd led the league in rushing) and valued team member of the Cleveland Rams' 1946 championship team, was a better artist than football player. In 1948, the art history major and technical illustrator from the University of Utah hand-painted ram's horns on either side of his helmet. Owner Dan Reeves loved the painted emblem and, after receiving permission from the league, commissioned Gehrke to hand-paint the team's new logo on the sides of all the team's helmets. And that in turn would start a frenzy of organizational logo invention across the National Football League -- the Baltimore Colts' horseshoe the first to appear after Gehrke's horns.

The Los Angeles Memorial Coliseum, home to both UCLA and USC football, was a huge venue accommodating 103,000 fans. Even in the late 1950s and very early 1960s, when the Los Angeles Rams were no more than a mediocre team, and one of five professional sports teams in Southern California, they were extremely popular, regularly drawing 10,000 to 40,000 (and more) fans above league average. In a 1957 game against the San Francisco 49ers, the Rams drew 102,368 fans. In 1958, the Rams' home attendance averaged 83,681, twice drawing more than 100,000 fans.

And yet Dan Reeves would struggle financially for years at a time, with the Rams operating at a loss. Despite these difficulties, Reeves would in 1962 acquire a 51 percent equity position in the team through paying out $4.2 million to the partners (mainly oil company magnate Edwin Pauley) he'd taken on in 1948.

By the mid-1960s, the Los Angeles Rams would experience a renaissance of sorts. The franchise that had built its reputation on its high-octane offense during the preceding 15 years now featured one of the greatest defensive lines in the history of the NFL. With this newfound star power on both sides of the ball, the Rams would in 1967 (the year Dan Reeves was enshrined in the NFL Hall of Fame) become the first NFL team to surpass one million spectators in a season, and would, in fact, duplicate that feat the following season.

Consistent winning, however, would not yield playoff success, and the Rams won nothing in this time. Dan Reeves died in 1971, leaving the team to his widow, Mary. Two years later she would sell her 51 percent of the Rams to a wealthy Chicago businessman named Robert Irsay, who had made his fortune in his family's heating and ventilation business.

On that same day, Irsay would trade the franchise he'd just purchased to Carroll Rosenbloom, who bought the NFL's Baltimore Colts in 1953. A straight-up trade of franchises, there was enough sleight-of-hand deception to make the world's greatest three-card monte dealer doff his cap in admiration. Carroll Rosenbloom, wanting to move to warmer climes, not to mention a bigger, glitzier, and more profitable market, had engineered the selling of one franchise, the acquisition of another, and the payment of not one cent of capital gains tax. Seemingly beloved and despised in equal measure, Rosenbloom could be, as they say, a good friend and a bad enemy. He was a colorful character that enjoyed living large in Southern California and Las Vegas, with many movie star and show business friends.

Rosenbloom's football legacy is ofttimes obscured by gossip and innuendo regarding his gambling, including betting on football games. There is certainly enough smoke to fairly deduce fire, but there have never been any definitive or declarative pronouncements on the subject -- just any number of juicy anecdotes and unsubstantiated second and third-party accounts. This even extends to the events of his death -- drowning while swimming in the ocean near his home in Golden Beach, Florida. Suspicions persist that he may have been the victim of foul play having to do with his unsavory activities, though it is all speculation and conjecture.

At the time of his death in 1979, Carroll Rosenbloom, the owner of two NFL franchises (at different times), held the highest winning percentage (.660) of any owner in the history of the NFL.

For the decade of the 1970s, Rosenbloom's Los Angeles Rams would be an elite team. As any casual fan of the NFL well knows, the 1970s had any number of great, short-term dynastic teams (dynastic with a small 'D') in that while not reeling off multiple Super Bowl victories, they would be dominant: namely, the Dallas Cowboys and the Minnesota Vikings. And so, despite winning seven consecutive NFC West divisions, the Rams, under head coach Chuck Knox, would lose their first four conference championships, twice each, to the Cowboys and the Vikings. And of course, in their first Super Bowl appearance in 1979, they would meet the real deal in terms of a 1970s dynasty, losing to the Pittsburgh Steelers.

Upon his death, Rosenbloom's second wife, the seven-times married former Las Vegas showgirl and television personality Georgia Frontiere inherited 70 percent of the team, with Rosenbloom's five children inheriting the remaining 30 percent.

During the decade of the 1980s, the Rams would continue their practice of making the playoffs and then falling short. Frontiere relocated the team to Anaheim, a plan that Carroll had initiated in 1978. Anaheim Stadium (baseball home of the Angels) was retrofitted and enclosed to accommodate football.

Making the playoffs seven times between 1980 and '89, the Rams continued their long-held practice of being good enough to make the post-season and then losing. By the early 1990s, with the team's stature (and attendance) diminishing, Frontiere, who in 1980 had bought from her children an additional 30 percent of the team, sought to relocate the Rams to her hometown of St. Louis, Missouri, enticed in part by a guaranteed yearly profit of $20 million from season-ticket sales, as well as a favorable lease with the Trans World Dome, still under construction at the time.

When the league did not approve her request, Frontiere threatened to bring an anti-trust lawsuit, and the league capitulated, allowing the move in 1995. At this time, Stan Kroenke of Missouri, quite wealthy in his own right before marrying a Walmart heiress, purchased 40 percent of the team from Frontiere, with the proviso that upon her death he would retain the right of first refusal to purchase the remainder of the team from her estate.

It would not take long for the now St. Louis Rams to reverse their fortunes. In 1999, head coach Dick Vermeil led the Rams to another NFL championship appearance. These Rams would make a return trip to the Super Bowl in 2001, losing to the New England Patriots on a last-second field goal by Adam Vinatieri.

In 2010, exercising his right of first refusal, Kroenke purchased the remaining shares of the team from Frontiere's children upon her death. He would transfer ownership of the Denver Nuggets of the NBA and the Colorado Avalanche of the NHL to his wife, Anne Kroenke Walton, to comply with a league rule that prohibited owning professional teams in other NFL markets. He would also go to arbitration (and win) over a clause in his stadium lease stating that the Rams' current stadium must be in the top 25 percent of all NFL stadiums. This would allow Kroenke to break his long-term lease and switch to a year-to-year lease arrangement.

In 2016, Kroenke received permission from the NFL to relocate the Rams back to Los Angeles. They are currently playing in their old and "original" venue, the Los Angeles Memorial Coliseum, while Kroenke is constructing a new, 70,000-seat stadium on the site of the old Hollywood Park racetrack that will be the centerpiece of the new Los Angeles Entertainment Center in the Inglewood section of the city.

How long of a run will the Rams have in Los Angeles this time around? While nothing is certain, with a brand-new stadium, an owner worth an estimated $7.4 billion, and a second chance for Los Angeles to reclaim its historic NFL franchise, a run equaling (if not surpassing) the 48-year tenure of the first Los Angeles Rams is a bet Carroll Rosenbloom would surely have placed.

Super Bowl Appearances: 3   Wins: 1
Forbes 2017 Valuation: $3.0 Billion

Miami Dolphins

Year	Owner(s)	Purchase Price
1966-1989	Joe Robbie	$7.5 Million
1990-1993	Tim Robbie	Inherited
1994-2008	Wayne Huizenga	$140 Million
2009-	Stephen Ross	$1.1 Billion

The Miami Dolphin franchise was founded in 1966 when Joe Robbie, an American politician and lawyer, teamed up with fellow Lebanese-American friend, actor and comedian, Danny Thomas, to raise $7.5 million for the AFL expansion franchise.

Robbie was born and raised in South Dakota to immigrant parents. From humble beginnings, he worked his way through the Great Depression, sending most of his pay as a lumberjack back to his family. It's no surprise this future politician won a debating scholarship to Northern State Teachers College, which paved the way for him to go to the University of South Dakota and later graduate from law school.

In 1948, Robbie entered politics. He eventually moved his family to Minneapolis where he was a protégé of Hubert Humphrey, the 38th Vice President of the United States. It was there he started his own law firm.

Robbie fell into owning a professional football team. One of his clients had requested his counsel about the possibility of putting an AFL team in Philadelphia. The plan fell through and AFL Commissioner Joe Foss, an old friend, suggested Miami as an alternate site. Robbie's client wasn't interested, but Robbie was.

Unlike some other franchise owners, Robbie wasn't a millionaire. He was a lawyer, a politician, the father of 11 children, and a self-proclaimed shrewd businessman. He is credited with being the Dolphins' first owner because, after pooling together the funds for the expansion fee, it was only a matter of time until he bought out the other investors to gain full ownership.

One of Robbie's best decisions was to hire head coach Don Shula in 1970. Robbie surreptitiously romanced Shula away from the Colts in 1969 just before the two leagues merged. Upset about his tactics, the NFL charged the Dolphins with tampering. For compensation, Miami had to surrender a first-round draft pick to Baltimore. It was worth it because Shula immediately took the team to its first winning season, and in year two the team made it to the '72 Super Bowl only to lose to the Cowboys 24-3. The next year history was in the making as the 1972-'73 Dolphins went undefeated (17-0), beating the Redskins in the '73 Super Bowl 14-7.

The Dolphins are still the only NFL team to end the season with a perfect 17-0 record. The Dolphins repeated as NFL Super Bowl champions in 1973-'74 and, get this: *the Dolphins have pro football's best record since 1970.*

Having one of the best teams in the NFL wasn't enough for Joe Robbie. He was adamant about financing a new stadium for the Dolphins and pledged his assets, including the Dolphins, as collateral for it. He believed the self-financed Joe Robbie Stadium, which cost $115 million, would not only host a Super Bowl (which it did in 1989) but would also be unique and accommodate future Miami professional sports teams including baseball and soccer. Eventually it did when MLB's Marlins came to Miami in the '90s. While the stadium was quite an accomplishment, it soon became a thorn in the side of Robbie's heirs when he died in 1990.

Before Robbie's death, he set up a living trust to ensure that the Dolphins would be kept in the Robbie family for at least another generation. But, with $90 million in stadium debt and looming estate taxes due, the Robbie family was in a bind. In what has been called one of the worst estate planning fiascos in sports ownership history, they were forced to sell shares of the franchise and stadium for bottom basement prices. Who was there to scoop them up? None other than garbage-king-billionaire Wayne Huizenga, the investor who bought 15 percent of the team for $12 million and 50 percent of the stadium for $5 million.

Huizenga was born in 1937 to Dutch parents and grew up in the suburbs of Chicago. A college dropout and a self-made man, he got his start by borrowing $5,000 from his father to start a garbage pick-up company in 1968. By 1971, he had a strong hold on garbage hauling companies and founded Waste Management, Inc. which he took public in 1983. It was his first of three Fortune 500 companies, the other two being Blockbuster Video and AutoNation.

In 1994, Huizenga agreed to purchase the remaining shares of the Dolphins, and the stadium, for a total of $140 million. He already owned two other Florida expansion teams: baseball's year-old Florida Marlins, which he acquired for a $95 million fee, and the NHL's Florida Panthers, which cost $50 million.

In 2008, after being sole owner of the Dolphins for 18 years, Huizenga decided it was time to bring in a partner. He was 70 and felt the need to focus on estate planning, saying, "We don't need some old guy limping around here trying to run this franchise."

Huizenga negotiated with real estate developer Stephen Ross who would acquire 50 percent of the franchise, Dolphin Stadium, and surrounding developable land for $550 million. One year later, Ross purchased another 45 percent of the team and stadium, making the total price tag $1.1 billion. Not a bad win for Huizenga! In 2016, Forbes put his worth at $2.6 billion.

Stephen Ross grew up in South Florida. Owning a Florida franchise like the Dolphins had been a lifelong dream. In 1972, he borrowed $10,000 from his mother, launched his own company, and made a fortune as a real estate developer. After acquiring the Dolphins, Ross brought in celebrities Gloria Estefan, Marc Anthony, Venus Williams, Serena Williams, Jimmy Buffett and others as minority owners. He wanted the glitz.

At one point, he considered investing $400 million to make major improvements to the stadium. Before agreeing to invest his own funds, he argued with the City of Miami that the cost of such repairs should be shared by the public, using taxpayer dollars. The city refused and so did the fans who saw Ross as a rich opportunist. Ross wasn't too pleased and dropped a few hints that perhaps the Dolphins should be moved up the road to Palm Beach, where he had a home. In the middle of this controversy, Ross donated $200 million to his alma mater, the University of Michigan. Fans couldn't help but feel a little slighted that Ross should be so generous at a time when Miami and the Dolphins needed him to spruce up their stadium. Ouch!

While Ross loved South Florida and spent much of his youth there, he resided full time in New York City. which was another point of animosity with Dolphin fans. After all, Ross had originally tried to buy the N.Y. Jets but lost the bid to Woody Johnson. It was difficult for fans not to blame him, an absentee owner, for the Dolphins' poor performance on the field since he took over. The Dolphins hadn't made it to the playoffs or even had a winning season until 2016/17 when they made the playoffs but lost in the first round.

Super Bowl Appearances: 5   Wins: 2
Forbes 2017 Valuation: $2.575 Billion

Minnesota Vikings

Year	Owner(s)	Purchase Price
1961-1964	Bill Boyer & Max Winter	$1 Million
1965-1986	Max Winter	
1987-1990	Wheelock Whitney	
1991-1997	Roger Headrick	
1998-2004	B.J. "Red" McCombs	$250 Million
2005-	Zygi Wilf	$600 Million

The Minnesota Vikings were originally slated to be one of the first eight AFL franchises. But in 1961, a group of Minnesota businessmen, led by Bill Boyer and Max Winter, were approached by the NFL and offered the 14ᵗʰ NFL franchise. The investment group pulled out of the AFL deal and instead went with the NFL, paying an expansion fee of $1 million. The Vikings were owned by different groups of minority investors over their first 30 years.

One noteworthy minority owner, Ole Haugsrud, who (for $1) founded the Duluth Eskimos, an NFL team of the late-1920s, struck a unique and interesting deal. When he sold the Eskimos back to the NFL, he was guaranteed first rights to any future NFL team in Minnesota. While he passed on the Minneapolis Red Jackets in 1929, he exercised his option in 1960 when the Vikings came to town. He was given, at no cost, 10 percent ownership of the Vikings, which he held until his death in 1976. Otherwise, control of the team bounced around over the years.

Bill Boyer was in control as the team's first president but was replaced by Max Winter in 1965. Winter remained the team's president until 1987, when Wheelock Whitney replaced him. Roger Headrick took over for Whitney in 1991. Until 1998, no single owner ever stood out, but their collective efforts got something right because the Vikings are considered one of the most successful teams in NFL history. Even though they never won the Super Bowl, they qualified for the playoffs 26 times, third-most in the league. The team, like the Buffalo Bills, has played in four Super Bowls without a win.

The Vikings' fans are as loyal and passionate as any in the league. Often seen dressed in Viking costumes with purple and yellow face paint, there is nothing dull about this group. The Viking name was chosen to represent the Nordic tradition of strength and perseverance. There is a strong sense of Scandinavian pride and camaraderie among fans who share a history of team success and deep-rooted heritage.

There have only been two majority owners in the team's history. Red McCombs, a billionaire out of San Antonio, Texas, bought a majority stake in the Vikings from a group of 10 co-owners for a reported $250 million in 1998. McCombs was also a former owner of the NBA's San Antonio Spurs and Denver Nuggets. He originally made his fortune founding Red McCombs Automotive Group, and later co-founded Clear Channel Communications, now called I Heart Media, Inc. After an unsuccessful attempt to replace the Hubert H. Humphrey Metrodome, McCombs sold the team for $600 million in 2005 to a group of investors led by Zygi Wilf.

Zygi Wilf, whose parents survived the Holocaust, became a successful real-estate developer. His company, Garden Commercial Properties, owns more than a hundred commercial properties and 90,000 apartment units around the country. A savvy developer and businessman,

Wilf's leadership and lobbying resulted in plans for a $1 billion stadium being passed, finally, by the state senate in 2012.

The stadium took nearly four years to build, during which time, Wilf and his business partners (his brother and cousin) were found guilty of racketeering by a New Jersey court for keeping a separate set of books to hide shared revenues from former business partners in a 1980 real estate deal. The judge ordered the Wilfs to pay $84.5 million in damages. Wilf's lawyers promised the fine would have no bearing on the ability to meet a $477 million commitment to fund the Wilfs' share of the new stadium, which was already under construction. In the end, the Wilfs will pay about $550 million of the stadium's costs. The balance of the funds will come from public and city revenues, naming rights, sponsorships, licensing fees, and a nifty $200 million loan from the NFL.

Finally, the Viking players and fans alike can bask in the glory of their new state-of-the-art U.S. Bank Stadium, located in downtown Minneapolis. Their first regular season game was held on September 18, 2016, when they beat the Green Bay Packers. The new stadium will be the second one in the NFL to have a fixed and translucent roof, the other being Detroit. However, the Vikings stadium will have the five largest pivoting glass doors in the world. This feature will allow natural light to enter the stadium and provide a view of downtown Minneapolis. These operable glass panels can swivel to allow the outside to come in, if desirable. Game day in the Twin Cities just got a whole lot better (and warmer). U.S. Bank Stadium is scheduled to host Super Bowl LII in 2018.

Super Bowl Appearances: 4   Wins: 0
2017 Forbes Valuation: $2.4 Billion

New England Patriots

Former name: Boston Patriots 1960-70

Year	Owner(s)	Purchase Price
1959-1988	Billy Sullivan	$25,000
1988-1991	Victor Kiam	$85 Million
1992-1993	James Orthwein	$23.5 Million
1994-	Robert Kraft	$172 Million

In the NFL, the term "dynasty," as applied to certain franchises, has a fairly simple and inexact (if not formal) definition: any team that has won multiple championships in a relatively short period of time is considered a dynasty: the Green Bay Packers, who won five titles in seven years; the San Francisco 49ers, winning five Super Bowls in 13 years; and of course, the Pittsburgh Steelers winning four Super Bowls in four years.

Beyond that metric, the one other defining characteristic of an NFL "dynasty" is the presence of a Hall of Fame tandem of head coach and quarterback: Lombardi and Starr; Walsh and Montana; and Noll and Bradshaw. This is the reason other great teams with multiple championships such as the Dallas Cowboys and the Baltimore Colts don't quite rise to this exalted status -- the same quarterback with different head coaches, or the inverse, does not a dynasty make.

However, the New England Patriots have complicated this notion by, frankly, becoming a category unto themselves. Through an unprecedented and sustained period of excellence of 14 years (2001 to 2015) in which they have four Super Bowl victories in six Super Bowl appearances in addition to division and conference championships in all but two of those years (2002 and 2008), the New England Patriots have literally redefined what it means to be an NFL dynasty. Likewise, a category unto themselves is the duo of head coach Bill Belichick and quarterback Tom Brady, whose Hall of Fame credentials make their election a mere formality (five years after their careers are over).

The last original AFL franchise, the Boston Patriots, starting play in 1960, were certainly embraced by the city of Boston although they remained very much the "new kid" in town. Remember the transformational nature of Boston pro sports in the decade of the 1960s: the Celtics were becoming *those* Celtics of Bill Russell; Bobby Orr was becoming a Boston deity leading the Bruins, and Carl Yastrzemski was becoming a Hall of Famer and winning the Triple Crown.

By the time William (Billy) Sullivan secured the AFL Boston franchise in 1959, Boston had seen five professional football teams come and go -- the Boston Bulldogs, Braves, Shamrocks, Redskins, and Bears.

The American Football League (AFL -- aka the Grange League) was founded in 1926 by Charles C.C. Pyle and General Charles X. Zimmerman, featuring legendary running back Red Grange, the "Galloping Ghost." Pyle was Grange's agent and the two co-owned the New York Yankees football team for which Grange was also the star playing attraction. The AFL was formed to rival the older and already established National Football League, competing against them not only for players but for fan bases as well. The league would only last one season (1926) before folding and because of subsequent iterations is also referred to as the "AFL I". It was in this league in that year (1926) that Boston would have its very first professional football team, the Boston Bulldogs (formerly the Pottsville Maroons of Pottsville, Pennsylvania founded in 1920). And just three years later, in 1932, Boston would get its second pro football team when George Preston Marshall would be awarded an NFL franchise, naming his team the Boston Braves.

A common practice of the time was to give a city's professional teams from different sports the same name -- the Boston Braves baseball team was one of two in the city (along with the Red Sox) during this era. In 1936, the second American Football League (aka AFL II) would be created and last all of two seasons with a Boston franchise called the Boston Shamrocks.

Thus, Boston had two professional football teams playing in rival leagues at the same time. To make matters worse, the AFL Shamrocks outdrew the NFL Braves, prompting Marshall first to rename his team the Boston Redskins and then, in 1937, to move the team to Washington, D.C. (In 1940, again just for one season, a third League (aka the "AFL III") would be created.

There is more than a little controversy as to Marshall's reasons for the name change, which reverberates to this day given the ongoing debate over the political correctness of retaining "Redskins" as the Washington franchise's team name. Briefly, Boston's head coach, William "Lone Star" Dietz, also a fine player in his own right, always claimed Native American heritage (as a member of the Sioux Nation). Additionally, there were several other Native American players on the Boston team. The popular mythology is that Marshall changed the name of the team in deference to Dietz and the other Native American players. The factual reality is that his decision to rename his team had more to do with wanting to maintain the American Indian motif and association from the Braves name, than relating directly to Lone Star Dietz, who eventually was proven not to be Native American at all. That Marshall's decision in rebranding his team was motivated more by business than any genuine attempt to honor or recognize Native Americans seems entirely consistent with his well-known and indeed infamous reputation as the most racist owner in professional football.

The West Virginia native steadfastly refused to sign a black player to the Redskins for decades, only doing so, finally, when coerced in 1962, under threat by then Attorney General Robert F. Kennedy of having the 30-year lease to the Redskins' D.C. stadium revoked if he failed to comply. That player, Syracuse All-American running back Ernie Davis ultimately refused "to play for that S.O.B.," and was subsequently traded for the Cleveland Browns' All-Pro halfback and wide receiver, Bobby Mitchell.

At first glance, Billy Sullivan, a native of Lowell, Massachusetts, graduate of Boston College, and son of a Boston Globe correspondent, had all the credentials to be the successful owner of a Boston franchise, with deep local roots and family connections -- his father was good friends with John Francis "Honey Fitz" Fitzgerald, the mayor of Boston (and maternal grandfather of John F. Kennedy). Sullivan was a beloved raconteur in Boston -- a larger-than-life storyteller; founder of the Jimmy Fund, a charity for the treatment of children's cancer, and a local benefactor to many. Yet, upon closer inspection, there was always something of a "day late and dollar short" aspect to Sullivan. He was the lovable comic strip character that always has the rain cloud suspended above his head. For all his family connections, Sullivan did not come from serious wealth nor would he ever amass any during his lifetime. Quite the opposite -- as the joke goes, Billy Sullivan was called the only man ever to parlay his life savings of $8,000 into a $100 million debt.

At various times, a sportswriter, college sports publicist (Boston College and Notre Dame), printer, and oil company executive, Sullivan wanted to acquire an NFL franchise for Boston. The NFL commissioner at the time, Bert Bell, had promised Sullivan that he would introduce the idea at an upcoming NFL meeting, but Bell died before that meeting would take place. Undeterred, Sullivan next arranged a meeting with an NFL patriarch, Tim Mara, founder and owner of the New York Giants; Mara died on the day of that meeting.

Eventually, the NFL would decide against having a franchise in Boston, pointing to the city's unenviable track record regarding professional football: five franchises that had either left town or folded. Thus, when the opportunity arose for Sullivan to acquire an AFL franchise, he took it, kicking in his life savings of $8,000, and joining a group of eight investors. Of the original AFL "Foolish Club" owners, half of whom were seriously wealthy like Lamar Hunt, Bud Adams, Ralph Wilson, and Barron Hilton, and half of whom were seriously NOT wealthy, like Harry Wismer, Bob Howsam, and F. Wayne Valley, Billy Sullivan was most certainly in the latter category.

Sullivan would immediately install his two sons in key team positions: Chuck as executive vice president, and Patrick as general manager. In these early years, the Boston Patriots would play home games in Nickerson Field, Harvard Stadium, Fenway Park, and Alumni Stadium before Sullivan would decide to relocate to Foxborough, Massachusetts, pretty much equidistant (20 miles) from both Boston and Providence, Rhode Island. He would get the Schaefer Brewing Company to pay for 25 percent of the construction cost and privately fund the rest for a new stadium there.

To coincide with moving into the new Schaefer Stadium in 1971, Sullivan decided to rename his team to better regionalize the franchise, choosing the Bay State Patriots as the new name. It was swiftly rejected by the NFL, though they would approve his second choice, the New England Patriots. In one stadium or another, Foxborough, Mass., would remain the home of the New England Patriots to this day: from the original Schaefer Stadium that was renamed Sullivan Stadium and then renamed Foxboro Stadium, to a new facility (in the same area) in 2002, Gillette Stadium, which the Patriots presently call home.

Through a variety of manipulations, Sullivan would throughout the 1960s grow in power, consolidate his ownership position, and accumulate a massive debt burden by continually borrowing from banks against projected team revenues that never materialized. Nonetheless, in 1975, Sullivan was named the majority owner of the New England Patriots.

In 1984, the Sullivans underwrote and bankrolled the Jackson Five Victory Tour featuring Michael Jackson, at the time the biggest music star in the world. In typical Billy Sullivan fashion, it was the "can't miss" venture … that missed. He'd put up Sullivan Stadium as collateral and by the end of the tour his losses were said to equal his net worth. In 1985, after multiple attempts to borrow more money from the banks, and then seeking assistance from private people including Michael Jackson himself and Reebok chairman and CEO, Michael Fireman, all to no avail, Sullivan sought permission from the NFL to sell 49 percent of the team in a public offering, which the NFL refused. With no alternatives left, Sullivan was forced to put both Sullivan Stadium and the New England Patriots up for sale.

At this exact time, a totally under the radar and seemingly unrelated transaction occurred. Robert Kraft, a magnate in the paper industry and member of an orthodox Jewish family in Brookline, Mass., quietly purchased a 10-year lease option on the Foxboro Raceway (situated on land directly adjacent to Sullivan Stadium).

In the ensuing years, Sullivan would experience several aborted attempts to reach a sale agreement with, among others, Donald Trump; Marvin Davis, the Denver oil billionaire who'd owned 20th Century Fox; and former Attorney General of the United States, Bob Tisch (who would later purchase a half-interest in the New York Giants). By 1988, the downward spiral had reached critical mass and the Sullivans, to stave off a court-mandated auction of Sullivan Stadium, filed for protection from creditors under Chapter 11 in bankruptcy court in Boston. They would also have to borrow $4 million from the NFL just to make payroll.

In 1988, Sullivan would sell the New England Patriots to Victor Kiam, President and CEO of Remington Products (according to the famous commercial, he liked the electric shaver gifted to him by his wife so much, he bought the company). It is important to note that Victor Kiam bought the team but *not* the stadium, which was still in receivership. And finally, in 1988, when the bankruptcy court did put Sullivan Stadium up for auction, Kiam (and all other interested parties) were outbid by one Robert Kraft who bid (and won) the auction for $22 million.

While the stadium itself was relatively worthless, the buyer would also be purchasing an ironclad 10-year lease with the New England Patriots, which ran until 2001. By 1991, Kiam himself was in severe financial distress from a series of bad investments and owed a lot of money. When he and Sullivan (who retained a small piece of the team) decided to relocate the franchise to Jacksonville, Florida, Mr. Kraft simply refused to let them out of their lease.

One of the people to whom Kiam owed money was James Orhtwein of St. Louis, Missouri, whose mother, Clara, was the granddaughter of Adolphus Busch, the founder of Anheuser-Busch. Orthwein, who'd made another fortune in the advertising agency business, was also the second-largest stockholder in Anheuser-Busch with 1.6 million shares, second only to his first cousin, chairman and president, August Busch III.

In 1992, Kiam would sell the team to Orthwein (who would in turn additionally pay off approximately $90 million of Kiam's personal debt). Orthwein's ownership tenure was short-lived. Wanting to relocate the franchise to St. Louis, he offered $75 million to Kraft to buy out the remainder of the lease but Kraft again refused. Initiating a hostile takeover bid with an offer of $172 million for the franchise he knew Orthwein no longer wanted, Robert Kraft, in 1994, assumed sole ownership of the New England Patriots, successfully completing a brilliant, long-term acquisition strategy that had begun nine years earlier.

And even though Orthwein's time was indeed brief, history duly notes that it was he who redesigned the team's uniform and color scheme, changing their longstanding red, white, and blue to silver and blue; and also that it was he who brought in Bill Parcells as head coach. Despite dramatically improving the fortunes of the team and making it to the 1997 Super Bowl (a loss to the Green Bay Packers), a case can be made that Bill Belichick, who'd been with Parcells in New York City with both the New York Giants and New York Jets, would never have ended up in New England had Parcells gotten along better with Robert Kraft and not left the Patriots to join the Dallas Cowboys.

And what became of Billy Sullivan? It would be just his (bad) luck that his one and only trip to the Super Bowl would be a 46-10 dismantling by perhaps the greatest single-season defense in the history of the sport: the 1985 Chicago Bears. But good-guy that he was, that rain cloud over his head would finally break and give way to sunshine, in 1995, in the form of an $11.5 million judgment in his favor from the 1991 anti-trust lawsuit he'd brought against the NFL for refusing to let him sell stock in his team to raise capital back in 1985.

Today, in 2017, the New England Patriots' dynasty continues unabated, but with Tom Brady approaching age 40, and Bill Belichick, 65, there are more glorious years behind them than in front of them, or so one would think. Yet every pre-season the New England Patriots are odds-on favorites to win their division, conference, and to make it back to another Super Bowl. As Tom Brady and Bill Belichick continue to ply their trade(s) in New England, we don't see that changing any time soon.

And we didn't. On Feb. 5th, 2017, Kraft's Patriots came from 25 points behind to humiliate the Atlanta Falcons in overtime, winning the Super Bowl in dramatic Tom Brady-come-from-behind fashion.

Super Bowl Appearances: 9   Wins: 5
Forbes 2017 Valuation: $3.7 Billion

New Orleans Saints

Year	Owner(s)	Purchase Price
1967-1984	John Mecom	$8.5 Million
1985-	Tom Benson	$64 Million

The New Orleans Saints were the brainchild of David Dixon, a Louisiana businessman and sports executive. His mission to bring a professional football team to New Orleans began in 1961 when he nearly bought the losing Oakland Raiders for $236,000. The city of Oakland interceded and the Raiders were never moved to New Orleans. To compete with the AFL and NFL, Dixon proposed another new league, the United States Football League (USFL), with a spring season instead of fall.

It was 1965 and discussions of the AFL-NFL merger had already begun. The NFL needed congressional approval to pass the merger, and as luck would have it, two members on the Congressional board of approval represented Louisiana. Pete Rozelle, then NFL commissioner, met secretly with Dixon and the congressmen in a closed-door meeting, which resulted in both the approval of the merger and the award to New Orleans as the sixteenth NFL franchise.

John Mecom Jr., son of a wealthy Houston oilman, became the team's first majority owner at the tender age of 26. He and a group of investors (Dixon included) purchased the New Orleans Saints for the $8.5 million expansion fee. It was no surprise when the team was named after a New Orleans favorite, "When the Saints Come Marching In," a tune made famous by trumpeter Al Hirt, also a minority owner of the team. The news of the Saints' birth was announced on November 1, All Saints Day, which fit perfectly with New Orleans' Catholic history. Mecom, sometimes referred to as a spoiled rich kid, is credited with selecting the team's black and gold colors to reflect the state's rich oil history, not to mention his own oil-based inheritance.

In 2008, long after he sold the Saints, he was sued by his four children for squandering funds left in trust by his mother, a portion of which were supposedly meant to be distributed to them upon adulthood. Their complaint claimed he hadn't distributed a nickel. Strange behavior with a fortune estimated at around $200 million.

Aside from that, Mecom was an unpopular, hands-off owner with poor leadership skills. Throughout the 18 seasons he was in charge, the Saints were the worst team in the league with a winning percentage of .311 – aka dead last. Mecom's reputation was further tarnished by his adversarial relationship with the press, the league, and especially the Saints fans when rumors suggested he was thinking about selling to parties interested in relocating the Saints to Jacksonville, Florida.

Luckily for Saints fans, Mecom sold the team in 1985 to a New Orleans native, Tom Benson, for a reported $64 million dollars. Benson was a savvy businessman who used profits from his successful Chevrolet dealerships to purchase small Southern banks. He later formed Benson Financial, which he sold in 1996 to Norwest Corporation, which merged with Wells Fargo in 1998. Benson knew the state's economy was suffering from a deep economic recession, and, to help his beloved Louisiana, he stepped up and saved the Saints from "marching out."

Tom Benson, although a popular owner at first, lost his luster after he made the tough decision to temporarily move team operations to San Antonio in the wake of Hurricane Katrina. The Superdome suffered extensive damage from the storm and was used to house thousands of displaced residents for many months following the statewide crisis. While most of the 2005 season was played in San Antonio and Baton Rouge, Benson ultimately committed to moving the team back to Louisiana for the 2006 season, which kicked off in the newly renovated Superdome, now the Mercedes-Benz Superdome. Ever since, the team's record has steadily improved. In 2010, with Drew Breeze throwing touchdowns, the Saints won the Super Bowl, defeating the Colts 31 – 17.

Tom Benson has had controversy follow him throughout his ownership of the Saints. First, he was constantly threatening to relocate the team to San Antonio and he used that threat publicly to negotiate better deals with the city, which angered New Orleans officials and fans. Second, under his watch as owner, the "Bountygate" scandal broke out in 2012 and became the biggest news in the NFL. The defensive coach was exposed for offering cash bounties to defensive players for intentionally trying to injure key opposing players. Specifically named were quarterbacks Kurt Warner, Brett Favre, Cam Newton, and Aaron Rogers. Several coaches and players were suspended and the NFL fined the team $500,000. Third, Benson became embroiled in bitter lawsuits with his children and grandchildren when they sued him for cutting them out of what they felt was their inheritance in both the Saints and the NBA Pelicans (which Benson had acquired in 2012). The case settled in early 2017.

Meanwhile, since the 2010 Super Bowl win, the Saints, under the cloud of Benson's notoriety, have been middle-of-the-road in team performance, but with the exciting Drew Brees at quarterback there is never a dull moment when the Saints play… win or lose.

Super Bowl Appearances: 1 Wins: 1
Forbes 2017 Valuation: $2.0 Billion

New York Giants

Year	Owner(s)	Purchase Price
1925-1929	Tim Mara	$500
1930-1964	Jack Mara & Wellington Mara	Inherited
1965-1990	Wellington Mara & Tim Mara	
1991-2005	Wellington Mara & Bob Tisch	$80 Million
2005-	John Mara & Steve Tisch	Inherited

One of the NFL's most venerable families, on par with surnames like Rooney and Halas, the Mara family has owned the New York Giants since patriarch Tim Mara paid $500 for them in 1925, just five years after the NFL started. Mara, needing to establish and differentiate his team, and his sport for that matter, named the franchise the New York National League Football Giants. In 1937, the team's legal corporate name would be modified to the New York Football Giants, Inc., under which they continue doing business to this day.

Given the NFL's preeminence today -- it is the most popular and wealthiest of all American professional leagues -- it is interesting to note that a scant 90 years ago, Mara's imperative in naming his team was to popularize the sport. At that time, professional football team needed all the help it could get. While collegiate football was an established part of the sports culture and landscape, well-reported and attended, in the professional realm, the three most popular sports were baseball, boxing, and horse racing.

Even "Tiffany" franchises such as the Pittsburgh Steelers, Chicago Bears, Green Bay Packers, and New York Giants, struggled mightily in often-dire financial circumstances. In fact, Tim Mara in 1931 transferred ownership of the team to his two sons to insulate himself from creditors (although he continued to run the team). At that time, Jack Mara was 22 years old and Wellington Mara, 14.

With the most NFL championship appearances (19) and eight championships -- four pre-Super Bowl ('27, '34, '38, and '56) and four Super Bowls ('86, '90, '07, and '11) -- from a historical perspective, the

Giants' winning history does not eclipse perhaps their greatest contribution to the modern-day NFL. Their televised overtime loss to the Baltimore Colts in Yankee Stadium in the 1958 championship, often called "the greatest game ever played," is credited with bringing NFL popularity to unprecedented heights and providing traction for the marriage of television and NFL football, which would prove to be worth billions of dollars.

The Maras were known as true sportsmen and gentlemen amongst NFL owners. Their head coach was Steve Owen, who coached the team for 24 years without a contract, but on a handshake deal with Tim Mara. It was Wellington Mara, in the early 1960s, who took the unpopular stance of pushing hard for revenue sharing even though his big-market Giants received $175,000 per game (four times as much as small-market teams). This forward thinking is perhaps the single greatest factor responsible for the NFL's geometric growth and prosperity. Upon Tim Mara's death in 1959, Jack and Wellington ran the team together until Jack's death in 1965. Leaving his share of the team to his son (named after his grandfather), Wellington had a new co-owner and partner, his nephew, Tim Mara.

The strained relationship between Wellington and Tim, never good to begin with, would worsen year by year and degrade to the point where the two men refused to speak to each other an the Giants' fortunes on the field reflected this dysfunction, with mediocre and losing seasons piling up throughout the late 1960s and 1970s.

Because it's never healthy for a league when one of its tent pole franchises is in a decade-long decline, NFL Commissioner Alvin (Pete) Rozelle interceded and with Wellington Mara's blessing, recommended George Young for the front office. Young, a highly-regarded executive from the Baltimore Colts, assumed the duties of general manager in 1979, auguring a renaissance for the franchise. Drafting players such as Lawrence Taylor and Phil Simms, along with promoting defensive coordinator Bill Parcells to head coach in 1983, who in turn would promote linebacker coach Bill Belichick to defensive coordinator in 1985, would quickly yield two Super Bowl victories, in 1986 and 1990.

Wellington Mara would have one last partner and co-owner when Tim sold his share of the team to Preston Robert (Bob) Tisch in 1991. Part owner of Loews Corporation with his brother Lawrence, Tisch was formerly Postmaster General under President Ronald Reagan. Mara and Tisch would die within three weeks of each other in 2005. The New York Giants won their most recent Super Bowl in 2011 with partners John Mara (Wellington's son) and Steve Tisch (Bob's son) leading the organization.

Super Bowl Appearances: 5   Wins: 4
Forbes 2017 Valuation: $3.3 Billion

New York Jets

Former name: New York Titans 1960-62

Year	Owner(s)	Purchase Price
1959-1963	Harry Wismer	
1963-1968	Sonny Werblin, Townsend Martin, Donald Lillis, Phillip Iselin, Leon Hess	$1 Million
1968-1976	Donald Lillis, Townsend Martin, Leon Hess, Phillip Iselin	N/A
1976-1981	Leon Hess, Townsend Martin, Donald Lillis	N/A
1981-1984	Leon Hess, Donald Lillis	$5 Million
1984-1999	Leon Hess	$5 Million
2000-	Robert Wood "Woody" Johnson IV	$635 Million

In the centuries-old German legend of Faust, a young man strikes a bargain with the devil through which, to experience worldly pleasures for a limited time, he will forfeit his soul to eternal damnation. He gets his deal and after a time is carried off to Hell.

This tale has been the basis for countless novels, short stories, dramatic plays, musicals, symphonies, operas, poems, and movies. And if one were to give Faust a name and face in the NFL, it might well be the New York Jets. While we neither believe in nor endorse the notion of a "cursed" franchise, there are more than a few lifelong New York Jets fans who have likely considered the possibility.

Surely one of the most glorious and iconic moments in the history of the National Football League, and indeed across the landscape of professional sports, was when the young and brash Joe Willie Namath guaranteed a victory over the superior and heavily favored Baltimore Colts in Super Bowl III, and then made good on it. At that moment, the notion of the New York Jets not returning to the Super Bowl for the next 48 years would have seemed nonsensical.

With that 1969 Super Bowl victory, the New York Jets not only stimulated the NFL-AFL merger of 1970, but also finally shed their image as the comical "Titans of New York," personified by their founder, Harry Wismer. Granted a charter in the new American Football League in 1959, Wismer would name his team the Titans because titans are bigger and stronger than giants ... as in the New York (football) Giants.

Beginning play in 1960 in the (baseball) Giants' recently abandoned Polo Grounds, the AFL New York Titans would not only have

149

an inferiority complex with regard to the NFL in general, but to the New York (football) Giants in particular -- not only in terms of reputation and swagger, but even regarding their respective venues: the rotting Polo Grounds in Upper Manhattan compared to the venerable Yankee Stadium in the Bronx.

Harry Wismer had a made a name for himself in sports broadcasting, with stints doing football at Michigan State University and for a short time, the University of Notre Dame, before moving on to the Detroit Lions, and then finding his greatest fame as the longtime voice of the Washington Redskins. A larger-than-life character well known for name-dropping celebrity "friends" during broadcasts, drinking and partying, and becoming embroiled in many public feuds, Wismer, a self-proclaimed hustler, nevertheless was able to secure the rights to the new AFL's New York franchise. In stark contrast to his fellow owners, all extremely successful with their considerable wealth derived from businesses outside of sports, whatever money Wismer did have he'd made from working as a broadcaster and through his relationships with team owners Ralph Wilson of the Detroit Lions and George Preston Marshall of the Washington Redskins -- both of whom, at various times, had given Wismer small ownership percentages in their respective clubs.

With Wismer flat broke within two years of the beginning of play, the other owners of the AFL assumed the operating costs of the Titans, as losing a flagship New York City franchise would have been disastrous for the upstart league, jeopardizing its very existence.

In 1963, the AFL would sell the New York Titans to the Gotham Football Club, Inc., a five-man ownership syndicate headed by David "Sonny" Werblin (president, Television Division, MCA). The other four members were Townsend Martin (investment banker and racehorse owner), Donald Lillis (Wall Street financier), Leon Hess (oil executive), and Phillip Iselin (women's apparel manufacturing and chairman of Monmouth Park Racetrack).

Werblin, a native New Yorker with a big reputation in the worlds of television and media who was known as a great star-handler, wasted no time in remaking the team with a swift succession of transformative actions: renaming the team the New York Jets; relocating their home field to the new Shea Stadium in Queens; changing the team colors from blue and gold to green and white; hiring Weeb Ewbank (formerly of the Baltimore Colts) to be head coach and general manager; and in 1965, signing to a then-unprecedented $427,000 rookie contract, quarterback Joe Willie Namath from the University of Alabama.

Utilizing his vast knowledge of television entertainment and manipulation of media in the manufacture of celebrity, especially in New York City, Sonny Werblin created the public persona of the first television-age star player.

150

Coming from Beaver Falls, Pennsylvania, by way of Tuscaloosa, Alabama, Joe Namath had no trouble adapting to life in the big city (thank you very much). Fur coats, drooping Fu-Manchu moustache, piercing blue eyes, drink in hand, beautiful women always on his arm, Namath's bachelor lifestyle perfectly aligned with Werblin's show-biz expertise.

Fortunately, that's not all Joe Namath brought to the never-ending party. A tough and very gifted player, for all the glitz and glamour, when Joe Namath took the field he was all business (he'd played for Paul "Bear" Bryant, after all). Hailing from hardscrabble western Pennsylvania, which has produced the likes of Johnny Unitas, George Blanda, Dan Marino, Joe Montana, and Jim Kelly, Joe Namath could throw the football with anybody (in either league), even while enduring tremendous pain from chronic knee injuries that would both diminish and shorten his career.

Sonny Werblin, who ran the team as an autocrat, making unilateral decisions without consulting his partners, would fall out with other owners who wanted to dissolve the partnership. And so, in 1968, despite his many accomplishments and contributions to the success of the New York Jets, Sonny Werblin was essentially forced out. He agreed to sell his shares of the team to his four partners. It is the greatest irony that Werblin was not part of the organization when Namath made his famous guarantee while lounging poolside in Miami prior to Super Bowl III.

Over the next 16 years, Leon Hess would gain sole ownership of the Jets, incrementally, by purchasing his partners' shares upon their deaths -- Iselin in 1976; Martin in 1981; and finally, from Lillis's daughter, Helen Dillon, in 1984.

Leon Hess, in both public profile and personal temperament, was quite the opposite of Sonny Werblin. A self-made man from Asbury Park, New Jersey, who'd built his fortune in the oil refinery business, Hess had served in World War II as a major who was the fuel supply officer for General George S. Patton. A soft-spoken man who preferred to remain behind the scenes, Hess was very much a hands-off owner who would always hire "football people" to run his franchise. Unfortunately, over his decades of owning the Jets, the name of Leon Hess would almost become synonymous with the Jets' prolonged futility. The football people he hired would come and go, and with them, countless "new eras" promising change and progress, then delivering nothing of the sort. Head coaches from Joe Walton to Bruce Coslet to Pete Carroll to Rich Kotite to Bill Parcells during the Hess era would all experience varying degrees of success, but none were able to play their way back to the Super Bowl.

And in perhaps the greatest infamy for the franchise, exactly one day after accepting the head coaching job after Parcells "retired," Bill Belichick would famously scrawl on a piece of paper, "I resign as HC of the NYJ" before conducting a terse press conference. If that was not enough of a slap in the face, Belichick taking up residence in New England

and coaching in the same division where he would torture the Jets for years to come only added insult to injury.

When Leon Hess died in 1999, he had stipulated in his will that none of his family could inherit the New York Jets, and so the team was put for sale. In 2000, "Woody" Johnson, great-grandson of Robert Wood Johnson (co-founder of Johnson & Johnson), would purchase the team. Well known as a philanthropist, and the owner of a private investment firm (Johnson Company, Inc.), at the time of the purchase, Woody Johnson was an unknown quantity in terms of the sports world, having had no prior involvement in professional sports. In Johnson's 17 years of ownership, the Jets have hired five more head coaches: Al Groh, Herman Edwards, Eric Mangini, Rex Ryan, and Todd Bowles. Making it to the AFC championship game two years in a row under coach Ryan, they would lose both times.

The New York Jets have surely had their share of great players: Joe Namath, John Riggins, Don Maynard, and Joe Klecko come to mind. And despite not having a stadium of their own since Shea (they've been co-tenants in two stadiums in New Jersey with the New York Giants), theirs is a proud franchise with an unusually loyal, stalwart, and patient fan base. The question remains: What is one of the greatest upsets in the history of American professional sports worth?

Forty-eight years is an awfully long time … but it is not *eternal* damnation. We suspect that any true New York Jets fan, if asked would they trade 1969 for a few more rings, would let you know (in very colorful terms) that they are one of only three teams in NFL history to have played in the Super Bowl and never lost … even if it was only once. The Tampa Bay Buccaneers and the New Orleans Saints are the others.

Super Bowl Appearances: 1 Wins: 1
Forbes 2017 Valuation: 2.75 Billion

Oakland Raiders

Former name: Los Angeles Raiders 1982-94

Year	Owner(s)	Purchase Price
1960	Chet Soda, Wayne Valley & partners	
1961-1965	Wayne Valley & E.J. McGah	
1966-1971	Wayne Valley, E.J. McGah, Al Davis	$18,000
1972-2011	Al Davis	Undisclosed
2011-	Mark Davis	Inherited

In 1959, when the AFL first emerged on the football scene, one of the original eight "Foolish Club" owners, Max Winter, who had been awarded an AFL team for Minneapolis, changed his mind and accepted a last-minute offer to join the NFL as an expansion team. The AFL, having been trumped by the NFL, needed to find a new city and group to buy into the budding league. As AFL owners hustled to find the perfect city, the Los Angeles Chargers' founding owner, Barron Hilton, threatened to forfeit his franchise unless a second team was placed on the West Coast.

Even though Oakland didn't ask for a team and there wasn't even a stadium in which to play, the AFL settled on the location because it rounded out the west coast division. The Oakland city leaders formed a limited partnership and found the investors.

Charles (Chet) Soda, a local real estate developer, and Wayne Valley became the general partners along with several limited partners. The Raiders played their first two years in the San Francisco Kezar Stadium, and eventually found a semi-permanent home in a converted high school stadium in Oakland. The Raiders would eventually open the doors to Oakland Alameda County Coliseum in 1966, where they would play until their move to Los Angeles in 1982.

The Raiders went 6-8 their first year and lost $500,000, a lot of money in the '60s. The ownership group felt the financial squeeze and began to bail. Soda bolted, which left Wayne Valley to take over the reins. To the rescue came Buffalo Bills founder Ralph Wilson Jr., who loaned Valley $400,000 to keep the franchise afloat. Then entered Al Davis, pro football's "Bad Guy," who would become a legend in his time.

Davis grew up in Massachusetts, the son of a successful garment manufacturer. As much as he might have tried, Davis was never a great athlete in school. Although he never played football, you could always find this "football junkie" on the sidelines or in the football strategy classes typically offered to players only.

Davis first got into coaching football at Adelphi College on Long Island. In 1952, he was drafted into the U.S. Army, where he quickly secured the coaching spot for his military outpost's football team. In 1954, he became a freelance scout for the Baltimore Colts and helped recruit Weeb Ewbank to become the Colts' head coach. Weeb, who later made a name for himself as the Jets' head coach, in turn helped Davis secure a position as assistant coach for The Citadel in South Carolina. Determined to make bigger splash, Davis then headed west to the University of Southern California (USC) as assistant coach and recruiting specialist.

At a coach's conference, Davis gained the attention of Los Angeles Rams coach Sidd Gillman, who was impressed with Davis's football acumen, enthusiasm, and eagerness to learn. When Gillman was hired by the Los Angeles Chargers in 1959, he brought Davis along as backfield coach. Al Davis had a keen eye, a kind of sixth sense, for selecting players who would fit with some team's system.

In 1962, Davis began negotiations with the Raiders' owner, Wayne Valley, who knew they needed a great head coach, one who could stop the bleeding. In 1963, Davis negotiated a three-year deal (at $20,000 a year) as head coach and general manager with complete control over football operations. Davis became the youngest NFL coach.

One of the first orders of business for Davis was to give the Raiders a new look. The iconic silver and black, Darth Vader-esque uniforms gave the team an intimidating presence that paired nicely with their pirate mascot. Al Davis began to make his mark. The team started winning. After the 1965 season, Davis was named AFL Commissioner and stopped coaching. When he returned to the team after the NFL/AFL merger, he purchased a 10 percent interest in the team for $18,000, and became the team's general partner in charge of football operations.

The team continued to rise under Davis's leadership, and so did tensions between the three owners – Valley, McGah, and Davis. Valley was less likeable and frequently absent from day to day operations. As far as McGah and Davis were concerned, Valley was dead weight. In 1972, when Valley was out of town, Davis had his attorneys draft a revised partnership agreement giving him total control over all Raider operations. McGah, a supporter of Davis (at that time), signed the agreement. By a 2–1 vote of the general partners, the new agreement was authorized. Valley immediately filed suit to have the new agreement overturned, but the court sided with Davis and McGah ... and Valley was toast.

In 1982, Davis, after a series of lawsuits, moved the Raiders to Los Angeles. There the team's great success began to decline. Dissatisfied with the L.A. Coliseum relationship, Davis began making noises about moving the team back to Oakland, citing the fact that Oakland had spent $200,000 on stadium improvements to lure Davis back "home." Al Davis had had enough of L.A. In 1995, Oakland and its die-hard fans had their Raiders back home.

In 2003, Al Davis was sued by the heirs of Raiders minority owner E.W. McGah, for financial mismanagement. The suit was finally settled in 2005 with Davis buying the McGah family's interest for an undisclosed amount, which gave Davis majority control for the first time. It was speculated he acquired 31 percent, which gave him approximately 67 percent overall. Later, he sold 20 percent to investors to bring his interest to approximately 47 percent. For 35 years, from 1966 to his death in 2011, he filled the role of co-owner and general manager.

During the first 20 years of Davis's ownership, the Raiders became one of the most successful teams in the league. (A good part of that success was attributable to Hall of Fame coach John Madden who went on to become a well-known announcer as well as spokesman for the popular video game *Madden NFL*). The Raiders made 15 playoff appearances and won 3 Super Bowls, one AFL Championship, and 13 Division Championships. He was the only executive in NFL history to be an assistant coach, head coach, general manager, commissioner, and owner. His smarts, coupled with his persuasive ball-busting ways, made him a key negotiator in the NFL/AFL merger.

Upon Al Davis's death in 2011, his son Mark Davis became the principal owner and managing partner of the team. He and his mother own a controlling interest, with 47 percent.

Mark Davis was raised alongside the Raiders and has always considered the team like family. Davis is known for his bowl-cut hairdo and his simple non-pretentious ways, like choosing to drive an inexpensive mini-van when he can afford a Tesla. Like his father, who moved the team to L.A., Davis Jr. has obtained approval from the NFL to relocate the team to Las Vegas, Nevada. Oakland Raider fans mourn the loss.

Super Bowl Appearances: 5   Wins: 3
2017 Forbes Valuation: $2.38 Billion

Philadelphia Eagles

Year	Owner(s)	Purchase Price
1933-1940	Bert Bell	$3,500
1941-1949	Alexis Thompson	Unknown
1949-1963	"Happy Hundred"	$250,000
1964-1969	Jerry Wollman	$5.5 Million
1969-1984	Leonard Tose	$16 Million
1985-1994	Norman Braman	$65 Million
1994-	Jeffrey Lurie	$195 Million

When considering the most heated (and hated) rivalries in professional football, the Philadelphia Eagles vs. the New York Giants is often cited near the top of the list, followed closely by the Philadelphia Eagles vs. the Dallas Cowboys, followed closely by the Philadelphia Eagles vs. the Washington Redskins.

The Philadelphia Eagles just can't get along with anybody, which suits their loyal and famously inhospitable fan base just fine. Voted by NFL players as the most intimidating fans in the league, Eagles fans have bought out every seat at every home game since 1999, including the notorious 700 Level. In the bad old days at Veterans Stadium, a judge was installed in the stadium to preside over a temporary court adjudicating sometimes up to 20 suspects during a single game for "hostile taunting, fighting, public urination, and general strangeness," among other indiscretions -- and that was just Eagles fans (let alone the visiting teams' fans).

Things have mellowed just enough so that "Eagles Court"' ended in 2003 -- not that Lincoln Financial Field is anybody's idea of a day at the beach. Yet the Philadelphia Eagles are perennially ranked as one of the top three NFL teams in attendance. And for all the sound and fury of their fierce rivalries, the Philadelphia Eagles are the only team in the NFC East to have never won a Super Bowl -- the Giants, Cowboys, and Redskins all, of course, having multiple Super Bowl victories.

Appearing in two and losing both (in 1980 and 2004), the Philadelphia Eagles are nonetheless an iconic franchise with three NFL championships on their resume: consecutive titles in 1948 and '49, and their last in 1960, when they were the only to team to ever defeat Vince Lombardi's Green Bay Packers in the playoffs. Then, as today, no team ever looked forward to seeing the famed green and white colors of that uniform or to the inevitable tussle that would await them.

A bankruptcy declaration by the NFL's Philadelphia Yellow Jackets (1924 to 1931) presented both a problem for the league and an opportunity for a young man named Bert Bell. Wanting to replace the franchise and maintain an NFL presence in the Philadelphia market, the NFL in 1933 granted Bell the new Philadelphia franchise for the standard expansion fee plus Bell's assuming the Yellow Jackets' debt of $11,000 to three other NFL franchises.

Bert Bell, a native Philadelphian who'd been a star quarterback at the University of Pennsylvania, would borrow money from his girlfriend, actress Martha Upton (whom he would later marry), to acquire the team, partner with his college football teammate, "Lud" Wray, and name his new team the Philadelphia Eagles. Bell would buy out Wray and be the sole owner by 1936. In 1940, Bell's good friend, Art Rooney, would sell his team, the Pittsburgh Steelers, to Alexis Thompson for $160,000. Thompson, 28 years old, scion of the family that founded Republic Iron and Steel, had made his own fortune selling eye care products after returning home from serving in World War I. Rooney would use the proceeds from his sale of the Steelers to buy a half-interest in Bell's Philadelphia Eagles. And as these things sometimes go, the respective owners, the Eagles' Bell and Rooney, and the Steelers' Thompson, having second thoughts, would end up trading back their cities (Philadelphia and Pittsburgh) but retaining their former rosters. Although not quite through with each other, they would in 1943, due to a manpower shortage because of World War II, merge their two teams (players as well as coaches), which was officially referred to as the "Phil-Pitt Combine," to create a team otherwise known as the "Steagles" for just that one season.

In 1949, Thompson would sell the Philadelphia Eagles to a group of Philadelphia-based investors popularly referred to as the "Happy

Hundred" and headed by James P. Clark, a Philadelphia trucking magnate, who along with Frank McNamee (named team president), assembled a hundred people, investing $3,000 each, to form the group.

The Happy Hundred would own the team until selling it in 1963 to Jerry Wolman, a Washington, D.C., builder and developer. In 1969, Wollman, facing bankruptcy, would in turn sell the team to Leonard Tose, another trucking magnate who'd originally invested $3,000 in the team as one of the Happy Hundred.

Tose, well known for having an extravagant and somewhat conspicuous lifestyle, and addicted to both gambling and alcohol, would in 1985 have to sell the team in part to pay off a gambling debt of some $25 million to Atlantic City Casinos.

Under the new owners, Norman Braman and Ed Liebowitz, car dealers from Florida, the Eagles would continue to be a mediocre football team. Their last highlight was a 1980 Super Bowl loss to the Oakland Raiders, after which head coach Dick Vermeil (brought to the Eagles from UCLA by Leonard Tose), would resign, introducing to the world the word "burnout," which he cited as the reason for his resignation.

In 1994, Braman would sell the franchise to Jeffrey Lurie, whose family wealth came from ownership of a national chain of movie theaters. In addition, Lurie founded a Hollywood production company for both film and television.

As a franchise, while not particularly blessed with stable ownership over the years -- one owner selling the team to avoid bankruptcy and another to clear millions in gambling debts -- throughout their history the Philadelphia Eagles have usually featured a handful of the toughest players in the league at any given time, on both sides of the ball: Hall of Famers such as running back Steve Van Buren, defensive end Reggie White, and perhaps the quintessential Eagle of them all, Chuck Bednarik. Pennsylvania born and bred, Bednarik was a college star at Penn, World War II combat hero, one of the hardest hitters and tacklers ever, and last of the full-time, two-way players (center and linebacker). "Concrete Charlie" is forever remembered for his clean hit on the New York Giants "golden boy" running back Frank Gifford, who was knocked unconscious and carried off the field on a stretcher in a game in 1960, not to return to game action for over 18 months.

At present, after many years of playoff failures, near misses, and bitter disappointments, the Philadelphia Eagles acquired what they hope will be their franchise quarterback for years to come, using their second overall pick of the 2016 NFL Draft to select Carson Wentz of North Dakota State University.

Super Bowl Appearances: 2   Wins: 0
Forbes 2017 Valuation: $2.65 Billion

Pittsburgh Steelers

Year	Owner(s)	Purchase Price
1933-1987	Arthur J. Rooney, Sr.	$2,500
1988- 2008	Dan Rooney	Inherited
2008-2017	Dan Rooney & Family	Divestiture
2017-	Art Rooney, Jr.	Inherited

The Pittsburgh Steelers evoke labels such as the "gold standard" and the "Tiffany" of NFL franchises. In the modern era (since the merger in 1970), the Pittsburgh Steelers have compiled a regular season record of 363–235–2 (.607) and an overall record of 394–253–2 (.609) including the playoffs; reached the playoffs 25 times; won their division 20 times; played in 15 AFC championship games, and won six of eight Super Bowls.

One of a handful of "national" franchises, in much the same way as the Oakland Raiders or Dallas Cowboys are, the Pittsburgh Steelers occupy a niche unto themselves. While "Steeler Nation" is indeed a national entity, the team is also quite provincial -- identified with, and representative of, its local region, hardscrabble western Pennsylvania.

They are the black and gold that makes the AFC North division black and blue. Other attributes of this unique franchise have to do with its single-family ownership from its inception; its coaching continuity (only three head coaches in over 40 -- unheard of!); its dynastic history from the mid-'70s; its selecting four future Hall of Famers in one draft, and its consistent winning tradition through the decades.

But it wasn't always that way. For a franchise that has been owned by just one family, the history of the Pittsburgh Steelers is as colorful as any in the history of American sport. Founding owner and one of the NFL's patriarchs, Art Rooney, born and raised in the Pittsburgh area, was an exceptional all-around athlete, recruited to play football at Notre Dame, baseball for the Boston Red Sox, and invited to join the 1920 Olympic boxing team. He was also known to heartily partake in another lifelong passion: handicapping and betting on horse racing -- but that would not fully flower until the 1930s.

Prior to that, Pennsylvania's puritanical history and traditions were still evident: the so-called "Pennsylvania blue laws," for example, prohibited play on Sundays. The NFL having chosen Sundays for their sport so as not to conflict with college football, played on Saturdays. A leading figure in repealing the Pennsylvania blue laws was Bert Bell, a rather unremarkable student and football player at the University of Pennsylvania who never graduated. Bell tried his hand as a stockbroker but encountered devastating losses in the Crash of '29. After returning to Penn as an assistant coach and then moving on to Temple in the same capacity, Bell finally took a job with the Ritz-Carlton Hotel in Philadelphia. By all accounts, Bell's true gift was in socializing at venues such as the racetrack at Saratoga, where he would easily mingle with the likes of Tim Mara and Art Rooney.

In 1933, Bell was first in line and borrowed funds from his future wife, the actress and Broadway star Frances Upton, to secure the rights to an NFL franchise in Philadelphia that he named the Philadelphia Eagles. Art Rooney, second in line (with a $2,500 check in hand), applied for and received an NFL franchise for Pittsburgh, which was first called the Pittsburgh Professional Football Club, Inc. and then the Pittsburgh Pirates (named after the city's baseball team, a common practice of the day). Later the team was called the Rooneymen (a nickname given by local media that stuck because two Pirates teams was confusing), and then the Pittsburgh Steelers, prior to the 1940 season.

However, with players in short supply during World War II, in 1943 the Steelers became the Phil-Pitt Combine, affectionately called the Steagles (a short-lived merger with the Philadelphia Eagles); and in 1944, Card-Pitt, which became Car-Pitt, which affectionately became the Carpets (a short-lived merger with the Chicago Cardinals). Finally, in 1945, there was a return to the Pittsburgh Steelers, once and for all.

Between the Great Depression of the 1930s followed by the World War II years of the 1940s, Mr. Rooney's football team struggled just to make payroll on a weekly basis and fared no better on the field, the Steelers being perennial losers for some four decades, posting only eight winning seasons in those 40 years.

And while Mr. Rooney undoubtedly loved his Steelers, they were not his only love: his Rooney-McGinley Boxing Club promoted fights, and there was his preoccupation with thoroughbred horse racing as well. In 1936 alone he is said to have won $300,000 betting on the ponies (which would be approximately $5 million today). But as these things are wont to be, there are no records of how much he may have lost at the track. Suffice it to say, the Pittsburgh Steelers were never able to compete against wealthier clubs like the New York Giants, Chicago Bears, or Green Bay Packers when it came to signing premier players coming out of college.

In 1936, it was Mr. Rooney's dissatisfaction with a system that allowed the winningest teams to sign the best players that led to the creation of the NFL Draft, thus providing a more equitable distribution of talent throughout the league. Another key figure in the creation of the draft was Bert Bell, co-owner of the Philadelphia Eagles, along with Alexis Thompson, grandson of the founder of Republic Steel and Iron.

Four years later, in 1940, Bell helped facilitate Rooney's sale of his Steelers to Thompson for $160,000. Rooney, in turn, acquired half of Bell's interest in the Eagles. Just a few months later, in a series of transactions that came to be known as the "Pennsylvania Polka," Rooney and Bell traded their entire roster of players plus their territorial rights in Philadelphia back to Thompson for his entire roster of players plus his territorial rights in Pittsburgh.

Rooney then named Bell head coach of the Steelers and assumed the title of general manager, in addition to being team president. And, since all these maneuvers occurred in the off-season, the NFL to this day only recognizes the Rooney family as the sole owners of the Pittsburgh Steelers since their inception in 1933. In 1946, Rooney bought out Bell's shares of the Steelers. As for whatever happened to Bert Bell, he was named NFL commissioner, serving from 1945 to his death in 1959, and was named a charter member in the very first NFL Hall of Fame class in 1963.

With the merger of 1970, fortunes turned for Art Rooney and his struggling franchise. His team was one of three old-guard franchises to join the new AFC; the Cleveland Browns and Baltimore Colts were the other two. Rooney was paid a $3 million relocation fee, which drastically improved the team's resources to field a more competitive product. While Art Rooney assuredly remained "the father" of the Pittsburgh Steelers, in 1975 he turned over day-to-day operations of the team to his son, Dan Rooney, naming him president. Dan Rooney presided over the franchise until naming his son, Art Rooney Jr., president in 2002.

Dan Rooney would be named the United States Ambassador to Ireland, serving from 2009 to 2012. The Pittsburgh Steelers' uniform, logo, and colors are amongst the most iconic in all professional sports. Black and gold have been their colors since the team's inception in 1933. In fact, all of Pittsburgh's professional teams' uniforms feature some combination of black and gold.

The Steelers' distinctive logo, too, is classic. Based on the "Steelmark" design of U.S. Steel, the logo debuted in 1962: the word STEELERS surrounded by three hypocycloids (diamond shapes). The colors are said to represent the ingredients used in the steelmaking process: yellow for coal, red for iron ore, and black for scrap metal.

Also unique, theirs are the only helmet in the NFL that has the team name on only one side (as per Art Rooney's dictum). And along with the New York Giants, theirs are the only uniforms to have the player's number on both the front and back.

In addition to their franchise, the Rooney family's other great legacy is their progressive, longstanding advocacy of civil rights. The Rooneys' decades-long insistence on equal opportunity for both minorities and women in the NFL ultimately found expression in the creation of the "Rooney Rule," named after Dan, longtime chairman of the league's diversity committee. The rule mandates that at least one minority candidate is given an interview in all NFL head coach hiring procedures.

As of 2008, the Rooney family restructured its ownership to comply with NFL ownership regulations. As two of the Rooney brothers own racetracks in Florida and New York, which feature video slot machine -- violating NFL policy that prohibits involvement with racetracks and gambling -- Dan and Art Jr. retain the league requisite minimum 30 percent-ownership and have made available small percentages of the team to various investors. Upon the death of Dan Rooney in 2017, Art Rooney, Jr. became the principal owner of the Steelers.

A note of football history: Although the Steelers did not enter the NFL until 1933, the City of Pittsburgh has been dubbed "the cradle of professional football" because the first professional game was played between the Pittsburgh Athletic Club and the Allegheny Athletic Club in 1892. The first football (non-pro) game was played between Princeton and Rutgers in 1869.

Super Bowl Appearances: 8   Wins: 6
Forbes 2017 Valuation: $2.45 Billion

San Diego Chargers / Los Angeles Chargers

Former name: Los Angeles Chargers 1960, San Diego Chargers

Year	Owner(s)	Purchase Price
1960-1965	Barron Hilton	$25,000
1966-1983	Eugene Klein	$10 Million
1984-	Alex Spanos	$48 Million

A hotel mogul, socialite, businessman, and philanthropist, William Barron Hilton was one of the founding members of the AFL and the original owner of the then Los Angeles Chargers. Born in Dallas, Texas, Hilton was offered the Los Angeles franchise by his friend Lamar Hunt in 1959. Being the son of Conrad Hilton, the founder of Hilton Hotels, Barron happily paid the $25,000 franchise fee and his team spent its first year playing in Los Angeles where they won the Western Division title. Despite the team's success, competing with the NFL's Rams for fans proved difficult. In 1961, Hilton moved the team to San Diego where they played as the San Diego Chargers.

Hilton not only served as the president of the AFL in 1965, he was a key negotiator in the AFL-NFL merger in 1966. Hilton was responsible for the development of a state-of-the-art San Diego stadium, now called Qualcomm Stadium, where the Chargers have played since 1967. Because of the new stadium, San Diego was also awarded a baseball franchise in 1969, the San Diego Padres.

In August 1966, Hilton was asked by the Hilton Hotel Corporation to succeed his father as president and CEO of the company on the condition he drop his football responsibilities. He sold the Chargers for $10 million to a group of Southern California businessmen led by Eugene Klein. Hilton is the last living member of the AFL's original founding member's "Foolish Club." Of his 23 grandchildren, Paris Hilton is the most famous. In 2007, Hilton donated 97 percent of his $2.3 billion net worth to his family foundation.

Eugene Klein was born in the Bronx. After serving as a bomber pilot in World War II, he settled in California where he owned one of the most successful used car dealerships and became the top western Volvo distributor. With this initial fortune, he became an investor in National General Corporation, a conglomerate that was involved in publishing and motion picture distribution. When Klein negotiated the sale of National General in 1973, it had $1.2 billion in assets.

Klein had always been an avid sports fan. Just as he had made his fortune bringing business to California, he also saw the potential in bringing professional sports teams to the western states. His first (unsuccessful) attempt to do so was in 1960 when he lobbied Major League Baseball owners to obtain an American League franchise for Los Angeles. Next up, Klein and partner Sam Schulman, along with other minority investors, did obtain the NBA franchise for the city of Seattle, Washington, the SuperSonics. In 1966, Klein led the charge to acquire the San Diego Chargers from Hilton.

Klein had a much-publicized longstanding feud with Al Davis, the managing general partner of the Oakland Raiders. Klein was a highly visible NFL spokesman against the Raiders' effort to move to Los Angeles. Al Davis didn't appreciate Klein's interference, and in his anti-trust suit against the NFL, Davis singled out Klein as the main culprit and ringleader in the NFL's refusal to grant Davis the right to move to L.A. While Klein was testifying on the witness stand in the anti-trust case, he suffered a heart attack. Davis and his Raiders won the suit, allowing the team to relocate to L.A.

Klein then sued Davis for $10 million, claiming Davis had no probable cause to single him out and blaming Davis for causing his heart attack. In 1986, the San Diego Superior Court awarded Klein $10 million in compensatory and punitive damages. Later, that award was reduced to $2 million. On appeal, a state Superior Court reversed the award and Klein was left with nothing but an eventual heart attack leading to his death in 1990.

The stressful ongoing lawsuits caused Klein to sell his majority stake in the Chargers. He had had it with Al Davis and football. In 1984, he sold his share to Alex Spanos for $48 million. Klein then devoted his energies to thoroughbred racing. His greatest achievement happened in

162

1988 when his filly, Winning Colors, captured the 1988 Kentucky Derby win. In 1989, Klein sold his 114-horse stable for $29.6 million.

Alex Spanos was born in California to Greek immigrant parents. His father owned a bakery where Spanos began working at age eight. He dropped out of college to join the U.S. Army Air Forces and served during World War II. Spanos made his first million after borrowing $800 from a local banker to buy a truck from which to sell sandwiches to migrant farm workers in the San Joaquin Valley. With his earnings, he invested in real estate and by 1977 became one of the nation's top apartment builders.

Spanos acquired the remaining shares in the Chargers in 1994. Since 1993, two of his sons helped him run the team. In 1995, the team finally made its first Super Bowl appearance, losing to the San Francisco 49ers 49-26.

Spanos wrote a book called, "Sharing the Wealth: My Story," which details his rise from a money-less man of 27 years to becoming a billionaire. And finally, after pleading with the City of San Diego for taxpayer help to build a new stadium but being rejected, Spanos decided to move the Chargers to L.A. and share Stan Kroenke's new L.A. mega-stadium with the L.A. Rams. Sadly, one of the original AFL franchises moved from its home of nearly 60 years, and left the San Diego fans in the dust.

Super Bowl Appearances: 1   Wins: 0
Forbes 2017 Valuation: $2.275 Billion

San Francisco 49ers

Year	Owner(s)	Purchase Price
1944-1957	Tony Morabito	
1957-1964	Josephine Morabito, Vic Morabito	
1964-1977	Josephine Morabito, Jane Morabito	
1977-1999	Edward J. DeBartolo Jr.	$16.5 Million
1999-	Marie DeBartolo York, John York	Inherited

The Gold Rush of 1849 in Northern California attracted a torrent of prospectors, miners, and fortune hunters that transformed the city of San Francisco and literally created statehood for California. Exactly 100 years later, the namesake San Francisco 49ers of the AAFC merged into the NFL, along with the Cleveland Browns and Baltimore Colts. Although the Gold Rush of 1849 was essentially over by 1850, a short two years in which $81 million was extracted from the ground, it is surely no coincidence that one of the San Francisco 49ers' two primary team colors is gold.

There has always been something just a little bit different, a little bit off-script, about the San Francisco 49ers. Presently they are the only professional sports team in America whose home stadium is more than 30 miles from their hometown, in a city larger than their own. They have also been solely owned by just two different families and in both, oddly, an in-law (one sister-in law and one brother-in-law) would become a principal. And while they have long been considered one of the upper-echelon franchises in the NFL, the San Francisco 49ers have been a fair-to-middling team like so many others: a few highlights and a few lowlights sprinkled in amongst mostly average seasons.

But as their lineage would suggest, *these* 49ers stumbled into a pitch-black space, struck a match, and found themselves in a goldmine, not once but twice: first, in 1977, when Edward J. DeBartolo Jr. purchased the team; and second, in fashioning a dynasty in which they would win five Super Bowls in just 14 years -- a championship run that compares favorably to any in the history of the NFL.

Original owner and founder Tony Morabito, who'd made his money in the lumber business in San Francisco, was rebuffed by the NFL on multiple occasions when applying for admission into the league. Finally, in 1946, he would take his team to the newly formed All-American Football Conference.

Upon merging in 1949, and starting play in the 1950 NFL season, the San Francisco 49ers would be a perennially second-division club for the next two decades. The 49ers were noteworthy in this era for their "Million Dollar Backfield" of the 1950s that featured four future Hall of Famers: quarterback Y.A. Tittle and three running backs, John Henry Johnson, Joe Perry, and Hugh McElheny -- to this day, the only "full-house" backfield inducted into the Hall of Fame.

Upon Morabito's death in 1957, the team passed to his widow, Josephine, and his brother Victor, who died in 1964, leaving his share of the team to his wife, Jane. Josephine and Jane Morabito would own the team until selling it in 1977 to Edward J. DeBartolo Jr. of Youngstown, Ohio.

Edward DeBartolo Jr. is the scion of one of the largest public real estate businesses in the country, the Edward J. DeBartolo Corporation, a family business that developed shopping malls and at one point controlled over two billion square feet of real estate throughout the United States. Running his football team as he did his other businesses, treating the players like family, DeBartolo became perhaps the most beloved and revered owner in NFL history -- not only by his players but by 49ers fans as well.

Five Super Bowl victories were the most ever celebrated by a single owner in NFL history until Robert Kraft won his fifth with the dramatic 2017 come-from-behind-victory. It was also the fifth Super Bowl victory for Tom Brady, who surpassed the record he held with the 49ers' great quarterback, Joe Montana. The debate as to who is the greatest quarterback of all time was settled on February 5, 2017, when Brady won his fifth.

In 1998, in a corruption case involving the former governor of Louisiana, Edwin Edwards, DeBartolo pleaded guilty to not reporting a felony – Edwards's attempted extortion of $400,000 from DeBartolo for granting him a gaming license for a Louisiana riverboat casino operation. DeBartolo was fined $1 million and given two years of probation in exchange for testifying against Edwards. He was further banned from the NFL for one year. Upon his return in 1999, he decided to restructure and reallocate his family's vast business interests and to divest himself of the 49ers in favor of other business endeavors. He ceded ownership of the team to his sister Marie DeBartolo York and her husband, John York, who both ran the team during his one-year suspension. It is no small measure of the esteem in which Edward J. DeBartolo Jr. is held that he would be inducted into the NFL Hall of Fame in 2016.

Super Bowl Appearances: 6   Wins: 5
Forbes 2017 Valuation: $3.05 Billion

Seattle Seahawks

Year	Owner(s)	Purchase Price
1976-1982	Lloyd Nordstrom & family	$16 Million
1983-1987	John Nordstrom	Inherited
1988-1996	Ken Behring	$80 Million
1997-	Paul Allen	$200 Million

Under the terms of the 1970 AFL-NFL merger, the NFL laid out plans to expand from 26 to 28 teams. In 1972, disgraced President Richard Nixon's brother, Edward Nixon, joined a group called the Seattle Sea Lions, led by Hall of Famer Hugh McElhenny, and applied for the NFL Seattle franchise. Their deal fell through. That same year, another consortium led by Herman Sarkowski that included the Nordstrom family also applied. In 1974, the NFL awarded the franchise to the Nordstrom group.

The Nordstrom brothers, majority partners in the consortium, had done well for themselves. Their father, John Nordstrom, started a shoe store with his partner, Carl Wallin, in 1901. That single shoe store grew into what would become Nordstrom department stores. By 1928, the Nordstrom brothers, Elmer, Everett, and Lloyd bought their father's (and his partners) shares and took over the family business.

In 1974, during the midst of a stock market crash that brought Nordstrom stock down from $24 to $8 a share, Lloyd, feeling the pinch, came to the family with an idea: to split the cost of their 51 percent ownership of the $16 million NFL expansion fee. The family agreed. Anxious to have a financially sound franchise in Seattle, the NFL agreed to help the owners pay the rent on the Kingdome, and because they had to pay the county 10 percent of ticket sales, gave the brothers eight years (interest free) to pay for the team. The brothers agreed and luckily too. Just a few months later the league negotiated a $5.5 million per-year per-team TV contract. With TV contract revenues flowing in, the Nordstroms barely had to borrow money from banks. "It was almost as if the team was free," said Lloyd's nephew John Nordstrom in an interview. Before the team ever took the field, Lloyd Nordstrom died and controlling interest of the Seahawks passed to his brother Elmer Nordstrom.

During the 1983 offseason, John Nordstrom (Elmer's son) became the managing general partner of the Seahawks. While the Nordstroms had loved owning a team, they couldn't face the possibility of yet another looming players' strike. The 1982 strike had been debilitating enough. Fighting with their players was awkward and upsetting and bumper stickers started showing up saying "Cheap Nordstroms." The family had to think of their company's reputation.

In August 1988, the Nordstroms sold the Seahawks to California real estate developer Ken Behring for $80 million. One of the main conditions in the sale to Behring was that the team remain in Seattle. Only agreed upon by a handshake, this proved to be a lie.

Ken Behring, also referred to as "the most hated man in Seattle" was an out-of-town owner and not well-received in Seattle. Behring had made his fortune as a real estate and land developer. Many Seattleites felt he would use the purchase of the team to pave the way to future real-estate ventures in the area. Behring was a heavy-handed, aggressive owner. He made decisions like a dictator. His worst was drafting Dan McGwire instead of the great Brett Favre. Because of his tyrant-like attitude, he was not popular with fans or the media.

Behring kept claiming the Kingdome was unsuitable for play and demanded a new public-funded stadium be built. The breaking point came in 1995 when city legislation approved a new baseball stadium for the Seattle Mariners and basically ignored the Seahawks' request. Behring was enraged. He and his lawyer met with King County officials to argue that the 20-year-old outdated stadium was now dangerous and unsuitable for play. "Tiles had fallen and the roof leaked," they argued, and it did not meet earthquake safety guidelines. Behring claimed the lease could be broken on these grounds.

By February 1996, Behring couldn't take it any longer. He ordered the team and the equipment be packed and moved to Southern California, ironically one of the great earthquake capitals in North America. While the Seahawks continued to play their games in Seattle, operations were moved to Anaheim where players did their off-season training in the old L.A. Rams facility. This was viewed in Seattle as an obvious step toward relocation. The city started to sharpen its legal swords.

The NFL, the city, the fans, the players (and especially John Nordstrom who had a handshake agreement with Behring to never move the team from Seattle) were in disbelief that this man could be so arrogant as to up and move the Seahawks without notice. The NFL threatened to fine Behring $500,000 plus $50,000 a week until he returned the team to its rightful home. And, King County filed a lawsuit against him for breaking the lease agreement with the Kingdome. Something needed to be done.

Enter Paul Allen, co-founder of Microsoft. Allen already owned one professional sports franchise, the NBA Portland Trail Blazers and was ranked by Forbes as one of the 50 wealthiest people in the world. He seemed a likely candidate to step in and save the day. Allen approached the purchase of the Seahawks as more of a civic duty than a great economic opportunity. He reached an agreement with Behring to buy the club on the condition with the city that a new stadium would be built.

Allen contributed $4.2 million to fund a special statewide election for stadium financing. Luckily, the vote came in at 51 percent in favor. Philanthropist Paul Allen purchased the team for $200 million in July 1997 – thus keeping the team in the Emerald City. In addition, Allen would put up $130 million of the $430 million stadium project cost, and taxpayers would contribute the rest. CenturyLink Field was completed in 2002.

Under Allen's ownership, the Seahawks have risen to the top. They have been to the Super Bowl three times, winning the 2014 Super Bowl by clobbering the Denver Broncos 43- 8. They should have won the 2015 Super Bowl, but blew it. Instead of handing the ball off to the unstoppable "beast" (Marshawn Lynch) for a one-yard plunge, coach Pete Carroll called for a short pass, which was intercepted, and the New England Patriots won the game.

Seattle is the only NFL franchise to have switched conferences twice. They started in the NFC West in 1976 then were switched to the AFC West in 1977 and switched back to the NFC West in 2002.

Super Bowl Appearances: 3   Wins: 1
Forbes 2017 Valuation: $2.45 Billion

Tampa Bay Buccaneers

Year	Owner(s)	Purchase Price
1974-1993	Hugh Culverhouse	$16 Million
1994	Stephen Story, Fred Cone, & Jack Donlan	NA
1995-2014	Malcolm Glazer	$192 Million
2014-	The Glazer Children	Inherited

Hugh Culverhouse was awarded the NFL's Tampa franchise for the $16 million expansion fee in 1974. Two years prior, he had tried to acquire the Los Angeles Rams on a $17 million handshake deal with then owner Dan Reeves. However, when Reeves learned he could make $2 million more selling the team to Robert Irsay – he did. Culverhouse wasn't pleased. And, when Irsay and Carroll Rosenbloom, then owner of the Baltimore Colts, traded teams for an even swap, Culverhouse sued, saying the whole transaction was a premeditated attempt to prevent him from purchasing the Los Angeles Rams. The case never made it to trial. Instead, the parties agreed behind closed doors that Rosenbloom (and the NFL) would help Culverhouse get an expansion franchise as soon as possible.

Culverhouse was a canny and successful tax attorney, but he made his fortune in real estate. After receiving a law degree from the University of Alabama, and a brief stint serving in the Korean War, he joined the legal team of the Internal Revenue Service where he served for 10 years. In 1962, he moved to Jacksonville, Florida, and became one of the nation's best-known tax attorneys. The one-time tax attorney for Richard Nixon and his buddy, Bebe Rebozo, Culverhouse's cases were often cited in the Supreme Court.

Known as a keen negotiator and the most frugal of NFL owners, he became head of the NFL's finance committee during the player's strikes of 1982 and 1987. To help modernize the NFL, Culverhouse introduced the use of computers to manage finances and scouting reports.

Culverhouse's reputation vacillated between extremes during his 20-year reign with the Buccaneers. While he was originally liked for bringing a major-league team to southern Florida, he was soon blamed for the team's laughable losing record. The Bucs were often the butt of late-night television jokes; they didn't even win their first game until the 13th week of their second season. The 1976 Bucs held the title as "the least-winning team" in NFL history until 2008 when the Detroit Lions took the title. Culverhouse just didn't seem to care about winning or losing. All he could see was the bottom line.

Culverhouse's motives came under question when the NFLPA (NFL Players Association) published reports revealing that while the Buccaneers had the fifth-highest gross income of all NFL teams, their average player salary was ranked 21st. That might not have looked suspicious except that in 1980, Culverhouse told players they were on one of the three highest-paid teams. Unfortunately for Culverhouse, the reports proved the Buccaneers were the third lowest-paid team. It became clear Culverhouse was much more concerned with profits than putting together a winning team.

A few more bad decisions followed. First, he guaranteed Coach John McKay employment for life, which fans couldn't fathom since his teams were losers. Next came the Bo Jackson draft debacle where Culverhouse's stinginess lost the Bucs the Heisman Trophy-winning running back from Auburn, the number-one player in the draft. Of course, Culverhouse wouldn't budge during negotiations. He even threatened cutting his offer in half if Jackson didn't accept the lowball number that he had offered. We all know how that turned out. Jackson chose baseball and signed a contract with the Kansas City Royals.

The straw that broke the camel's back came in 1986 when once again Culverhouse's frugal ways, while negotiating with quarterback Doug Williams, created resentment on and off the field. Williams had led the Bucs to the playoffs in three of his five years with the team. He was their most important player but only earned a salary of $120,000, which was lower than some third-string quarterbacks. Williams asked for $600,000. Culverhouse refused anything higher than $400,000 and, for insurance, traded that year's number-one draft pick for a back-up quarterback should Williams not agree. Williams walked and signed with the Oklahoma Outlaws of the USFL.

This infuriated fans and players alike. Adding insult to injury, the Buccaneers' losing streak prevented home games from being broadcast on television due to the NFL blackout policy. From 1982 to 1986, the Buccaneers had a streak of 32 consecutive blackouts. At one point, there were no Buccaneer games broadcast in the state of Florida.

Even though Culverhouse brought Super Bowl XXV to Tampa, it was too late. His reputation was tarnished. He didn't care. The Bucs, however bad they were on the field, were one of the more profitable teams in the NFL. In 1989, with a record of 5-11, and the league's second-lowest payroll, the Bucs ranked second in the league with $6.3 million in profits while the Super Bowl champion 49ers lost $16.2 million. Go figure.

In 1994, Culverhouse died and control of the team was handed to Stephen Story (Culverhouse's law partner), Jack Donlan, and Fred Cone. Ironically, when the team's books were opened after Culverhouse's death they showed a near bankrupt franchise. In March 1995, Malcolm Glazer, CEO of First Allied Corporation, outbid George Steinbrenner's group and paid $192 million to buy the Bucs, the highest sale price for a professional sports team at the time.

Glazer, another owner who made his fortune in real estate, immediately placed three of his sons in charge of the team and its finances.

Raymond James Stadium, supported by public taxes, opened in 1998. When Glazer took over operations, the team had a .300 winning percentage in its 19 years of play. In just two years, with a new coach on the sidelines and bold new uniforms on the players, a 16-year playoff drought was over.

Glazer was the light at the end of the losing tunnel. Perhaps it was from his humble beginnings when he inherited his father's wholesale watch and jewelry repair business that he gained the ability to fix things that had stopped working. And that's exactly what he did with the Bucs. When he came on board in 1995, Glazer approached rebuilding the team as he would one of his more difficult watch repairs. First, he had to figure out what wasn't working, and then rebuild the whole with new, functioning parts.

One of the biggest differences between styles of ownership was Glazer's interest and passion for the people in his organization. He prided himself on knowing each player face to face, and he cared about the fans and the community. He also better understood that creating a winning team wasn't just about the bottom line, but about empowering and mobilizing a group of parts to work together as a whole.

In January 2003, the moment everyone had been waiting for happened. Tampa Bay won Super XXXVII, defeating the Oakland Raiders 48-21. From there, positive momentum kept building. In 2006, the Buccaneers moved into one of the best new training facilities in the NFL and the team won three division titles in the next seven years. Glazer was revered among fans.

In 2005, Glazer paid $1.4 billion for one of the most valuable teams in the world, Manchester United of the English Premier League. In 1999, he set up the Glazer Family Foundation, donating millions of dollars to charitable initiatives for the community, including a $5 million Children's Museum that opened its doors in 2010.

Glazer died in 2014, leaving behind his wife and six children. The children will continue to own and operate the team as they have since Glazer took over in 1995. Upon his death, the Glazer fortune was valued by Forbes at $4.4 billion. Glazer's heirs continue to own Manchester United.

Super Bowl Appearances: 1   Wins: 1
Forbes 2017 Valuation: $1.975 Billion

Tennessee Titans

Former names: Houston Oilers 1960-96; Tennessee Oilers 1997-98

Year	Owner(s)	Purchase Price
1960-2013	Bud Adams	$25,000
2014-	Tommy Smith/KSA Industries	Inherited

Nashville has been known as "Music City" going back to its earliest settlers in the late 1700s. Even Nashville's first celebrity, pioneer and congressman Davy Crockett, was not only known for his story-telling, but for his talent with the fiddle. From Hank Williams to Bob Dylan to the Beatles to the Grand Ole Opry and beyond, music and songwriting have been the theme that gave Nashville its reputation as the music capital of the world.

When Nashville competed for one of the two 1995 NFL expansion franchises, they thought they had it in the bag until the NFL sang a different tune and awarded those franchises to Charlotte, North Carolina, and Jacksonville, Florida. The city's only option at this point was to see if they could orchestrate having an existing team relocate to Nashville. Two years later, in 1997, Bud Adams changed his tune about Houston and decidee on Nashville, giving the city something new to sing about.

Kenneth Stanley "Bud" Adams, Jr. was the founder of the Houston Oilers, one of the AFL's original eight teams. He was born in Oklahoma in 1923 to K.S. "Boots" Adams, one of the nation's youngest leaders of a major corporation, Phillips Petroleum Company. Adam's grandparents became involved in some of the first oil trade deals with Native American chiefs in early Oklahoma. It was this history and connection with the Cherokee tribe that helped establish members of the Adams family in the oil business.

After graduating from the University of Kansas, Bud Adams served in the US Navy during World War II. Following military service, he took after his ancestors and became involved in the oil business, eventually founding his own wildcatting firm known as Adams Resources and Energy. It was during this time he became fast friends with Lamar Hunt, a fellow Texas oilman. After Hunt had been rejected by the NFL for an expansion team in Dallas, he pitched the idea for a new league to Bud, who was all in. Because Hunt lived in Dallas and Adams in Houston, they felt their teams could strike up a good ole Texas rivalry to help make the league successful.

In 1960, Adams formed the second AFL team, the Houston Oilers, for the $25,000 franchise fee. Adams helped show the NFL that the AFL meant business when he landed LSU's All-American Heisman Trophy winner, Billy Cannon -- the top pick in the draft. Because of his good draft picks, Adams's early Oilers were one of the more successful teams in the AFL, winning the first two AFL Championships.

Several decades later, Adams began thinking about moving the Oilers to a new city because the mayor rejected his proposal for a new stadium in Houston. The Oilers had been playing in the Astrodome, but lackluster attendance with crowds usually no more than 20,000 made the team look even more pathetic than it was. Adams knew he needed a city with a larger stadium. In 1995, he negotiated with the City of Nashville, Tennessee. They were constructing Adelphia Coliseum, now known as Nissan Stadium. The deal with Nashville went through and the Oilers moved to Tennessee in 1997, but the stadium would not be ready for the '97- '98 season.

Adams was confronted with the difficult decision about where to play: in the bigger Memphis stadium or in Nashville's Vanderbilt stadium. Either choice was doomed. Memphis fans felt they were being *used* as a temporary city for Nashville's team and resented playing second fiddle and weren't going to cheer on another city's team. Nashville fans weren't about to drive down the under-construction I-40 to see their new team play in another city's stadium. Unfortunately, Bud chose Memphis and the season was a bust, drawing the smallest crowds in NFL history.

The next year he agreed to play in Nashville's Vanderbilt Stadium because the smaller stadium made it feel like they had more fans. In 1999, the gates to Nissan Stadium finally opened and Adam's team had its much-awaited home. It was then he decided to change the team's name to the Titans because he felt it better suited their titanic new home. The newly named Titans had their best season in franchise history that year, going 13–3. The team's success continued in 2000 when they made their first and only Super Bowl appearance, losing to the Rams 23-16.

Adams died in 2013 at the ripe old age of 90. Being one of the longest tenured owners in NFL history, his 409 wins were the most of any current NFL owner. His franchise made 21 playoff appearances in 53 seasons, eighth among NFL teams since 1960. He left the team to his three children (through his holding company, KSA Industries), who appointed Adams's son-in-law, Tommy Smith, as president and CEO. In 2015, Smith announced his retirement and appointed longtime Oilers/Titans senior executive vice president, Steve Underwood, to step in as president and CEO.

Super Bowl Appearances: 1   Wins: 0
Forbes 2017 Valuation: $2.05 Billion

Washington Redskins

Former name: Boston Braves 1932-1933, Boston Redskins 1933-1936

Year	Owner(s)	Purchase Price
1932-1961	George Preston Marshall	Unknown
1961-1997	Jack Kent Cooke	Unknown
1997-1998	Jack Kent Cooke Foundation	Inherited
1999-	Daniel Snyder	$800 Million

The Washington Redskins were founded as the Boston Braves in 1932 by a group led by George Preston Marshall. In 1933, after the 1932 first-year money-losing season, Marshall became the sole owner of the team and changed the name to Boston Redskins to distinguish the team from the well-known Boston Braves baseball team, while retaining the team's American Indian theme identity.

Along with the changes in ownership and name in 1933, the Boston Redskins agreed to play in Fenway Park, home of the Boston Red Sox, through the 1936 football season. At the end of the 1936 season, after dismal attendance at a home playoff game, Marshall decided to move the team to Washington, D.C., where he lived.

The Washington Redskins began their 1937 first season of play in Washington, D.C., at Griffith Stadium, the home of the baseball Washington Senators. They arrived with their recently drafted player, Sammy Baugh, who proved to be not only a gifted and versatile player, but also an innovator of the forward pass. The passing game became a signature feature of the Redskins' play during the era of "Slingin' Sammy Baugh". The Redskins won their first NFL Championship in 1937, their first year in Washington, and played for it again in 1940 but lost.

George Preston Marshall owned the franchise throughout the 1930s, 1940s, 1950s, and into the 1960s. The team was particularly successful during the early 1940s when they were regularly in contention, and won their second NFL championship in 1942. The team played in, but lost, the 1943 and 1945 championship games.

During that time, the franchise gradually became an entrenched and beloved part of the region, including throughout the southeastern United States, there being no other NFL franchise south of Washington and east of the Mississippi River. In fact, after establishing the team as part of an entertainment program with a college football atmosphere, with its own marching band and fight song, it considered itself to be the "Team of the South." This identity unfortunately mandated being an all-white team.

In 1944, Marshall established the first Redskins Radio Network throughout the South and in 1950 arranged for the team to be the first in the NFL to have all its games televised, sponsored by the American Oil Company. After the 1940s championships and near-championships until the 1970s, the team's success on the gridiron waned with a parade of unsuccessful coaches hired by Marshall.

In 1961, the Redskins moved into DC Stadium, later named Robert F. Kennedy (RFK) Memorial Stadium in 1969, where they played until 1996.

Also, in 1961 the Redskins drafted their first African-American player, Ernie Davis, who was traded to the Cleveland Browns for Bobby Mitchell, also an African-American and a future Hall of Famer. The Redskins were the last NFL team to integrate, having maintained an all-white roster due to owner Marshall's views. Mitchell was welcomed to the team only grudgingly, after pressure from the NFL (and the federal government) forced Marshall and the Redskins organization to give in.

After Marshall suffered a stroke in 1961, Jack Kent Cooke purchased a 25 percent interest in the Redskins. During this time, the team front office was affected by Marshall's aging decline, causing decision-making difficulties for the team's management and other stockholders.

Upon Marshall's death in 1969, Edward Bennett Williams, a minority stockholder and prominent attorney who lived in Washington, ran the franchise while Cooke lived in Los Angeles. Cooke owned the Los Angeles Lakers basketball team at that time. He became the majority owner of the Redskins in 1974. In 1985 he became the sole owner.

In 1977, Jack Kent Cooke moved from Los Angeles to Virginia and took over operations of the Redskins from Edward Bennett Williams. While Cooke was owner and operator of the Redskins, the team won three Super Bowls, in 1981, 1987, and 1991, the franchise's first championships since the 1940s.

Cooke completed a new stadium for the team in 1997 and died shortly after its opening. The stadium was posthumously named Jack Kent Cooke Stadium. In his will, the team was left to the Jack Kent Cooke Foundation with the direction that the team would be sold and the proceeds be used for education scholarships.

After the death of Cooke, his son, John Kent Cooke, announced his attempt to purchase the team. After two seasons, 1997 and 1998, John Kent Cooke was unable to purchase the Redskins from his father's foundation. In 1999, Daniel Snyder, an advertising executive, received unanimous approval from league owners to purchase the franchise for $800 million, at the time the highest price paid for a pro sports franchise. Shortly after purchasing the franchise and the Jack Kent Cooke Stadium, Snyder sold the naming rights to the stadium to Federal Express, changing the name to FedEx Field.

From 1999 to the present, the Washington Redskins have been owned by Daniel Snyder, a man who is not without controversy. Rolling Stone magazine ranked him number one in its list of the 15 worst owners of a professional sports team. The "Skins" play on the field has generally been mediocre and only in 2015 have they even won a division championship with a putrid .500 record. In 2016, the Skins blew a golden opportunity to make the playoffs by losing their final home game in lackluster fashion.

Super Bowl Appearances: 5   Wins: 3
Forbes 2017 Valuation: $3.1 Billion

Major League Baseball

Arizona Diamondbacks

Year	Owner(s)	Purchase Price
1997-2004	Jerry Colangelo	$130 Million
2005-	Ken Kendrick	$238 Million

The Arizona Diamondbacks were founded in 1997 by Jerry Colangelo for a fee of $130 million and began playing in 1998. Colangelo is most widely known for his connection to basketball, as he joined the Phoenix Suns NBA expansion franchise in 1968 to become the youngest general manager in professional sports.

Colangelo's basketball resume is extensive and it was that connection that sparked his interest in baseball when he attended a Chicago Cubs game while in town for the Suns. That was enough to get him hooked and inspired him to contact Major League Baseball about expanding in Arizona. He gathered a group of investors and inquired a year before the expansion meetings of 1995. His investment group was then granted the expansion team following the official meeting.

Getting a stadium built is always a first order of business with a new franchise and accomplishing this in Phoenix was no different. The county approved a quarter-cent increase in sales tax to fund a portion. The issue was controversial enough that the county supervisor was shot and injured while leaving a board meeting. Cost overruns of $85 million, also typical in such construction, placed owners in a tight financial bind. The additional financial stressor was that the agreements between the Diamondbacks and Devil Rays (the original name for the current Tampa Bay Rays) and MLB left them with no revenue sharing the first five years. That aside, the stadium was completed in time for the first season's opening day in 1998.

Colangelo, a shrewd businessman and excellent talent evaluator from all his years with the Suns, seized the opportunity to hire Joe Garagiola, Jr. as the general manager and Buck Showalter as the team manager. These decisions started the team off well and, except for the first and last years of Colangelo's leadership, the team had record-setting success and won their division in only their second season.

The winning continued and contributed to amazing attendance as the franchise averaged just under 3 million a year in its first seven seasons, while many expansion teams have struggled for years to hit the 2 million mark. The Diamondbacks went on to win their division in both 2001 and 2002 and brought the first professional sports championship to Phoenix with their 2001 World Series win over the New York Yankees.

In 2004, disagreements with the majority owners caused Colangelo to announce he would step down as managing partner at the end of the calendar year. Jeff Moorad, a 12 percent owner, would be named CEO. Moorad would hold that position until 2009 when he resigned to make a bid to buy the San Diego Padres. Ultimately, Ken Kendrick, Jr., a part owner, would lead a group to purchase the team for $238 million and become the managing general partner. The team was in debt from stadium overruns, five years without MLB revenue sharing, and high levels of investment in players to make the team competitive out of the chute. Through careful debt and equity restructuring, Kendrick eliminated more than $200 million in debt, which placed the team on stronger footing.

During Kendrick's leadership, the Diamondbacks won their division in 2007 and 2011. They reached the NLCS in 2007 but lost in the LDS in 2011. However, 2011 was important and successful in other ways. In February 2011, the team opened Salt River Fields at Talking Stick, a state of the art spring training facility they share with the Colorado Rockies. That same year, they hosted the All-Star Game at Chase Field. ESPN has ranked the Diamondbacks highly on their success both on and off the field and Yahoo! named them as the "best workplace in sports."

World Series Appearances: 1   Wins: 1
Forbes 2017 Valuation: $1.15 Billion

Atlanta Braves

Former names: Boston Braves -1953; Milwaukee Braves 1953- 1966

Year	Owner(s)	Purchase Price
1912-1923	George Washington Grant	
1923-1935	Emil Fuchs	$500,000
1935-1941	Charles Adams	
1941-1944	Bob Quinn	$750,000
1944-1951	Lou Perini, Maney, and Rugo	$750,000
1951-1952	Lou Perini and Maney	
1952-1962	Lou Perini	
1962-1976	William Bartholomay	$6.2 Million
1976-1996	Ted Turner	$11 Million
1996-2007	AOL Time Warner	Acquisition
2007-	Liberty Media Corp.	$450 Million

George Washington Grant was the owner of the Atlanta Braves, the then Boston Braves, during the beginning of the modern era of baseball. He purchased the team from the Percy Haughton estate for an undisclosed amount. Grant was a motion picture promoter in London and New York City. He had strong ties with John McGraw, manager of the New York Giants, and many believed he used his franchise ownership like a farm club for the Giants.

In 1923, he sold the team to a group led by Judge Emil Fuchs for $500,000. Probably not coincidentally, Fuchs was the attorney for the New York Giants, and close with McGraw. Much of the perceived farm team activities continued but he did try to bring interest to the team with Sunday baseball, ladies days, and radio broadcasts.

The Depression did not help and he found it difficult to pay the rent on Braves Field. He hired Babe Ruth in a leadership capacity but Ruth realized he was being used as a figurehead, and retired. Fuchs eventually turned over control to minority owner Charles Adams in 1935. Fuchs had held the team for 12 seasons and only started realizing .500-level baseball in the final three years, but overall they remained in the middle of the pack.

Charles Adams worked his way up in the grocery industry and parlayed that success into being a sports promoter and team owner. In addition to the Boston Braves, he owned the Boston Bruins and Suffolk Downs horse racing. In 1936, there was a fan poll that changed the name of the team to the Boston Bees but they reverted back to the Braves in 1941.

During his six years of ownership, the team continued to struggle and had a .428 win rate. The baseball commissioner, Judge Kenesaw Mountain Landis, had an issue with mixing horse racing and baseball, so Adams felt forced to sell the Braves. Thus, Adams's interest in the team was acquired in 1941 by a syndicate headed by Bob Quinn for $750,000. Quinn had recently owned the Boston Red Sox, from 1924 to 1932. He was only with the Braves for three years and team performance remained lackluster with a .412-win rate.

1944 began a 19-year reign with Lou Perini in the owner's seat. He initially led a group including Guido Rugo, Joseph Maney, and his brothers, to purchase the team from Adams for $750,000. By 1947, they achieved the club's first year with over one million fans in attendance. The next year they won the pennant but couldn't pull off the championship; however, attendance was up again.

The Braves signed Sam Jethroe as their first black player in 1950, nearly a decade before the Red Sox had any integration. In a racially divided city, it is hypothesized that this could have contributed to dropping attendance rates.

In 1951, Rugo sold his shares to Perini and Maney for an unknown amount. Their cross-town rivals were then owned by the wealthy Tom Yawkey, who was investing in their ballpark and players. At the same time, Perini and his brothers, known as the "Three Little Steam Shovels," gained complete ownership. They invested in an electronic scoreboard and targeted funds for player development but were unable to draw fans and were operating at a loss each year.

Perini also owned the team's Milwaukee minor-league club and that city was in the process of building a new stadium in hopes of landing a major-league team. Once Bill Veeck made a move to try to relocate the St. Louis Browns to Milwaukee (but was denied), Perini knew the time had come and he received the necessary votes to move the Braves to Milwaukee in 1953.

It was energizing to the team, as they drew 1.8 million fans their first year in Milwaukee – a National League attendance record – and had a .597-win rate. Perhaps most importantly, the struggling team turned a $1.5 million profit after operating at a loss for many years. The next year Hank Aaron was called up and the winning and rising attendance continued. They hosted the All-Star Game in 1955 and showed the baseball world what could be accomplished with a new stadium in a hungry market. They achieved two million in attendance for four consecutive years, won the World Series in 1957, and narrowly missed a repeat in 1958 when they lost four games to three.

Then the crowds stopped coming and attendance dropped below the million mark. Perini wanted to avoid the losses he had experienced in Boston and decided to sell the team. In total, Perini's Braves won three division titles, appeared in the World Series three times, and won the championship once. He also took the average Boston attendance of .79 million to 1.7 million in Milwaukee.

In 1962, the team was sold to a syndicate led by William Bartholomay for $6.2 million. Bartholomay was from Chicago and made his fortune in the insurance industry. When he bought the Braves, he already had a goal of moving them to Atlanta. He wanted to see the baseball footprint move south and had identified Atlanta as a growing regional center.

Milwaukee had long wanted baseball in their city and did not go down without a fight; thus, numerous lawsuits were filed when Bartholomay's intentions became known. The case went all the way to the US Supreme Court, but they upheld the Wisconsin Court decision that affirmed professional baseball's right to control its franchise locations.

The team was moved to Atlanta and renamed Atlanta Braves in 1966. The Braves were welcomed to Atlanta and the Atlanta Fulton County Stadium was filled with 1.5 million fans the first year. But like Milwaukee, attendance started to decline a bit over time, although they enjoyed six consecutive years at over one million and got a boost when the Braves won their division in 1969.

Ted Turner of Turner Broadcasting System approached Bartholomay in 1976 about buying the team and marketing them on a national scale and they reached an agreement to transfer controlling interest. In 13 seasons, Bartholomay moved the team from Milwaukee to Atlanta, had an average win-rate of .501, and an average attendance of one million. His legacy would be moving professional baseball into the Deep South.

Turner purchased the team for $11 million in 1976. Turner, a media mogul, started the Cable News Network (CNN), founded TBS, and established the superstation concept and revolutionized how people receive their news. His decision to buy the Atlanta Braves was influenced by his need to keep the Braves as a major piece of his broadcasting enterprise. His superstations became the talk of baseball and many owners were not happy that his broadcasts were seen locally more than their own teams, which could lead to a competitive imbalance.

In 1985, Commissioner Ueberroth convinced the Braves and Yankees to pay an annual superstation tax into a shared fund for other owners; hence, revenue sharing. While this debate and negotiation was happening off the field, the Braves started building momentum and hit over two million in attendance in 1983 for the first time in Atlanta.

The bottom dropped out and the Braves moved to be cellar dwellers in their division. The attendance tanked as well. They then brought in Bobby Cox to manage for what turned out to be 20 years of dominance. The Braves won their division 14 out of the next 15 years. They won the National League pennant in 1991 and 1992, and the World Series in 1995. Turner also saw the team achieve its first three million in attendance in 1992, and raised the average attendance during his 20 years to 1.57 million. In October 1996, Time Warner acquired Turner Broadcasting System and all assets, including the Braves. While Turner stayed on as vice chairman, his influence over the Braves diminished greatly. In 1997, Turner Field opened, after the conversion of the 1996 Olympic Stadium into a ballpark. Then in early 2001, AOL purchased Time Warner, becoming AOL Time Warner. While all this was going on, the team continued its domination, averaging a .603 win-rate with nearly three million in attendance, and won two more pennants.

In 2007, Liberty Media made a $1.27-billion purchase, which included cash, stock, and assets of Time Warner, one of those assets being the Atlanta Braves, valued at $450 million. As a part of the approval process with Major League Baseball, it was agreed that there would be no immediate changes to president, general manager, and manager. While the team performance has been solid with a .520 win-rate, and average fan attendance has remained consistent at 2.4 million annually, the Braves have only won their division once in the last 10 seasons while making it to the postseason three times.

Their slide to the bottom continued in 2016 with the second worst record in the 30-team league and coming in dead last in their division. 2017 showed solid improvement.

World Series Appearances: 9   Wins: 3
Forbes 2017 Valuation: $1.5 Billion

Baltimore Orioles

Former name: Milwaukee Brewers 1901, St. Louis Browns 1902-1953.

Year	Owner(s)	Purchase Price
1915-1933	Philip Ball	$525,000
1933-1936	Phil Ball Estate	NA
1936-1945	Don Barnes/William DeWitt, Sr.	$325,000
1945-1949	Richard Muckerman	$1.443 Million
1949-1951	William DeWitt, Sr.	$1 Million
1951-1953	Bill Veeck	$1.4 Million
1953-1965	Miles/Hoffberger/Iglehart	$2.5 Million
1965-1979	National Brewing Company	Unknown
1980-1988	Edward Bennett Williams	Unknown
1988-1993	Eli Jacobs	$70 Million
1993-	Peter Angelos	$173 Million

The Baltimore Orioles were the St. Louis Browns when the modern era of baseball began in 1920. The Browns were owned by Phil Ball (who made his money on the cold storage business) from 1915 until his death in 1933, at which time ownership passed to his estate.

In 1914, Ball and a partner, Otto Stifel, founded a team in the upstart Federal League, which meant yet a third team in St Louis. Inter-league lawsuits ensued, and in 1915, Ball, with the American League's support, negotiated an out-of-court settlement for Ball to purchase the Browns for $525,000, with the American League contributing $50,000 of Ball's cost.

The Browns performed well until Ball fired his business manager, Branch Rickey, in 1916. This forced Rickey, who became one of the best general managers of all time, to jump to the St. Louis Cardinals while Phil's St. Louis Browns jumped to mediocrity. Ownership of the team was held in the Ball estate until 1936, when the team was sold to Donald Barnes, majority owner, and William (Bill) DeWitt, Sr., his son-in-law, as minority owner. To finance the acquisition, Barnes sold 20,000 shares in the Browns to the public at $5 a share.

Bill DeWitt began his 60-year baseball career with the St. Louis Cardinals. His first job, at age 17, was selling soda pop at the ballpark. He

184

learned the ropes from Phil Ball's discard, Branch Rickey, who was the Cards' GM from 1916 to 1942.

DeWitt, as general manager of the St. Louis Browns, had to compete with the more established St. Louis Cardinals in a market that was relatively small in those days. In 1936, the Browns' annual attendance was less than 95,000. Bill was forced to pinch pennies and trade good players to make ends meet, the result being losing years and falling attendance.

In 1941, the Browns were planning to move to Los Angeles. The American League's vote to approve or deny the move was scheduled for the week of December 8, one day after the Japanese bombed Pearl Harbor and rushed the country into World War II … and kept the Browns in St. Louis for another 12 years.

Under Bill's leadership in the early '40s, with some money he raised to improve scouting, the team improved and the Browns won the 1944 World Series, defeating none other than his hometown rival Cardinals. It was not considered a "real" championship because so many good players were serving in the Armed Forces, but a win is a win in the record books. Bill's son, William DeWitt, Jr., is currently the principal owner of the St. Louis Cardinals. His grandson, William DeWitt III, is currently the Cards' president.

In 1945, Barnes and DeWitt sold control of the team to Richard Muckerman for $1.443 million. Then in 1948, Bill DeWitt and his brother, Charlie, paid $1 million to re-acquire control of the Browns from Muckerman, an owner who seemed to be more interested in improving the field (Sportsman's Park) than the team.

However, the DeWitts couldn't reverse a losing trend and could no longer afford to sustain the financial losses, and in 1951, sold the Browns to Bill Veeck, who had been the majority owner of the Cleveland Indians from '46 to'49.

Love him or hate him, as one did or didn't, Bill Veeck was a legend in baseball circles. Born in Chicago in 1914, Bill grew up with the Chicago Cubs. His father, William Veeck, Sr., was a sportswriter who claimed he could run the Cubs better than the current management. Hearing these taunts, the Cubs' owner William Wrigley, Jr. took heed and hired him.

Eventually William Veeck, Sr. became the Cubs' president. Bill Veeck, whose first job was selling popcorn at the ballpark, went to Phillips Academy in Massachusetts, then to Kenyon College, but left school when his father died and went back to work for the Cubs and eventually became treasurer. His first venture into franchise ownership (which seemed to be in his blood) came in 1942 when he left Chicago and co-invested (with former Cubs star and manager, Charlie Grimm) in the Milwaukee Brewers minor league team. They played well during those war years and he reportedly made a $275,000 profit when they sold the team in 1945, a hefty hunk of change in those days.

During World War II, and during his ownership of the Brewers, Bill served in a Marines artillery unit. His weapon recoiled, shot him in the leg and, after several surgeries, his leg required amputation. He wore a wooden leg in which he drilled holes and, as a chain smoker, used them as an ashtray.

Bill Veeck was indeed a showman and great promoter of the game, although many of his antics and promotional stunts angered other owners. When he acquired a controlling interest in the St. Louis Browns, he was hell-bent on driving the more popular St Louis Cardinals out of town.

Veeck's purchase of the Browns included ownership of Sportsman's Park, where both teams played, making the Cards his tenant. Veeck had balls. He went and stripped all Cards identity and promotional material from the ballpark, replacing them with material promoting the Browns; he hired former Cards pitching great, the ever-popular Dizzy Dean, to broadcast the Browns games; and he signed former Cards popular "retired" players to his roster, all of which bolstered his gate receipts at the expense of the Cardinals.

Veeck's most fabled stunt was in 1951. He signed a contract with a midget, the three-foot, seven-inch Eddie Gaedel, who came to the plate in a uniform numbered 1/8th and wore turned-up elf-style shoes. The umps balked, as did the opposing team, but Veeck showed them the signed contract. The fans loved it when Eddie, with zero strike zone, walked on four straight pitches. The commissioner nullified the contract the next day, but Veeck had his outlandish promotion and a good laugh. He also instituted a "fans day" whereby the fans could make managerial decisions by holding up a placard that said: "Take, Swing, Bunt".

Meanwhile in 1953, during this cross-town, inter-city rivalry, the Cardinals' owner, Alan Saigh, was being indicted for tax evasion and was on his way to jail. It seemed to Bill Veeck that his plan to run the Cardinals out of town was working.

Offers were made to buy the troubled Cardinals and relocate them but Anheuser-Busch trumped these offers and saved the St. Louis Cardinals for St. Louis. Veeck quickly realized his pockets weren't deep enough to compete with a beer dynasty and decided to get out while the gettin' was good.

But many of the other American League owners, who didn't appreciate Veeck's style and antics, wanted no more part of him as a minority owner (which he tried to negotiate) and vetoed his applications to sell, first to Milwaukee, then to Baltimore.

In 1953, Veeck sold Sportsman's Park to the Cardinals and sold the Browns for $2.5 million to a Baltimore group initially led by attorney Clarence Miles and brewery owner Jerold Hoffberger. That's how the St. Louis Browns became the Baltimore Orioles.

Bill Veeck, who owned three different major league teams over the course of his career (Cleveland Indians, St. Louis Browns and Chicago

White Sox), did much to promote and make innovations to the game. He was elected to the Hall of Fame in 1991. (He is also credited with getting the ivy planted on the brick walls of Wrigley Field in 1937). He died of cancer in 1988.

The team was moved to Baltimore in 1954 and the name was changed to the Baltimore Orioles (the Oriole being the official Maryland state bird). Jerold Hoffberger was initially a silent partner with Clarence Miles (1954 to 1955), James Keelty (1955 to 1960), and Joseph Iglehart (1960 to 1965).

In 1965 Joseph Iglehart, then the largest shareholder of the Orioles (32 percent) and board chairman since 1955, was facing a conflict. Since he had a large holding of CBS shares, and CBS bought the Yankees, he had to sell one or the other to avoid a conflict of ownership. He kept the Yankees shares and sold the Orioles shares to the National Brewing Company.

Hoffberger, the brewery president, became the Orioles' new chairman of the board. From 1964 to 1983, the team experienced its greatest success when they won nine division championships, six pennants, three World Series championships, and had five Most Valuable Player awards won by four players (Cal Ripken won twice).

In 1975, the National Brewing Company merged with the Canadian brewer Carling. In 1980, Hoffberger sold his share to Edward Bennett Williams, the prominent Washington, DC lawyer who was a minority owner of the Washington Redskins NFL football team. At that time, Williams bought back the shares that Donald Barnes sold to the public in 1935, making the franchise privately held again.

Williams owned the Orioles through the successful years in the early 1980s (the Orioles won the World Series in 1983) until his death in 1988. Despite fears in Baltimore that he would move the team to Washington, D.C., Williams signed a long-term lease with Baltimore that would pay for a new stadium, which would become Oriole Park at Camden Yards. He would not live to see the new ballpark.

After the death of Edward Bennett Williams, the team was purchased from the Williams estate by Eli Jacobs, a secretive New York venture capitalist who acquired an 87 percent ownership share for $70 million. His other partners included Larry Lucchino (a holdover from the Williams regime and current owner of the Boston Red Sox), and Sargent Shriver and his son Bobby. (Shriver, part of the Kennedy family through marriage, started the Peace Corps under JFK's administration).

The American League franchise owners unanimously approved the sale in April 1989. Jacobs became chairman of the board, with Lucchino managing the organization. In the first year of Jacobs's ownership, the Orioles went from the worst team in the major leagues in 1988 to falling just short of the American League Eastern Division championship.

In 1992, the team moved to Oriole Park at Camden Yards, its current home. The new stadium, which hosted the 1993 All Star game, was an instant success, providing the prototype for ballparks throughout the major leagues over the next two decades, utilizing a design that harkened back to a traditional baseball stadium feel but with contemporary accoutrements. After moving into the new stadium, the team achieved moderate success and was in contention in the first two seasons.

In 1993, Eli Jacobs was forced to divest his interest in the Orioles when seven banks filed petitions to force him into bankruptcy (no wonder he was secretive). In a 1993 auction held in bankruptcy court in New York, the team was sold for $173 million to a group of Baltimore investors led by Peter Angelos, a prominent Baltimore trial attorney. The Orioles franchise had not been in the hands of local ownership since 1979. Peter Angelos, born of Greek parents who immigrated to America, grew up in a working-class neighborhood in Baltimore. He made a name (and money) for himself as a personal-injury trial lawyer whose firm represented the State of Maryland in suits against "big tobacco" (Philip Morris) and "big pharma" (Wyeth). He also represented some 9,000 blue-collar workers in their claims of asbestos poisoning and reportedly received more than $300 million for that endeavor alone. Of the $173 million price tag for the Orioles, Peter invested $40 million, making him the principal owner with well-known minority owners such as tennis great Pam Shriver, film producer Barry Levinson, and author Tom Clancy.

The Orioles have a burgeoning rivalry with the nearby Washington Nationals, which developed after the Montreal Expos were moved to Washington as the Washington Nationals in 2006. Until that time, the Baltimore Orioles had become the defacto home team for the Washington regional market. The rivalry has been nicknamed the "Beltway Series" or the "Battle of the Beltways."

World Series Appearances: 7   Wins: 3
Forbes 2017 Valuation: $1.175 Billion

Boston Red Sox

Year	Owner(s)	Purchase Price
1917-1923	Harry H. Frazee	$500,000
1923-1933	J.A. Robert Quinn	$1.15 Million
1933-1976	Thomas A. Yawkey	$1.2 Million
1976-1977	Jean R. Yawkey	Inherited
1978-1980	JRY Corp	Transferred
1981-2002	Jean R. Yawkey Trust	Held in Trust

| 2002- | John Henry, Tom Werner, Larry Lucchino | $660 Million |

At the onset of the modern era of baseball, Harry Frazee and Hugh Ward were the owners of the Boston Red Sox. In their second season, the Red Sox won the World Series. It was just a year later that finances became an issue and Frazee began selling players to the New York Yankees, Babe Ruth being the most famous of all the deals.

Even after raising capital, the team was still on the verge of bankruptcy. Many were up in arms that Frazee and Ward were funding Broadway productions versus putting money into the team. The other contentious issue was Fenway Park. It was owned by the publishers of the Boston Globe, and team owners simply rented it from the Fenway Realty Trust each season. Frazee wanted to own the ballpark to have more leverage against Ban Johnson, the American League president, and tried to negotiate a buyout of controlling shares. Much drama ensued but eventually Frazee became the sole owner of Fenway Park. During turbulent times coupled with a divorce and the death of his father, Frazee felt compelled to sell the team to a group of investors for $1.15 million, more than doubling his initial investment.

The investor group was headed by Bob Quinn, but it was Palmer Winslow, of the Winslow Glass Company, who had the deep pockets. This became a concern when Winslow became ill a year later and withdrew most of his ongoing financial support. Quinn was a longtime baseball man who even had a stint as a minor-league catcher early on and served in numerous minor league leadership capacities. Success in baseball does take money; the team was not receiving adequate investments for players and Fenway was in a state of disrepair.

Winslow died in 1926 and his wife inherited his shares but didn't invest any more than her husband had. Team performance was lackluster and they finished last in their league seven of nine seasons, had a horrid 43-111 record in 1932 (still the worst in franchise history), and accumulated a .348 win rate overall.

Bob Quinn was ready to sell the team after that season and he did. He went on to be the general manager of the Brooklyn Dodgers, president of the Boston Braves, and president of the Baseball Hall of Fame.

On the advice of his friend Eddie Collins, Tom Yawkey bought the franchise and Fenway Park for $1.2 million in 1933. Yawkey's family had substantial wealth from the timber and mining industries. His father died when he was a baby and his mother moved them to live with her brother, William Yawkey, who was co-owner of the Detroit Tigers. Thus, Tom Yawkey grew up around major league baseball team owners. It was supposedly Ty Cobb who suggested he consider buying a team one day.

When Collins suggested the Red Sox, the team was in dire straits in both performance and finances. Yawkey made Collins vice president and general manager and tasked him with building the team's talent and farm system. Within two years, the Red Sox were playing .500-level baseball. They were competitive but not pennant-worthy.

Yawkey never hesitated to invest in the team and invest in a big way. Fenway Park, in great disrepair, required massive renovations. He spent money so freely the team was nicknamed the "Gold Sox" and the "Millionaires."

World War II sent many of his star players off in service to the country. The stars returned and Yawkey saw the team win its first pennant in 1946 and hit over one million in attendance for the first time. Amid many cherished and heralded accomplishments during Yawkey's tenure, the one negative was being the last major league team to field a black player. Nevertheless, he was popular with his players, many of whom considered him a father figure. His team went on to win two more pennants, 1967 and 1975, but did not experience a championship. Yawkey died in 1976 after quietly battling leukemia. He loved the team, invested in its success, and took a fledgling team to average a .520 win-rate during his 43 seasons at the helm. Yawkey was posthumously inducted into the Baseball Hall of Fame in 1980.

The Yawkey name continued at the forefront of Red Sox ownership through 2002. Jean Yawkey, Tom's widow, took over immediately upon his death in 1976. A year later, a partnership of Haywood Sullivan and Buddy LeRoux wanted to buy the team but the American League would not approve it until Yawkey agreed to be the third general partner. Jean bought out LeRoux in 1983 and was as active an owner as her husband. She attended nearly every game (and kept a scorecard) and participated in the management of the team. When Jean Yawkey died in 1992, her shares – now two of the three voting shares – transferred to the Yawkey Trust that was managed by John Harrington. Led by Harrington as the CEO, the Yawkey Trust bought out Sullivan in 1993 and held control of the franchise until it was sold in 2002. During the 26 seasons when Jean Yawkey was associated with the Red Sox, the team had a .531 win-rate, achieved its first two million attendance year in 1977, and averaged 2.1 million overall, and won the pennant in 1986. In total, the Yawkey name was associated with Red Sox ownership for a staggering 69 seasons.

In late 2001, a group led by John Henry, Tom Werner, and Larry Lucchino, won the bid to purchase the Red Sox for $660 million. The sale was approved and closed in February 2002. John Henry was the principal owner, Werner the chairman, and Lucchino the president and CEO. Each member brought previous ownership experience to the franchise. Henry had owned the Marlins, Werner, the Padres; and Lucchino, the Orioles and Padres. Together, they are part of the Fenway Sports Group, LLC (FSG), which owns not only the Boston Red Sox and Fenway Park, but also the New England Sports Network (NESN), Roush Fenway Racing, Fenway Sports Management, and Liverpool F. C. of the English Premier League.

The leaders of FSG brought with them experience and deep pockets to raise the team to new heights. Within three seasons, in 2004, the team won the World Series championship for the first time since 1918 and the mythical "Curse of the Bambino" was lifted. They won two additional championships in 2007 and 2013 after earning a berth in the post-season seven of 14 years. The ownership group committed to staying at Fenway Park and invested $285 million in improvements. Attendance has been over two million each year, achieved three million for the first time in 2008, and has averaged 2.9 million in their first 14 years of ownership. The .550 average win rate has brought with it three championships thus far. Thanks, "Big-Papi!"

World Series Appearances: 12   Wins: 8
Forbes 2017 Valuation: $2.7 Billion

Chicago Cubs

Year	Owner(s)	Purchase Price
1918-1932	William Wrigley, Jr.	Not Available
1932-1977	Phil Wrigley	
1977-1981	Bill Wrigley	
1981-2009	Tribune Company	$20.5 Million
2009-	Thomas Ricketts	$642 Million

Most people coming from the Judeo-Christian tradition are familiar with the Ten Commandments. For most of the 20th century and well into the 21st, citizens of Chicago and Boston lived with an eleventh commandment: THOU SHALL NEVER WIN THE WORLD SERIES.

In a secular sense, this was the indisputable law of nature in the ecosystem that is Major League Baseball. Transcending earthly bonds of physical competition, this "law" would become metaphysical, involving a portly left-handed pitcher (who also played a little right field), a billy goat, a black cat, and a guy named Steve Bartman -- call it a curse if you must, but the Chicago Cubs and the Boston Red Sox don't win the World Series, thus had it ever been and thus would it ever be. Luckily, a young man from Brookline, Mass., named Theo Epstein never got the memo.

In 2011, after delivering unto Boston, after an 86-year drought, not one but two world championships, there was only one logical destination for the man who was now a certified and credentialed miracle worker. Named the Chicago Cubs' president of baseball operations, Epstein brought with him from Boston Jed Hoyer, who he immediately installed as general manager.

If a team, rather than a person, could be called quirky, it would be the Chicago Cubs. At the start of the 2016 season, they held (or shared) two all-time records: oldest sports franchise in the United States (along with the Atlanta Braves, doing business in 1876 as the Boston Red Stockings), and had all to themselves the record for being the most futile of any American (and North American) sports franchise, with 108 years (and counting) without a championship.

In 2015, having hired manager Joe Maddon, he of the brilliant baseball mind and quirky personality and demeanor, the Chicago Cubs would make it all the way to the NLCS before being swept away by the New York Mets. Yet even with that defeat, the City of Chicago was strangely optimistic about the upcoming season. They'd merely run into the buzz saw of a starting rotation that was throwing great, and that's just baseball.

The north side of Chicago, specifically 1060 West Addison Street, is home to some of the most loyal and passionate fans in all of sports. In a world where every team pursues and covets new, state-of-art venues, Chicago Cubs fans continue to fill a rickety old structure that opened in 1916, where ivy covers brick walls, and which didn't even have lights until 1988 --Wrigley Field, which was named after the Cubs' owner, William Wrigley Jr.

Mr. Wrigley founded his company, the Wm. Wrigley Jr. Company, in Chicago in 1891. The company sold a product called Wrigley's Scouring Soap. As an added inducement to buy the soap, Wrigley threw in a free can of baking powder with each purchase. In short order, he found the baking powder was more popular than the soap and abruptly got out of the soap business and into the baking powder business. Wanting to incentivize sales, with each can of baking powder sold, he threw in two packs of chewing gum. Once again, he found that the chewing gum was more popular than the baking powder and so got out of the baking powder business and into the chewing gum business, which is where he would make his vast fortune.

In 1916, William Wrigley, Jr., and William Weeghman, who owned a lunch counter business, bought a minority interest in the Chicago Cubs, whose majority owner was Albert Lasker, often referred to as the "founder of modern advertising." Over the next four years, as Weeghman's lunch counter business kept failing, he continued selling his shares of the Chicago Cubs to his partner, Wrigley, who by 1921 was the majority owner, and by 1924, sole owner, having bought out Lasker.

The Cubs would be run by the so-called "Double-Bills," William Wrigley and team president Bill Veeck, Sr., until their deaths, Wrigley in 1932, and Veeck in 1933, respectively.

William Wrigley's son, P.K. Wrigley, and the Wrigley family, retained control of the Chicago Cubs until selling the team in 1981 to the Tribune Company.

The Tribune Company, always in financial distress, eventually declared bankruptcy and in 2007 was acquired by Chicago real-estate mogul, Sam Zell, who, having no interest in one of his new assets, the Chicago Cubs, sold the Tribune Company to the Ricketts family (four siblings and both parents) for $900 million, a significant portion of which represented 95 percent ownership of the Cubs and Wrigley Field (along with 25 percent of Comcast SportsNet Chicago).

Family patriarch Joe Ricketts is the founder of TD Ameritrade, one of the largest online discount brokerages in the world. His son, Tom, who'd attended the University of Chicago, shared an apartment with his brother on the "sports corner" of Addison and Sheffield right across from Wrigley Field, and met his future wife, Cecilia, in the bleachers of Wrigley, is the owner and chairman of the team.

Come 2016, both the Chicago Cubs and their fans found themselves in the uncharacteristic position of being not only a National League power but also a pre-season favorite to win their division and then the pennant. In what would be an epic World Series, the Chicago Cubs faced off against the Cleveland Indians, virtually guaranteeing one of the cities a historic outcome -- whoever won would end their city's longstanding drought.

In a rare instance of the game(s) living up to the hype, Chicago and Cleveland battled to three victories apiece featuring outstanding pitching (both starting and relief) and setting up a Game 7 for the ages featuring a little bit of everything including a rain delay and extra innings.

On November 4, 2016, the Chicago River was dyed a light shade of blue (Cubs' blue), an estimated five million people (twice the city's population) crammed the city's seven-mile parade route (starting at Wrigley Field and ending in Grant Park), and cheered each and every Cub player, coach, and executive as they rolled by in open double-decker buses. Manager Joe Maddon, wearing a stocking cap, sunglasses, and a T-shirt that read, "We Didn't Suck," thanked everyone for their "patience," as Joe and Tom Ricketts and Theo Epstein and Jed Hoyer each took their turn raising the World Series trophy above their heads.

For all of Chicago's illustrious sports history encompassing championships and parades for the Bears, Bulls, White Sox, and Blackhawks, this was a spectacle never-before seen and never to be seen again. Ask any Cubs fan, anywhere, and they will tell you it was truly worth the wait.

World Series Appearances: 11   Wins: 3
Forbes 2017 Valuation: $2.675 Billion

Chicago White Sox

Year	Owner(s)	Purchase Price
1900-1931	Charles Comiskey	
1931-1939	Lou Comiskey	Inherited
1939-1956	Grace Comiskey	Inherited
1956-1959	Dorothy Comiskey Rigney	Inherited
1959-1961	Bill Veeck	$2.7 Million
1961-1969	Arthur Allyn & John Allyn	$2.94 Million
1969-1975	John Allyn	Unknown
1975-1981	Bill Veeck	$8.55 Million
1981-	Jerry Reinsdorf & Eddie Einhorn	$19 Million

The Chicago White Sox are one of the original American League franchise teams, founded by Charles Comiskey. He was born in Chicago, the son of a politician. Comiskey was a baseball player, pitcher then first baseman, with the St. Louis Brown Stockings. He initially bought a club in Iowa and moved it to Minnesota. The National League approved his proposal to move that team to Chicago. At the same time, in 1900, he and Ban Johnson, the AL's first president, positioned the Western League (renamed the American League) to challenge the National League monopoly. They became the chief architects of getting the NL to accept the AL as an equal. The NL eventually agreed and the two-league MLB structure began.

Comiskey's White Sox won the pennant in 1901 and the World Series in 1906. Comiskey spent $750,000 building White Sox Park, which debuted in 1910. The Sox won the World Series again in 1917.

Charlie Comiskey was a benevolent owner, known for giving away thousands of tickets to kids and servicemen. However, like other owners trying to keep their teams afloat, he needed to keep player salaries in check and was called a miser by the players. There was no players' union at the time and contracts and the reserve clause prevented players from changing teams without the current team's permission. It was not uncommon in this era for gamblers to find players looking for extra cash, and clubhouses were often divided by those who would and wouldn't fix a game.

In 1919, the White Sox won the pennant and headed to the World Series once again. This was the year of the Black Sox scandal when eight players were accused of throwing the championship. (They were first dubbed the "Black Sox" because their white socks were always dirty, but after the gambling scandal that name had a second meaning). While the players were acquitted of conspiracy charges, they were banned from baseball for life and the White Sox never won a pennant again during Comisky's lifetime. He died of heart complications following the 1931 season. During his 31 years of ownership, his team had a .507 win rate and two championships. Comiskey was posthumously inducted into the Baseball Hall of Fame in 1939.

After Charles's death, his son Lou took over as the team's owner. He had worked for the organization since 1910 and knew the team well. In his first year of ownership, the team had a dismal 102 losses.

In 1933, the White Sox hosted the first All-Star game as part of the World's Fair. Lou Comiskey died of heart disease in 1939 at the age of 53. Less than a month following his death, the White Sox hosted their first night game at Comiskey Park. In Lou's seven-plus seasons of ownership, the team's win rate was .459.

Following his death, his widow Grace Comiskey and their children took over the team's ownership. Grace Comiskey had an uneventful ownership. The team did host the All-Star game again in 1950 and reached one million in attendance for the first time in 1951.

In 1956, Grace died of a heart attack. Her death led to Lou's daughter, Dorothy Comiskey Rigney, becoming the majority owner. At the helm for only two seasons, she was frequently embroiled in a battle for control with the team's next largest stockholder, her brother Chuck. This acrimony prompted Dorothy to sell the team at the end of the 1958 season. She hoped to sell it to Chuck but he made such an insulting lowball offer she thought 'blood-be-damned' and sold controlling shares in 1959 to a group led by Bill Veeck for $2.7 million, thus ending the 58 years the Comiskey family controlled the franchise. During that time, they had a .498 win rate, made three World Series appearances, and won the championship twice.

Bill Veeck was not new to baseball ownership. Prior to becoming the majority owner of the White Sox, he had already attempted to buy the Phillies, had owned the Cleveland Indians, and had an 80 percent share of the St. Louis Browns. In his first season of owning the White Sox franchise, they won the pennant but lost the championship. Health issues drove Veeck to sell his shares in 1961 to minority owner Arthur Allyn, who bought Hank Greenberg's shares.

A year later, Chuck Comiskey sold his minority interest to Allyn. Over the next eight years, Allyn acquired the remaining franchise shares from the various minority owners. In 1969, he sold his shares to his brother John for an undisclosed amount. In 1975, due to financial troubles, John

Allyn sold the team back to Bill Veeck for $8.55 million. During the 15 seasons of the Allyn brothers' ownership, the White Sox never finished better than second in their division, had no post-season play, and, with Comiskey Park deteriorating, average attendance dropped below the million mark. However, they did have a .503 overall win rate.

Bill Veeck had never truly lost his lust for baseball after selling the White Sox in '61. He loved the action and tried buying the Seattle and Baltimore teams without success. Determined, he gathered more than 40 investors to buy back the White Sox in 1975.

His first order of business was what many called a publicity stunt. Veeck and his general manager, Roland Hemond, held trade meetings in a hotel lobby. What had always been private was now public. Ironically, two weeks later the era of free agency began when Peter Seitz ruled against the reserve clause and ended the perpetual player renewal rights by the teams. Veeck was a captain of marketing and publicity and never missed an opportunity. He reactivated Minnie Minoso in 1976 and 1980 to give him claim to having played in five decades. Veeck was the one who originally requested that Harry Caray sing, "Take Me Out to the Ball Game," over the loudspeaker during the seventh inning stretch.

With dwindling funds and declining health, Veeck decided to sell the team in 1981. During his second tenure with the White Sox they didn't perform as well, with a .457 win rate, but the fans returned and the average attendance rose to 1.3 million. Bill Veeck was elected to the Baseball Hall of Fame in 1991.

A group led by Jerry Reinsdorf and Eddie Einhorn purchased the team from Veeck for $19 million. Reinsdorf, a certified public accountant and tax attorney, made his fortune in real estate tax shelters. He has also been the owner and chairman of the Chicago Bulls since 1985, one year after the Bulls drafted Michael Jordan.

Eddie Einhorn and Jerry Reinsdorf were buddies in college. Eddie had a successful career in broadcasting and became a minority owner of the White Sox when Reinsdorf led the 1981 acquisition. Eddie was a popular owner and served 25 seasons as vice chairman. Under their ownership, they quickly increased the team's promotional budget and nearly doubled the number of scouts. By 1983, they achieved two million in attendance for the first time and had the best record in Major League Baseball at .611, but didn't make it to the World Series.

After 81 seasons at the original Comiskey Park, a new Comiskey Ballpark opened in 1991 at a cost of $167 million. The new ballpark attracted just under three million fans in its inaugural year. In 2003, U.S. Cellular bought the naming rights for the stadium and the All-Star game was played there that year. In November 2016, naming rights passed to the White Sox landlord and mortgage lender, Guaranteed Rate. In his 35 seasons as owner, Reinsdorf's White Sox have earned six division titles and a 2005 World Series championship, and have averaged 1.9 million in attendance.

World Series Appearances: 5   Wins: 3
Forbes 2017 Valuation: $1.35 Billion

Cincinnati Reds

Year	Owner(s)	Purchase Price
1920-1929	Julius and Max Fleischmann	Unknown
1929-1933	Sidney Weil	$640,000
1933-1934	Central Trust Company	Bankruptcy
1934-1961	Powell Crosley	$175,000
1961-1962	Crosley Foundation	Donated
1962-1966	Bill DeWitt	$4.63 Million
1966-1984	617, Inc.	$7 Million
1984-1999	Marge Schott	$24 Million
1999-2005	Carl Lindner, Jr.	$67 Million
2005-	Robert Castellini	$270 Million

When the modern era of baseball began, a syndicate headed by Julius and Max Fleischmann owned the Cincinnati Reds. Julius and Max were the sons of Charles Fleishmann, who was a manufacturer of yeast products. Max innovated a method to produce yeast in a manner that revolutionized baking. Julius left college to run the family business and later was elected mayor of Cincinnati in 1900, making him the youngest person to hold that position, at age 28. The Fleishmann family first got involved with baseball by financing a semiprofessional team in the late 1800s. During their 10 seasons of owning the Reds, they never finished better than second in the National League but did manage a .518-win rate overall.

In 1929, controlling ownership of the team was sold to Sidney Weil for $640,000. This was accomplished through a series of secret deals over time. He targeted the smaller shareholders first and then those who disagreed with a principal stockholder, Lou Widrig.

Weil gained control of the team in October 1929, with just three days left in the season. He invested heavily in the team but the stock market crash reduced his net worth into the depths of bankruptcy. The Reds were not doing well, having come in last three years in a row and carrying a four-year average of .381. Ownership of the Reds was subsequently relinquished to the Central Trust Company in 1933. Central Trust hired Larry McPhail to lead the franchise and in less than three months, he had convinced Powell Crosley to purchase the team for a rumored $175,000.

Crosley was born in Cincinnati and grew up fascinated by vehicles – automobiles, airplanes, and ships. He graduated from the Ohio Military Institute and studied engineering for two years. Throughout his life, he was trying to invent something that would work better and be more affordable. Much of this started when he attempted to build his own car. Later, his son wanted a radio and he was stunned to learn they cost $100. Naturally, he built his own and found a way to manufacture them for $7 so everyone could afford one. In addition to radios, he had an appliance company, led an aircraft company, and started Crosley Motors. With Crosley, it seemed important to always have a new and interesting endeavor.

Crosley also brought innovation to baseball by gaining permission to hold the first night game, held under electric lights in May 1935, against the Philadelphia Phillies. Under Crosley's ownership, the franchise started to perform well. The Reds won the National League in 1939 and 1940 and the World Series in 1940. Another important milestone was achieved when the Reds surpassed one million in attendance for the first time in 1956.

Crosley died of a heart attack before the start of the 1961 season and the team was left to the Crosley Foundation. In the 28 seasons of Crosley ownership, the team went from a sub .400 performance to a .486-win rate, three pennants, and one World Series championship. They started playing under the lights and increased attendance in a manner that brought relevancy to the franchise. All this from an individual who never set out to own a baseball team but who had a deep curiosity and just wanted to build cars.

A syndicate led by Bill DeWitt purchased the team in 1962 for $4.63 million. DeWitt was raised in St. Louis, Missouri, and earned a law degree. Most of his adult life involved working in professional baseball. DeWitt was treasurer of the St. Louis Cardinals starting in 1926. He won a World Series as the general manager of the St. Louis Browns in 1945 and became their majority owner a few years later. He then spent a decade with the Yankees and Tigers. In 1961, he joined the Reds as general manager, the same year they won a National League pennant.

Moving into the ownership role of the Reds seemed like a rather logical transition. DeWitt had built a great team as the general manager and that came to fruition with nearly 100 wins in 1962. While they performed well with a .545-win rate overall, and attendance was mostly on the rise, he is most remembered for what is often referred to as one of the worst trades in history. DeWitt traded Frank Robinson, the future Hall of Fame outfielder, to the Orioles for two pitchers and a minor-league player because he felt Robinson was at the end of his prime, at 30 years old. The following year, Robinson won the Triple Crown, was voted in unanimously as the American League Most Valuable Player, and was on the Orioles' first World Series championship team.

DeWitt's group sold its shares in December 1966, to a syndicate titled, "617, Inc.," which was led by Francis Dale and Louis Nippert.

The 617, Inc. ownership group had two primary goals: keeping the Reds in Cincinnati and building a riverfront stadium. Dale, an attorney and publisher of The Cincinnati Enquirer, served as Reds president for six years. During his tenure, Riverfront Stadium was built and opened in time for the 1970 season. This also marked the start of the "Big Red Machine," as they achieved 102 wins that year, won their division and the National League pennant, but lost in the World Series. In 1972, there was similar success with winning the pennant but losing in the World Series. Dale sold his shares to minority owner, Louis Nippert, in 1973.

Nippert, a Proctor & Gamble heir, was at the helm of the Reds during an incredibly successful era. In his first year, the winning continued and attendance achieved over two million for the first of eight consecutive years. The Reds won back-to-back World Series championships in 1975 and '76. The winning continued but no additional pennants were earned. In February 1981, Nippert sold his shares to minority owners, the William brothers.

After the 1981 season, the wheels started to come off the "the Big Red Machine." The Reds experienced their first 100-loss season in 1982 and there wasn't much change after that. Overall though, in 18 seasons with the 617, Inc. group, they realized a .550 -win rate, seven division titles, four pennants, and two world championships. They got Riverfront Stadium built and enjoyed an average 1.7 million in annual attendance.

In 1984, majority ownership of the team was sold to Marge Schott, who was a minority owner since 1981, for a reported $24 million. Schott was the first woman to buy, versus inherit, a franchise and manage it. Schott is remembered for many things but several of them are not positive. For example, she loved her St. Bernards and allowed them to have free rein of the stadium, forcing the players to sidestep their droppings. There were other issues such as not believing scouts should be paid for watching baseball, and she fostered disagreements and disrespect toward team managers. On one hand, she was kind toward children, who often flocked to her box seats at the stadium, and she was a champion of the everyday fan. On the other hand, she had strong opinions and lacked a filter for many of her offensive thoughts and remarks.

During her tenure, she offended people regularly with derogatory statements. Baseball suspended her from daily operations for the 1993 season but racist remarks continued and she was again forced to surrender daily control in 1996. She sold team control to Carl Lindner Jr., already a limited partner, for $67 million in 1999. During her 15 seasons of ownership, the franchise performed well despite the drama. The team won three division titles, had a .520-win rate, average attendance of 2.04 million, and won the World Series in 1990.

Carl Linder dropped out of school as a young teen to help in his family's dairy store, which he helped grow to a chain of 100 stores. Being both street-smart and numbers-smart, Lindner founded American Financial Group and other enterprises that made him a billionaire. With junk bond financing from Michael Milken, Lindner got his financial hands into many business pies. One adversary called him a "shark in sheep's clothing." But Lindner was popular. With a net worth of $2.3 billion way back in the mid-'80s, Carl could write his own ticket. Frank Sinatra sang at one of his birthday parties. George W. Bush was a recipient of Lindner's generosity, as was the Republican Party. His philanthropy has been well noted.

Notable during his franchise ownership was the 2003 opening of the Great American Ballpark, home of the Reds and the NFL's Bengals, financed by the Great American Insurance Company, a Lindner-controlled company. Team performance under Lindner's reign was rather lackluster, with an overall win rate of .459. However, fans remained loyal and attendance averaged 2.15 million. By the end of the 2005 season, Lindner was prepared to sell controlling shares of the franchise.

In January 2006, Major League Baseball approved the purchase of controlling shares (approximately 70 percent) of the Reds to Robert Castellini for $270 million. Lindner retained a minority share along with several others. Castellini was previously part of an ownership group with the Cardinals and Rangers and had a prior investment with the Orioles. However, as a native of Cincinnati, he proclaimed himself a lifelong Reds fan. After a long streak of losing seasons, the Reds won their division in 2010 and 2012. Thus far, under Castellini's leadership, the team has an average of only .494 but managed to maintain strong average attendance of 2.2 million. The Reds continued as bottom feeders in 2017.

World Series Appearances: 9   Wins: 5
Forbes 2017 Valuation: $915 Million

Cleveland Indians

Year	Owner(s)	Purchase Price
1916-1922	James Dunn	$500,000
1922-1927	Edith Dunn	Inherited
1927-1946	Alva Bradley	$1 Million
1946-1949	Bill Veeck	$1.6 Million
1949-1952	Ellis Ryan	$2.5 Million

1953-1956	Myron Wilson	Unknown
1956-1962	William Daley	$3.96 Million
1963-1966	Gabe Paul	Unknown
1966-1972	Vernon Stouffer	$8 Million
1972-1975	Nick Mileti	$10 Million
1975-1978	Ted Bonda	Unknown
1978-1983	Steve O'Neill	$11 Million
1983-1986	Estate of Steve O'Neill	Inherited
1986-2000	Richard and David Jacobs	$35 Million
2000-	Larry Dolan	$323 Million

The American League president, Ban Johnson, sought a syndicate to purchase the Cleveland Indians in 1916. A group headed by James Dunn paid Charles Somers $500,000 to gain ownership of the franchise. Dunn renamed League Park to Dunn Field and in 1920 the Indians won their first World Series championship. Dunn passed away in 1922 and the control of the team went to his widow, Edith Dunn. She was one of the first women to own a major-league franchise. She held onto the team until after the 1927 season. Together, the Dunn family had a .533-win rate during its 12 years of ownership.

Alva Bradley was president of a group that purchased the Indians franchise in November 1927 for $1 million. While he maintained the top role with the group, he was never a majority shareholder. It was during this time that the Cleveland Municipal Stadium opened. It was one of the earlier multi-purpose stadiums and had an enormous seating capacity of 78,000, one of the largest in baseball. It was during Bradley's tenure that Hall of Fame pitcher Bob Feller was signed with the team in 1936. Although the Indians played winning baseball during his 18 years, (a .517-win rate), they never earned a trip to the post-season.

Bradley's group sold the team in 1946 to a group headed by Bill Veeck for $1.6 million. Veeck immediately started broadcasting the games on radio and moved the team to Cleveland Municipal Stadium full time. Veeck was a longtime fan of the Negro League and was quick to sign Larry Doby, the first black player in the American League. The next year he signed Satchel Paige, the oldest rookie in major league history.

In 1948, Veeck saw the Indians break the two million attendance mark, win their division, and take the World Series championship for the first time since 1920. A divorce from his first wife led to selling the team to fund the divorce settlement. He only had the team for four years but they had a .536-win rate, averaged 1.86 million in attendance, and won a championship.

Veeck's group sold the team for $2.5 million to a syndicate headed by Ellis Ryan. He was a Cleveland native and an insurance executive. Ryan had a brief tenure as owner of the Indians as he sold his shares to Myron

Wilson in 1952. Although he only controlled the team for three seasons, they had a .598-win rate, but without a postseason berth. Ryan owned shares of the Cleveland Browns from 1953 to 1961.

Myron Wilson was also a native of Cleveland and served three seasons as president and principal owner. The team continued to win and went to the World Series in 1954 after a 111-win season, but lost in four straight games. Overall, Wilson enjoyed a .637-win rate. In 1956, Wilson's shares were sold to a group led by William Daley for $3.96 million. Daley held the team for seven seasons with limited success. While the overall win rate was .516, they didn't fare well in the division and had no post-season opportunities. In addition, attendance only surpassed the million mark one year and averaged .88 million overall.

Following the 1962 season, Gabe Paul became part-owner, president, and general manager. He brought with him a near lifetime of experience in baseball, starting as a batboy at age 10. He was vice president of the Cincinnati Reds and was brought to Houston for the Houston Colt .45s start-up but clashed with ownership.

In 1966, Vernon Stouffer bought an 80 percent share of the Indians for $8 million, $2.5 million of which he borrowed. He retained Gabe Paul as president. Stouffer was a pioneer in the frozen food industry as he played a significant role in developing frozen and microwavable foods. Stouffer's earlier merger with Litton Industries became an issue when the stock lost more than half its value, causing Stouffer difficulty in making payments on the $2.5 million note. This resulted in him cutting the player development budget of a team that was already performing poorly. He even attempted to sell 25 percent of the team to another investment group that wanted the team to play part of the season in the New Orleans Superdome, but the American League rejected the proposal. The poor performance, .444-win rate in five years, and average attendance of .69 million led Stouffer to sell the team.

In 1972, Nick Mileti's syndicate purchased the Indians for $10 million. Mileti served in the military and then opened a law practice. Mileti was an author, businessman, lawyer, and property developer. He first bought the Cleveland Arena, then sought an expansion team to keep the arena busy, which brought the Cavaliers into the NBA in 1970. The year following, after acquiring the Indians, he formed Ohio Communications, acquired several radio stations, and moved the play-by-play rights for the Cavaliers and Indians to his 50,000-watt channel.

Mileti's creditors forced him to sell his shares of the Indians in 1973. Ted Bonda became the top executive of the syndicate and Mileti sold his last remaining shares to Bonda in 1975. Bonda and the other main syndicate partner, Howard Metzenbaum, owned an airport parking company and the Cleveland Stokers soccer club. Notable during Bonda's leadership, Frank Robinson became the player-manager in 1975, making him the first African-American manager in Major League Baseball. The syndicate didn't bring the performance level of the team up, as the seven years resulted in a .465-win rate and continuing low attendance, with .85 million average.

In 1978, the team was sold to a syndicate headed by Steve O'Neill for $11 million, which included $5 million in assumed debt. The O'Neill family prospered through the trucking business. O'Neill had been a minority partner in the Indians during the Daley, Paul, and Stouffer years but sold his interest in 1973 to become a limited partner in the Yankees. He sold his Yankees shares to become a 63 percent owner of the Indians. O'Neill died in 1983 and the team was held by his estate for three more years.

In 1985, Peter Bavasi was hired as president. He was frustrated when the team lost 102 games that season and he knew great change was needed. He sought the expertise of management guru Peter Drucker as an organizational consultant to get the team on track. They quickly discovered that Drucker's approach with "Management By Objective" (MBO) was a perfect fit for baseball. The results were indisputable. They won 84 games after winning only 60 the prior year, and attendance went from 655,000 to nearly 1.5 million. Unfortunately, Bavasi left after the 1986 season and Drucker no longer consulted for the team. The O'Neill years, with few exceptions, continued the mediocre performance with a .468-win rate and lackluster attendance with .92 million average.

The O'Neill estate sold the franchise to Richard and David Jacobs in 1986 for $35 million. The Jacobs brothers founded a real estate development company in Akron, Ohio, that focused on building strip malls. They eventually owned 40 malls, 31 Wendy's fast-food restaurants, and numerous Marriott hotels. David Jacobs died in 1992. Two years later, the Indians played their first game in their new ballpark, Jacobs Field. This seemed to be a turning point as they had a winning season that same year. From 1995 to 1999, over five consecutive seasons, the Indians won their division. In 1995 and 1997, they made it to the World Series but couldn't win. 1996 was the Indians' first time to break the three million attendance mark. During the Jacobs' 13 seasons of ownership, the team finally had a winning record with a .508-win rate and average attendance of 2.15 million. Revenues were also up thanks to the new Jacobs Field.

Larry Dolan, an attorney by trade, bought the Indians for $323 million in 2000. In 2006, Dolan started SportsTime Ohio to broadcast the Indians games. It was sold to Fox Entertainment Group in 2012. Jacobs Field was renamed Progressive Field in 2007 but most fans still call it "The Jake." In the last 16 years, the Indians have won their division twice and made it to the post-season three times. The .498-win rate and 2.02 million average attendance are both lower than under the previous ownership. Dolan plans to keep the team ownership in his family long-term.

In 2016, the Indians, behind great pitching, returned to the World Series, only to lose to the destined Chicago Cubs in seven games.

World Series Appearances: 5   Wins: 2
Forbes 2017 Valuation: $920 Million

Colorado Rockies

Year	Owner(s)	Purchase Price
1991-	Colorado Baseball Partnership	$95 Million
1990-1992	John Antonucci	
1992-2003	Jerry McMorris	
2003-	Dick and Charlie Monfort	

In 1990, Colorado Governor Roy Romer formed an advisory committee to recruit an ownership group that, it was hoped, would acquire a team for Denver in the 1993 MLB expansion. The group's efforts were successful and Colorado was granted a franchise for $95 million, with play beginning in 1993 as the Colorado Rockies. The other expansion franchise was awarded to south Florida and became the Florida Marlins.

The first chairman of the Colorado Baseball Partnership was John Antonucci, a wholesale beverage distributor in Ohio. Antonucci led the charge to sell season tickets, and helped choose the site for the anticipated ballpark to be named Coors Field. Although Antonucci led most of the tasks required to prepare for a Major League Baseball franchise, his name isn't mentioned in the team's official timeline and he wasn't present for the team's first opening day. Less than a year before the inaugural season, the vice-chairman of the Colorado Baseball Partnership, Michael Monus, was indicted for embezzlement from his pharmacy chain, Phar-Mor. Even though Antonucci was not a party to the embezzlement charges, the stigma attached to his longterm business partner caused him and his father to sell all their shares in the partnership. The Colorado Rockies organization does not mention this in their official timeline; instead, it is recorded as locals acquiring interests that had been "previously owned by non-Coloradoans."

With the inaugural season upon them, the partners restructured and named Jerry McNorris as chairman, president, and CEO in January 1993. Oren Benton and Charles Monfort became vice-chairmen. McNorris graduated from the University of Colorado's School of Business. While attending the university, he purchased a small trucking company for a mere $7,000 and turned it into a $400 million trucking empire. However, McNorris is most fondly remembered as the savior of Major League Baseball in Colorado.

When things became complicated after the Monus indictment, the partnership faced a $20 million shortfall and Major League Baseball was prepared to pull the Denver franchise. McMorris pledged to make up half the deficit himself and acquired the rest of the funds from Oren Benton and Charlie Monfort. It was all worthwhile when the Colorado Rockies hosted their first game on April 9, 1993 at Mile High Stadium. The record-setting opening day attendance of 80,227 was just the beginning. The Rockies went on to reach the one million mark in early May, two million before the end of June, three million before July concluded, and four million before the season was over. Not only did they establish the single-season attendance record with 4,483,350, but they also achieved the most wins by a National League expansion team in their first season.

While the Rockies certainly enjoyed the incredible attendance at Mile High Stadium, they were excited to welcome Coors Field at the start of the 1995 season. This was an exciting time for McMorris to be leading the Rockies as they played in their first post-season competition. Although they lost in the first round to the Atlanta Braves, it was a milestone that the partnership leaders were proud to claim. In 1999, for the seventh consecutive season, the Colorado Rockies led the major leagues in attendance, with 3,481,065 entering the gates of Coors Field.

Even with respectable win-loss records and amazing attendance, operating a Major League Baseball team can cause a financial drain. Cash-strapped, the partnership group brought Rupert Murdoch into the fold in 2004 as a limited partner. In return, Murdoch's Fox Sports invested $20 million in the franchise. The valuation was questioned and it seemed that Murdoch got his shares at about 50 cents on the dollar; thus, he agreed to invest another $200 million over 10 years for the rights to broadcast Rockies games on Fox Sports Net-Rocky Mountain.

During the 12 seasons McMorris was at the helm of the Colorado Baseball Partnership, the team began play, Coors Field was opened, attendance records were consistently achieved, and the Rockies enjoyed four seasons over .500, including one post-season appearance. In 2005, McMorris sold his share of the franchise to the Monfort brothers. Jerry McMorris died in May 2012, after a battle with pancreatic cancer.

Both Dick and Charlie Monfort were considered to be club founders although they were not named as original members of the Colorado Baseball Partnership. They were, however, very early financial supporters of the team. Charlie Monfort joined the partnership in 1992, at the same time as Oren Benton, following the Monus/Phar-Mor scandal. Dick Monfort later replaced Benton. The Monfort brothers made their fortune through the family meatpacking business that was acquired by ConAgra. The brothers have been contributors to the community through their Monfort Family Foundation.

Charlie Monfort earned a Bachelor of Science degree in marketing and business Management from the University of Utah. He became the

CEO of the Colorado Baseball Partnership in 2003 and his brother Dick served as his vice-chairman. Dick Monfort is a 1976 graduate of the University of Northern Colorado with a B.A. in business management. Dick followed Charlie as CEO in 2011. During the Monfort brothers' ownership, the Rockies made the World Series in 2007 by making one of the greatest comebacks in MLB history.

After trailing by six games on September 1, they won 14 of 15 games, including 11 in a row, and finished the season tied with the San Diego Padres for the National League Wild Card playoff spot. The game was a nail-biter played in front of a sell-out crowd at Coors Field. After nine innings, the game was tied. In the top of the 13th, the Padres scored two runs, but the Rockies followed in the bottom of the 13th with three runs to win the game 9-8. The Rockies' amazing win streak was dubbed by the press as "Rocktober," as the team went on to win the NLCS and made the World Series, only to get swept by the Boston Red Sox.

Rockies fans are not supportive of the Monfort brothers and some have named them an affliction: "The Curse of Monfort." The Monfort brothers have led the partnership for the past 13 seasons and have an overall winning percentage of .460. Only two of the 13 seasons can boast a winning record. But 2017 shows dramatic improvement.

World Series Appearances: 1   Wins: 0
Forbes 2017 Valuation: $1 Billion

Detroit Tigers

Year	Owner(s)	Purchase Price
1908-1935	Frank Navin	Unknown
1935-1952	Walter Briggs, Sr.	$1 Million
1952-1956	Walter Briggs, Jr.	Inherited
1956-1983	John Fetzer	$5.5 Million
1983-1992	Tom Monaghan	$53 Million
1992-	Mike Ilitch	$82 Million

Frank Navin owned the Detroit Tigers when the modern era of baseball began. Born in Michigan, Navin attended the Detroit College of Law and became a lawyer and accountant. When Samuel Angus originally purchased the Tigers in 1902, Navin was working as the bookkeeper in his insurance office. Angus brought him over to team operations where Navin served in nearly every capacity.

Navin enjoyed gambling and used winnings from a card game to invest $5,000 in the team in 1903. He ran the farm system with a great eye for talent and signed legendary Hall of Famer, Ty Cobb, who led the Tigers to the World Series in three consecutive seasons. But the team was losing money so Angus directed Navin to secure a buyer. Lumber baron William Clyman Yawkey died before the purchase was closed but Navin convinced his son, Bill Yawkey, to buy the team. Yawkey didn't want to be involved with team operations and left Navin in charge. By 1908, Yawkey sold Navin half the club and he took over officially as team owner and president.

By the end of 1911, the wooden Bennett Park no longer felt relevant. A new concrete and steel structure, with a 23,000-seat capacity, was named Navin Field and was the original Tiger Stadium. It was opened in April 1912, the same day as Boston's Fenway Park. When Yawkey died in 1919, Navin acquired Walter Briggs, Sr. as a 25-percent partner and later a full partner; however, Navin continued running the club. Navin also played a key role, along with Barney Dreyfuss of the Pirates, in the establishment of the office of Commissioner of Baseball in 1920 with the appointment of Judge Kenesaw Mountain Landis. In 1927, Navin served as acting American League president until Ernest Barnard was elected.

Between gambling and the Depression, Navin was nearly broke in the 1930s but relied heavily on Briggs's financing to keep the team afloat and competitive. In October 1935, the Tigers finally won their first World Series championship. A mere six weeks later, Navin had a fatal heart attack while riding one of his horses. As the early father of Tigers baseball, he accumulated a .517-win rate, ushered them into the World Series four times, and finally got the win before he died.

Following Navin's death, Walter Briggs, Sr. bought Navin's 50-percent share for $1 million, making him the sole owner. Briggs was the owner of Briggs Manufacturing Company, which manufactured automobile bodies for the auto industry. In 1935, the Briggs Dream Car design was patented and became the prototype for the 1936 Lincoln Zephyr, an instant sensation.

Briggs quickly made Mickey Cochran vice president. His first undertaking was to complete a major renovation and expansion to Navin Field. In 1938, the park was converted into a bowl with a double-decker grandstand, which more than doubled the seating capacity to 58,000. The park was renamed Briggs Stadium and the structure remained unchanged for the next 60 years. With the new design and capacity, Briggs made a deal with the Detroit Lions to play their games in the stadium starting in 1938. In 1948, the Tigers became the last AL team to install lighting to enable night games.

Briggs never took a salary while he was an owner of the team. He paid his players well and was known for his generosity, sportsmanship, and business acumen. In 1941, he was named baseball's top executive by

Sporting News. However, he would not allow black fans to sit in box seats, and a black player was never signed during his tenure.

After his death in 1952, his son, Walter "Spike" Briggs, Jr., assumed the ownership post. Although he wanted to keep the Tigers and Briggs Stadium, the family estate administrators ordered him to sell both in 1956. The Briggs family had a positive influence on the Tigers during its 20 years at the helm, and accumulated a .514-win rate as well as two World Series appearances and a championship in 1945.

Radio executives John Fetzer and Fred Knorr assembled a syndicate of 11 to purchase the franchise for $5.5 million in 1956. By 1960, Fetzer had purchased the entire club and was president. The following year he renamed Briggs Stadium to Tiger Stadium. Fetzer had a long fascination with communication and broadcasting and bought his first radio station in 1930. His innovation led to the creation of a directional antenna for broadcasting at night and placed him on the map as a pioneer in the industry. He later acquired the Muzak franchise and began Fetzer Cablevision. His knowledge and positioning in the communications industry provided an excellent platform for broadcasting Tigers baseball games even before he was the owner.

In 1962, he became the chairman of the Baseball and Television Committee for the American League and negotiated baseball's first national TV contract in 1967, which changed access to baseball.

The farm system paid off as the Tigers were winning year after year and won their third World Series title in 1968. That year also marked the first time their attendance surpassed the two million mark. All in all, Fetzer led the team for nearly 30 years with a .517-win rate overall, and one championship.

In 1983, Tom Monaghan, founder of Domino's Pizza, bought the team for $53 million, the most paid for a baseball franchise at the time. It had been a great year for Domino's as they opened their 1,000th store.

Fetzer wasn't necessarily looking to sell the team but he was aging and knew the time was near. When Fetzer and Monaghan met, they found they had much in common and talked for hours. Each had lost their father at a young age and built businesses from scratch. Monaghan and his brother borrowed $900 to buy a small pizza store. He revolutionized the pizza business by offering fast delivery and creating the insulated pizza box to enable multiple stops per delivery trip while still keeping the pizza warm. He eventually sold his controlling stake in the company for an estimated $1 billion.

Owning a baseball team was a dream come true for him. One of his first actions was to offer team stock to the executives, as that aligned with how he had always run his businesses – rewarding people who perform and making them part of the business.

Monaghan was a flamboyant owner, helicoptering in from the Domino's headquarters to attend Tigers games. Everyone liked that he was visible, approachable, and personable. In 1984, his second year of ownership, the Tigers roared their way through the competition, winning 104 games. They won the World Series and became the first team since 1955 to command first place from start to finish. Winning brought fans to Tiger Stadium and a club record of 2.7 million fans attended games. During his nine seasons of ownership, he accumulated a .532-win rate and average attendance of 1.95 million.

When Monaghan decided to sell the Tigers, it was less a conscious decision and more of a spiritual epiphany. His strong Catholic faith had him questioning whether he had too much, and how he might use his wealth to do more "good" versus merely show off by having more than others. It seems somewhat ironic that he chose to sell the team to the owner of his main business competitor.

Monaghan sold the team in 1992 to Mike Ilitch, founder of Little Caesars Pizza, for $82 million. After serving in the Marine Corps, Ilitch was offered a minor league contract to play for the Detroit Tigers. He played mostly as a second baseman in the farm systems of three teams but a knee injury ended his playing career in 1955. A few years later, he and his wife started a pizza business. Little Caesars didn't grow through delivery but with fresh dough baked a golden brown. Ilitch's business model was based on quality and value; coupons were king. The business took off when they promoted two-for-one pizzas and coined the phrase, "Pizza! Pizza!" It worked so well that they had to install conveyor belt ovens for continuous baking. Ilitch had tried to buy the team previously when it went to Monaghan. He purchased the Detroit Red Wings hockey team instead.

The Tigers struggled during his first 14 years of ownership with only one winning season. Ilitch dreamed of a new ballpark. Groundbreaking took place in the fall of 1997 and boasted 60 percent private funding. Its unique design included a classic seating bowl, with the unique addition of family-friendly amusement park features. Comerica Park opened in April 2000. The team had a dismal 2003 with only 43 wins but went on to make an enormous comeback with 95 wins in 2006 and a trip to the World Series.

Excitement was renewed and the club had its first three million-fan attendance record in 2007. They later had four consecutive years in the post-season and another World Series opportunity in 2012 but no championship. Ilitch is considered one of the top owners in all of sports because he invests heavily in his teams as well as in his city. Players want to be on his team and win a World Series for him. Time will tell.

World Series Appearances: 11   Wins: 4
Forbes 2017 Valuation: $1.2 Billion

Houston Astros

Year	Owner(s)	Purchase Price
1960-1965	Houston Sports Association	$1.8 Million
1965-1976	Roy Hofheinz	N/A
1976-1978	General Electric Credit Co and Ford Motor Credit Co	$38 Million in Debt Transfer
1978-1979	Ford Motor Credit Co	
1979-1992	John McMullen	$19 Million
1992-2011	Drayton McLane, Jr.	$117 Million
2011-	Jim Crane	$680 Million

George Kirksey and Craig Cullinan wanted to bring baseball to Houston. They originally tried to purchase the St. Louis Cardinals in 1952 but when that didn't succeed, they teamed up with Bob Smith and Roy Hofheinz to form the Houston Sports Association. Major League Baseball was not interested in expansion during this time and the syndicate sought to form a new league – the Continental League. This fell through as well but in the fall of 1960, the National League granted one of the two expansion franchises to Houston for a fee of $1.8 million. The other expansion franchise was awarded to Joan Payson, an heiress and founder of the New York Mets. After a "name the team" contest, the Houston franchise was named the Colt .45s after the very popular gun. Colt Stadium was constructed as a temporary venue and used for the 1962 through 1964 seasons. The first game of the Colt .45s was played on April 10, 1962, when they defeated the Chicago Cubs 11-2.

Much of the momentum behind the franchise was driven by Roy Hofheinz, otherwise known as "The Judge." In addition to his work on the judicial bench, he was formerly both a state representative and the mayor of Houston. He was flamboyant, charismatic, and politically well connected, all of which contributed to his being able to get things done. It was his vision to have the first covered baseball and football stadium in the world. His vision, funding, and persistence through stadium issues led to the creation of the first domed stadium, which some called the "eighth wonder of the world." In 1964, it was named the Astrodome to align with the NASA space program. Additionally, the team name changed to the Astros.

Hofheinz, who became known as the "Father of Indoor Baseball," became the sole owner of the franchise in 1965. The first year in the new stadium boosted the Astros' attendance over two million for the first time. That was short-lived, as the team continued to struggle at the bottom of the National League. In 1969, they became part of the National League West and although they were fifth out of six teams in the division, they did have their first .500-win season.

Even with several years in the positive, attendance continued to drop and was sub-one million in the 1975 and 1976 seasons. Hofheinz's vision aside, the Astrodome accumulated $38 million in debt. In September 1976, Hofheinz suffered a stroke, which prompted creditors GE Credit Company and Ford Motor Credit Company to assume control to protect their assets. Two years later, Ford Motor Credit assumed full ownership.

In May 1979, the team was sold for $19 million to a group led by John McMullen. Before the Astros, McMullen had been a limited partner in the Yankees and had a very close friendship with Yogi Berra. When Berra was fired, he immediately offered him a job with the Astros. Under McMullen's leadership, the Astros offered the first $1 million free agent contract to the local player and future Hall of Famer Nolan Ryan. They also reached the post-season for the first time in franchise history in 1980 and again in 1981.

But the Astrodome continued to have issues and attendance averaged 1.6 million a year during his tenure. The GM, Tal Smith, had built an amazing farm system and helped get the Astros to the post-season, but McMullen fired him after the 1980 season. McMullen was despised locally because of his constant rifts with the media, his firing of the team radio announcer, and for having the balls to trade Nolan Ryan to the Rangers. McMullen decided to sell the team at the end of the 1991 season and concluded his ownership with a .510-win rate.

In 1992, Drayton McLane Jr. purchased the franchise for $117 million. McLane, a native Texan, worked his way up in his father's grocery distribution network. He sold the family business to Sam Walton in 1990 for $50 million plus 10.4 million shares of Walmart stock. Chaching! Much of those earnings were used to purchase the Astros.

McLane headed the franchise on the philosophy of "Be a Champion; Make a Positive Difference in the Community." During his tenure of 19 seasons, the Astros boasted a .525-win rate and reached the post-season six times, including a World Series appearance in 2005 where they were swept by the White Sox.

McLane also ushered in a new stadium in 2000 that featured a retractable roof and a more intimate feel than the Astrodome. It was initially called Enron Field but Minute Maid bought the naming rights in 2002 following Enron's bankruptcy. The success on the field, coupled with the new stadium, brought the fans out and the Astros enjoyed four seasons during which they broke the three-million attendance mark and averaged 2.4 million per year overall. Citing family reasons, McLane placed the franchise up for sale in November 2010.

A year later, McLane sold the team to Jim Crane for $680 million. Crane grew up outside of St. Louis and played baseball at Central Missouri State University. Crane moved to Houston in 1980, borrowed money from his sister, and founded a freight logistics business. After selling that business, he formed Crane Capital Group. Crane's goal for the Astros was to rebuild the franchise for sustained success. After a few losing years, it appears Crane's plan is finally coming together.

World Series Appearances: 1   Wins: 0
Forbes 2017 Valuation: $1.45 Billion

Kansas City Royals

Year	Owner(s)	Purchase Price
1968-1993	Ewing Kauffman	$5.55 Million
1993-2000	Greater Kansas City Community Foundation	Held in trust
2000-	David Glass	$96 Million

The Kansas City Royals were founded as an expansion franchise in 1968 by Ewing Kauffman for a fee of $5.55 million. Kauffman served in the United States Navy during World War II. He then worked in the pharmaceutical industry until he formed Marion Laboratories in 1950. The company was very successful, reaching $1 billion in revenues by 1989 and merging with Merrell Dow Pharmaceuticals.

Kauffman believed in service and giving back to his community. He established the Ewing Marion Kauffman Foundation in the mid-1960s to advance entrepreneurship and improve the education of youth. It remains one of the largest private foundations in the U.S., with assets of approximately $2 billion.

Kauffman used the same level of zest and entrepreneurial spirit as owner of the Royals. There were several innovations he brought to baseball during his tenure, all of which were good business practices in marketing, performance, and development. To generate season ticket sales, he created the "Royal Lancers," a group of supporters committed to selling at least 75 season tickets for the 1969 season.

Long before Sabermetrics were common, Kauffman used statistics to measure player contribution. For development, he formed the Royal Baseball Academy for elite athletes to refine their skills. His strong business acumen also enabled him to recognize in the early 1990s that Major League Baseball had issues with competitive balance. He sought to protect small market teams and recommended revenue sharing and/or a salary cap.

As the owner of an expansion team, getting a stadium built was a priority. Although the team had the Municipal Stadium, Kauffman's vision was to build a baseball-only stadium for the Royals. While this is common today, Royals Stadium, between 1962 to 1991, was the only MLB stadium built for baseball only. The 40,793-seat stadium opened in April 1973, as part of the Harry S. Truman Sports Complex. Less than four months later, Royals Stadium hosted the 44th All-Star Game.

In May 1993, Ewing Kauffman, in his last public appearance at the stadium, was inducted into the Kansas City Royals Hall of Fame. Shortly thereafter, the stadium was renamed in his honor (Kauffman Stadium) and is the only American League stadium named in honor of an individual. Just one month later, Kauffman died after a battle with bone cancer.

Under Kauffman's wise ownership, passion, and love for the team and community, the Kansas City Royals were incredibly successful, especially by expansion team standards and expectations. The Royals enjoyed an amazing 16 of 25 winning seasons with an overall winning record of 51.7 percent; they appeared in the World Series twice, winning in 1985.

Before Ewing Kauffman died, he recognized the value of succession planning and sought to secure an owner for the team who would guarantee that the Royals remained in Kansas City. Identifying such a candidate proved difficult, so he put together a group of boosters to help with funding in the short term.

The most creative piece of Kauffman's plan was to temporarily convert the team into a charitable organization so that he could gift the Royals to Kansas City. His only requirements were that the foundation would secure a buyer who would keep the team in Kansas City and that the proceeds from the sale would be donated to local charitable organizations. This was a carefully and brilliantly crafted plan that marked the first and only time a major-league sports team was donated to charity. Eventually, the IRS issued a private letter approving the transaction.

David Glass, as CEO of the Royals, and Michael Herman, as team president, led a group of limited partners to manage the team. To make the foundation a reality, local investors raised $50 million to start, and this provided approximately $3 million income a year to help cover operating losses. During the six seasons of foundation ownership, the Royals had one winning season (1994) and an overall winning record of 45.6 percent.

In 2000, David Glass purchased the team for $96 million. The approval for Glass to purchase the team came after Major League Baseball did not approve a $120 million offer by Miles Prentice, due to concerns with his overall net worth.

Glass amassed his fortune as a 25-year executive at Walmart. He held the position of president and CEO for 12 years until stepping down in 2000 to purchase the Royals. Glass is credited with creating the super-center concept at Walmart. Under his leadership, stock prices rose from

$3.42 to $55 a share, after splits. This is attributed to sales increasing tenfold to $5.4 billion, the number of stores tripling to 4,000, and employees increasing to 1.1 million. For his efforts, Glass was named Retailer of the Year in 1986 and 1991. In 1995, he was named Chief Executive of the Year. Glass served on the board of Walmart Stores, Inc. from 1977 to 2009.

That stated, David Glass is not well liked in baseball circles and it seems challenging for fans to comprehend the friendship of Kauffman and Glass. Unlike Kauffman, who continuously invested in the club, Glass has been known for applying Walmart style cost-cutting measures. And while Kauffman built relationships, Glass seems to find every opportunity to insert wedges. One widely publicized example was Glass revoking the press credentials of two journalists in 2006 because he didn't like their questions about his ownership approach. In 2012, a group of Royals fans put up $5,100 to publish an open, and critical, letter to Glass in the Kansas City Star. In the fall of 2014, even after the team appeared in the World Series, Rolling Stone listed Glass as one of the 15 worst owners in all of professional sports.

In perhaps Glass's most winning move, he was able to hire Dayton Moore in 2006 from the Braves to take the role of general manager. Through 2015, David Glass has owned the Royals for 16 years and they have had only four winning seasons and a 44.4 percent record. However, they do have two World Series appearances, including a championship in 2015.

World Series Appearances: 4   Wins: 2
Forbes 2017 Valuation: $950 Million

Los Angeles Angels of Anaheim

Former names: Los Angeles Angels 1961-1964; California Angels 1965-1996; Anaheim Angels 1997-2004

Year	Owner(s)	Purchase Price
1960-1998	Gene Autry	$2.1 Million
1998-1999	Jackie Autry	Inherited
1999-2003	The Walt Disney Company	$150 Million
2003-	Arturo Moreno	$184 Million

Given this team's proximity to Hollywood, and over their hundred-year presence (in one form or another) in Los Angeles, the history of the Angels is very much like a movie, a mixed-genre one, to be sure – equal parts science fiction, historical, caper, western, corporate satire and intrigue, and of course, sports, but a movie nonetheless.

The science fiction: Had the Brooklyn Dodgers and Chicago Cubs made a test-tube baby, it would be the California Angels, born in 1961 as part of MLB's expansion that year, with the Angels and the Washington Senators the two new franchises.

The historical: the Los Angeles Angels, of California's famed Pacific Coast League, can be thought of as Los Angeles's first professional sports team. Joe DiMaggio (from San Francisco) and Ted Williams (from San Diego) are just two players to have passed through the Pacific Coast League on their way to the majors.

Charter members of the PCL in 1903, the Angels had been playing in Los Angeles in Wrigley Field ever since. Lest there be any confusion, this minor league franchise was owned by William Wrigley, who also owned the major league Chicago Cubs, hence the familiar name of their Los Angeles ballpark, not to be confused with that other park, at 1060 Addison on the north side of Chicago.

The caper: The owner of the Brooklyn Dodgers, Wall Street attorney Walter O'Malley, was one of the sharpest and shrewdest executives in all of baseball. Given his difficulties with Robert Moses in getting a new ballpark built in Brooklyn, and knowing that he would soon be taking his team out of that borough, O'Malley in 1956 purchased the minor league Angels of the PCL from Wrigley's son, Phillip, because hidden in the transaction was the proviso that the owner held the MLB rights to any future franchise in Los Angeles -- such as the now Los Angeles Dodgers, circa 1958.

The western: A singing cowboy, sitting atop his pony with a guitar strung across his back, was only too happy to pay $350,000 for the minor league PCL Angels to O'Malley, who had absolutely no need nor use for them, with his Dodgers then firmly entrenched in Los Angeles. Gene Autry, "America's Singing Cowboy," was not only a major figure in popular entertainment, both film and television, but was also a major influence and catalyst for the popularity of country music. From 1934 to 1953, Autry had starred in 93 films as well as 91 episodes of his television series. It was Autry who was the subject of the Angels' famous World Series rallying cry, "win one for the cowboy," which, sadly, they would finally accomplish in 2002; four years after his death.

The Los Angeles Dodgers would play their first four seasons in the Los Angeles Memorial Coliseum before moving to their new home, Dodger Stadium, in 1962. The Los Angeles Angels played their inaugural season at Wrigley Field (their spiritual home) before sharing Dodger

215

Stadium with the Dodgers from 1962 through the 1965 season, referring to the stadium as "Chavez Ravine."

Fitting into Hollywood quite effortlessly, these early Angels didn't do too much winning on the field but off the field was another story -- perhaps best personified by pitcher Bo Belinsky. A journeyman with a career losing record, Belinsky did pitch the team's first no-hitter (in 1962) but is best remembered for being romantically linked with, among others, Ann-Margret, Connie Stevens, Tina Louise, Mamie Van Doren, and Playboy Playmate of the Year Jo Collins, who he married.

Corporate satire and intrigue: Autry changed the name of the team to the California Angels in September 1965, in anticipation of moving into their brand new ballpark, Anaheim Stadium, for the start of the 1966 season. In 1996, Autry sold a 25 percent interest in the team to the Walt Disney Company. Three years later, his widow, Jackie Autry, would sell the remainder of the team to the Walt Disney Company.

In conjunction with the city of Anaheim, Disney completely renovated the stadium for $118 million, with the city contributing $18 million. The refurbished stadium was christened the Edison International Field of Anaheim. The renegotiated lease between the Walt Disney Company and the City of Anaheim stipulated that not only the name of the ballpark but also the name of the team feature the word Anaheim -- hence the team's third name change to the Anaheim Angels.

In 2003, the Walt Disney Company sold the team to Arturo Moreno, the first Mexican-American and Latin-American owner of a major American professional sports franchise. Mr. Moreno, a combat veteran of the Vietnam War, went into the advertising field after returning home and graduating from the University of Arizona. In 1996, he took his billboard company, Outdoor Systems, public. In 1998, Mr. Moreno sold Outdoor Systems to Infinity Broadcasting for $8 billion (the hidden value in billboards being their real estate value). Wanting to embrace his team's history while also exciting the fan base of the country's second largest market, Los Angeles, Moreno renamed his franchise the Los Angeles Angels of Anaheim.

The sports: The Angels have, rather improbably, been one of the top-ranked professional sports teams in terms of attendance and fan popularity, not only in major league baseball, but in all of American professional sports. Improbable because since their inception they've lost more than they've won, although experiencing a few prolonged periods of success, culminating in their lone World Series victory in 2002, a seven-game affair against the San Francisco Giants.

Drawing three million fans for 12 straight seasons, and two million for 17 straight seasons, the Angels have always had star players on their rosters. From a past with the likes of Nolan Ryan, Rod Carew, Bobby Grich, and Vladimir Guerrero, to a present featuring Albert Pujols and Mike Trout, who is widely acclaimed as the best player in the game (at the moment), the Angels somehow remain impervious to the volatility associated with multiple changes in their team name and venue.

World Series Appearances: 1   Wins: 1
Forbes 2017 Valuation: $1.75 Billion

Los Angeles Dodgers

Former name: Brooklyn Dodgers -1958

Year	Owner(s)	Purchase Price
1912-1925	Charles Ebbets, Ed and Steve McKeever	
1925-1938	Steve McKeever, Ed McKeever heirs, Ebbets heirs	
1938-1944	Steve McKeever, Ebbets heirs	
1944-1950	Walter O'Malley, Branch Rickey, John Smith, Dearie Mulvey	$1.1 Million
1950-1958	Walter O'Malley, Mary Louise Smith, Mulvey heirs	$1.25 Million
1958-1975	Walter O'Malley, Mulvey heirs	
1975-1979	Walter O'Malley	
1979-1997	Peter O'Malley	
1998-2004	Fox Entertainment Group	$311 Million
2004-2012	Frank McCourt	$430 Million
2012-	Guggenheim Baseball Mgmt.	$2.15 Billion

The story of the Los Angeles Dodgers is one of the longest and most convoluted of all the professional sports franchises, yet we must necessarily begin and end with just one chapter: the momentous signing of Jackie Robinson in 1947, a watershed moment in the social history of this country, not only regarding the integration of baseball but more importantly as a defining moment in the civil rights movement.

In 1947, the Dodgers had already been around for 64 years, starting as the Brooklyn Atlantics and then becoming the Brooklyn Bridegrooms, Grooms, Superbas, Robins, Trolley Dodgers, and finally, in 1933, the Dodgers.

In 1912, owner Charles Hercules Ebbets, who'd started as a bookkeeper for the team, was running out of money in the middle of construction of his new ballpark in Brooklyn, and sold half his interest in the team to brothers Ed and Stephen McKeever to acquire the necessary funds to finish the ballpark. The McKeever brothers had made their fortune as construction contractors. Thus, in 1920, at the start of the so-called modern era, Charles Ebbets, Steve McKeever, and Ed McKeever were the principal owners of the Brooklyn franchise. Charles Ebbets died in 1925. As the story goes, while attending his funeral, Ed McKeever caught a cold; he died of pneumonia one week later. And so, in 1925, Steve McKeever and the heirs of Ebbets and Ed McKeever were the owners of the team. Steve McKeever died in 1938, leaving his shares, 25 percent of the team, to his daughter, Dearie Mulvey.

By the early 1940s, both Walter O'Malley and Branch Rickey were integral figures in the Brooklyn Dodger hierarchy. O'Malley, a prosperous and well-connected attorney in the employ of the Brooklyn Trust Company, which owned the estate of the late Charles Ebbets, had been looking after his company's Dodgers interests since 1933. In 1942, he was appointed an attorney for the Brooklyn Dodgers and shortly thereafter obtained a minority interest in the club.

Branch Rickey, who as general manager of the St. Louis Cardinals had built championship clubs, was brought in to replace general manager Larry McPhail, who'd enlisted in the army. There was immediate friction and strained relations between O'Malley and Rickey, which would steadily grow with each passing year. Other than both being shrewd baseball men, the two had nothing in common. The tension had as much to do with lifestyle, personality, and temperament as with business decisions. O'Malley was a boisterous sort who enjoyed a cigar and drink and nightlife, while Rickey, a very religious man, lived a quiet life.

Nevertheless, in 1944, O'Malley and Rickey became partners, along with John L. Smith, a chemist by trade and president of Pfizer. Each of the three men each purchased 25 percent of the team from the heirs of Ebbets and Ed McKeever, with Dearie Mulvey retaining her 25 percent share bequeathed by her father, Steve McKeever.

Several years later, 1950 would be a pivotal year in the history of the Brooklyn Dodgers as both John L. Smith and Dearie Mulvey died. Smith left his 25 percent to his wife, Mary Louise Smith, and Mulvey her 25 percent to her children. O'Malley would purchase both Rickey's and Smith's shares, assuming majority control of the team, with Dearie Mulvey's heirs retaining the rest.

In 1958, O'Malley wanted to build a new ballpark in Brooklyn and tried to invoke eminent domain in acquiring land in downtown Brooklyn. Unable to do so, he moved the Dodgers to Los Angeles, and enlisted Horace Stoneham to do likewise with his Giants, moving them to San Francisco. O'Malley's move would cement a divided legacy: to some, he was a forward-thinking visionary who brought big-league baseball to California, thus opening the vast western territory of the United States for expansion -- at the time, major league baseball's westernmost presence was in Kansas City. But for others, namely the residents of Brooklyn, he was scorned and reviled for absconding with their beloved "bums" like a thief in the dead of night.

It wasn't until 1975 that O'Malley finally purchased the rest of the team from Dearie Mulvey's heirs, consolidating his sole ownership of the team. Upon his death in 1979, his son Peter O'Malley assumed ownership. He would run the Los Angeles Dodgers until selling them to Rupert Murdoch's Fox Entertainment in 1998. Fox would own the team a scant five years before selling the franchise, including the ballpark and surrounding land, to Frank McCourt, a real estate developer from Boston whose wealth was accumulated by operating parking lots, among other ventures.

McCourt's tenure represents what many consider to be the nadir of this illustrious and historic franchise noted for NL Pennants; six World Series championships; being the first team to draw three million in attendance (1978); having a pitching-rich tradition from Koufax to Drysdale to Sutton to Valenzuela to Hershiser to Kershaw et al., and the highest fan attendance in total, 175 million, in all professional sports (since 1901), and of course, being the franchise that broke the color barrier with Jackie Robinson.

For a franchise known for its consistency and the longevity of its relationships with figures like manager Walter Alston (24 consecutive one-year contracts); the lifelong association with Tommy Lasorda as player, coach, manager, and executive; and with their incomparable broadcaster, Vin Scully, in the booth calling games since 1950, the volatility of McCourt's ownership was disheartening.

Having purchased the team mostly with debt, McCourt necessarily had to operate on a shoestring budget, which led to fielding a less talented team. McCourt had to borrow money from Fox on several occasions just to make payroll. McCourt would have an ongoing contentious relationship with MLB and its commissioner, Bud Selig, who, always citing the best interests of baseball, the Dodgers, and its fans, would not approve or otherwise block McCourt's various schemes through which he intended to divert funds from the Dodgers to alleviate his personal financial burdens.

After Selig did not approve a $3 billion television deal McCourt had in place with Fox in 2011, McCourt used that rejection as the basis to file for Chapter 11 bankruptcy protection and secure a $150 million loan from a JP Morgan Chase hedge fund, which he would then use to make payroll and cover other operating costs.

And when things could not get any worse, they did. In a highly publicized and salacious divorce proceeding between McCourt and his then-wife Jamie, who'd served as vice chairman, then president, and finally CEO of the team, McCourt's ownership of the Los Angeles Dodgers was contested, as it was considered community property in California.

After much legal wrangling, Frank McCourt paid Jamie McCourt $130 million in cash as part of the divorce settlement (the largest in California history) to retain ownership of the Los Angeles Dodgers. In 2012, Mark Walter, founder and CEO of Guggenheim Partners, a privately held global financial services firm with $170 billion in assets under management, headed a group called Guggenheim Baseball Management, which purchased the Los Angeles Dodgers, Dodger Stadium (aka Chavez Ravine), and the surrounding land. Other principals in the group were Magic Johnson, Peter Guber (a film producer and an owner of the Golden State Warriors), Todd Boehly (Walter's close associate and colleague at Guggenheim Partners), Stan Kasten (a veteran sports executive from the NBA as well as MLB), and Robert (Bobby) Patton from Texas (a rancher/investor with a background in oil, natural gas, and real estate).

Going forward, with now stable ownership and vast resources, the Los Angeles Dodgers are well positioned to prosper in their third century of existence. In fact, the 2017 Dodgers had the best record in baseball and are primed for a deep run in the playoffs.

World Series Appearances: 18   Wins: 12
Forbes 2017 Valuation: $2.75 Billion

Miami Marlins

Former name: Florida Marlins 1993-2011

Year	Owner(s)	Purchase Price
1993-1998	Wayne Huizenga	$95 Million
1998-2002	John W. Henry	$158 Million
2002-2017	Jeffrey Loria	$158.5 Million
2017-	Jorge Mas	$1.2 Billion

The Miami Marlins are the only pro team to have been owned and controlled by three dynamic billionaires, each of whom has owned multiple pro sports teams, and each of whom has been hated, or at best, strongly disliked by the Miami fan base. This adversarial relationship with Marlins owners extended to some Miami Dolphins owners as well. Much of the blame lies with the Miami fans and the city, for arguments over who should pay for new or renovated facilities.

Nevertheless, the Marlins are one of only two teams to have played in the World Series twice and won both times (the other being the Toronto

Blue Jays). The only other teams batting .1000 in World Series competition were the Los Angeles Angels of Anaheim and the Arizona Diamondbacks, but they each only made the Series once. There are only two out of the 30 MLB teams that never made it to the World Series: the Washington Nationals and the Seattle Mariners. There are seven of 30 teams that never won a World Series.

In 1990, shortly after Major League Baseball announced its intention to add two new teams to the National League, Wayne Huizenga began pursuit of a franchise for southern Florida. In 1991, beating out Orlando and Tampa Bay, he was awarded a Miami-based franchise for a $95 million expansion fee. Although they considered Flamingos as the team name, they settled on the Florida Marlins. The team's first season of play was in 1993.

Huizenga is a well-known entrepreneur who founded three highly successful companies that grew to make the Fortune 1000 list: Waste Management, Blockbuster Entertainment, and AutoNation. While those ventures made him extremely wealthy, he had also dominated the sports scene in southern Florida. In addition to the Florida Marlins, Huizenga was the owner of the Miami Dolphins NFL team and the Florida Panthers NHL team. He was unsuccessful in his attempt to purchase the NBA's Miami Heat team. Huizenga was inducted into the Florida Sports Hall of Fame.

After four seasons of team building, Wayne's Marlins not only pulled off a 92-win season (.568) in 1997 but also went on to win the World Series title in only their fifth season of play. This accomplishment was contradicted by Wayne's historic "fire-sale" in which he traded nearly all the team's best players. The result was one of the worst post-championship seasons in MLB history, which culminated in 108 losses and a .333 average.

Wayne was no dummy. One year later, in 1998, after cashing in on the player "fire-sale," he sold the team to John Henry for $158 million and concluded his Marlins ownership with an overall .450 win/loss record … and a nifty $63 million profit (pre-tax) in his pocket.

John Henry, the son of soybean farmers, was born in Quincy, Illinois, and grew up in Arkansas. He was weaned listening to the St. Louis Cardinals radio broadcasts and had baseball in his blood. He was also a numbers wiz who dropped out of college (where he got into guru philosophy) to play guitar and perform in '60s rock bands. In the mid-1970s, his father died, forcing him to take over the family farming business. That's when he learned that trading soybean futures was much better than farming them. He made his initial fortune trading commodities and used his intuitive mathematical acumen to formulate a trading method that relied on a system of metrics he developed, and it worked. His first professional baseball ownership was in 1989 with an AAA minor league team, the Tucson Toros, who competed in the Pacific Coast League. In

1991, Henry purchased a 1 percent interest in the New York Yankees for $1 million.

John Henry was successful in most everything he touched … except the Florida Marlins. Although to give Henry the benefit of the doubt, he may have been using the Marlins as a steppingstone to bigger things -- the Boston Red Sox franchise, which he knew was soon to be sold by the Yawkey Trust. He bought what Huizenga sold him, a team with little talent, and he made it worse by keeping the Marlins at the lowest player payroll in the MLB. During his three-year period of ownership, the Marlins never managed a winning record, which came as no surprise to the angry Marlins fans given his lack of investment in talent. For a competitive businessman, hell-bent on winning, a man who was banned from casinos for winning at blackjack by card-counting, Henry struck out with the Marlins. But he went on to achieve fantastic success as majority owner of the Boston Red Sox. To own the Red Sox, he had to sell the Marlins.

In 2002, Henry sold the team to Jeffrey Loria for $158.5 million, virtually the same price he had paid Huizenga three years prior. In 2007, John Henry bought the Brookline, Mass., home of Frank McCourt, a rival losing-bidder for the Red Sox (who owned the Dodgers at the time), and gutted it in favor of a 35,000 square-foot mansion. A man who has a zest for life, and for winning at all cost, John Henry seems to have much in common with Paul Allen, Microsoft co-founder and owner of the NFL's Seattle Seahawks and the NBA's Portland Trailblazers: they both were endowed with brilliant minds, they both dropped out of college, they both played guitar in rock bands, they both own mega-yachts and enjoy partying, they both sit in an owner's box, they both have championship rings and they both shun publicity, preferring the soft-light to the limelight. In 2016, Forbes valued Henry's net worth at $2.4 billion.

Jeffrey Loria, whose penny-pinching ruined the Montreal Expos, sold the franchise back to Major League Baseball for $120 million and used those funds, as well as a $38.5 million interest-free loan from MLB, to purchase the Marlins. Loria earned much of his wealth as an art dealer. Prior to owning the Marlins, Loria first owned the AAA minor league team the Oklahoma City 89ers, and won the American Association championship in 1992. Loria made an unsuccessful bid to purchase the Baltimore Orioles in 1994.

The Marlins were on the rise and finished second in their division in 2003. They continued that success in the post-season and went to win the World Series that year by defeating the New York Yankees.

In 2011, the team was renamed Miami Marlins due to an agreement with the city. The following year, Marlins Park opened in time for the 2012 season. Even with the World Series title and a new ballpark, the attendance at Marlins games remains low. They finally surpassed two million the year the new ballpark opened, but the average dropped again to approximately 1.7 million during the next three years. The constant selling of talent and poor performance on the field has made it nearly impossible to create a loyal following in the Little Havana suburb of Miami.

Loria is not liked or respected as an owner. Many have used the term "meddlesome," and he seems to make it challenging to succeed within the organization. The ESPN network called Loria "dishonest" in 2013 when he was ranked number 122 (last) on the professional sports list of owner (dis)honesty. The following year, Rolling Stone ranked Loria next-to-last on the 15 worst owners in sports. At one point, Loria started suing former season ticketholders for not continuing their multi-year contracts, which they claim should be void due to benefits being withheld.

In 2017, facing mounting operating losses and feeling the squeeze, Loria put the Marlins up for sale asking an exorbitant price of $1.6 plus billion. Future New York Yankee Hall of Famer, Derek Jeter, put together a group of investors led by Cuban American billionaire, Jorge Mas, who made a deal to buy the Marlins for $1.2 billion. Loria will be off the hook and the Marlins fans will have new hope.

World Series Appearances: 2   Wins: 2
Forbes 2017 Valuation: $940 Million

Milwaukee Brewers

Former name: Seattle Pilots 1968-1970

Year	Owner(s)	Purchase Price
1968-1970	Dewey Soriano and William Daley	$5.3 Million
1970-2005	Bud Selig	$10.8 Million
2005-	Mark Attanasio	$223 Million

The dream of baseball in Seattle was alive for many years prior to the granting of the franchise in 1968. A syndicate headed by Dewey Soriano and paid for by William Daley founded the Milwaukee Brewers as the Seattle Pilots for a $5.3 million expansion fee.

Dewey Soriano spent a decade as an accomplished minor league pitcher. Taking his passion for baseball into the business side of the game, he went on to own the Yakima Bears, a short-season Class A affiliate of the Arizona Diamondbacks. Dewey also served as general manager for the Vancouver Capilanos and the Seattle Rainiers. His experience and connections led him to become the president of the Pacific Coast League (PCL) in 1960. It was during his tenure as president of the PCL that the league expanded in both number of teams (12) and locations (Hawaii to Indianapolis). Dewey was nominated in 1965 to be major league commissioner but the position went to William Eckert. Instead, Dewey remained focused on securing a franchise for Seattle.

Finally, in 1968, Major League Baseball awarded expansion franchises to Kansas City, Montreal, San Diego, and Seattle. Conditions attached to the Seattle franchise included refurbishing Sick's Stadium for use while building a new domed stadium in Seattle. Dewey and his brother Max Soriano appeared to be ideal candidates to run the newly awarded franchise except that they did not have the funds to operate the organization. To help with capital, the Sorianos sold a 47 percent share to William Daley, former owner of the Cleveland Indians.

As happens too often, the expansion and refurbishment of Sick's Stadium fell behind schedule and they were unable to fully sell a planned 25,000 season tickets because they couldn't even seat that many until later in June. Couple that with the old stadium structure that lacked enough water pressure to flush toilets and such poor technology wiring that they couldn't broadcast locally, and there was little revenue flow. Stadium issues, lack of revenue, and a 98-loss season caused Daley to cease additional investment in the club. Unfortunately, this forced the Sorianos into bankruptcy. Dewey Soriano was diagnosed with Alzheimer's, and died in 1998.

Following the 1970 bankruptcy of the Seattle Pilots, the franchise was sold to a group led by Bud Selig for $10.8 million. Immediately after acquiring the franchise, Selig moved it to Milwaukee and renamed it the Milwaukee Brewers. The acquisition brought Selig back full circle to his childhood when his mother took him and his brother to see a minor- league team, the Milwaukee Brewers, and fulfilled his quest to bring Major League Baseball back to Milwaukee.

In 1953, the Boston Braves franchise had relocated, becoming the Milwaukee Braves. Selig later became the team's largest public stockholder and minority owner of the club. Rumors indicated the team would be moved to a larger market, but Selig was determined to keep the Braves in town, forming Teams, Inc. The group's efforts failed and the Braves moved to Atlanta after the 1965 season. He changed the group's name to Milwaukee Brewers Baseball Club, Inc. and became focused on getting baseball back in his town.

Selig was brilliant at keeping baseball alive and top of mind in Milwaukee. He arranged for games to be played at the Milwaukee County Stadium and managed to draw a crowd of over 51,000 for a pre-season game between the White Sox and the Twins. In 1968 and 1969, he hosted a total of 20 regular season White Sox games in Milwaukee, with amazing attendance. His group attempted to buy the White Sox in 1969 but the sale was vetoed. Regardless, the excitement for baseball in Milwaukee was solidified and this helped with the purchase approval for the Pilots the following year.

During Selig's tenure as owner and club president, the Brewers had 11 winning seasons of 28 and one World Series appearance in 1982, although they were not victorious. Notably, the club won Organization of the Year seven times. On another note, Selig was named as part of an owner's collusion in 1985 through 1987, which resulted in owners paying $280 million in damages to players. After serving as acting baseball commissioner for six years, the owners officially named Selig commissioner during the 1998 season.

To avoid technical conflicts of interest, Selig transferred his ownership interest to his daughter, Wendy Selig-Prieb, who was already involved with the Brewers as general counsel since 1990. During her tenure, she hired Doug Melvin as general manager in 2002 and he rebuilt the minor-league system. However, the most notable accomplishment came in 2001 with the opening of Miller Park. The state-of-the-art ballpark attracted nearly three million fans in its first season and set a MLB record for largest attendance increase during the first year of a new ballpark.

Under her leadership, the Brewers created Brewers Charities (now the Brewers Community Foundation), which supported programs such as the Girls of Summer Softball League and the establishment of the Selig Scholarship Fund. In 1994 and 1995, Selig-Prieb was the first woman to represent Major League Baseball during collective bargaining. Unfortunately, this did not translate to success on the field, as the Brewers had no winning seasons during Selig-Prieb's seven years at the helm.

The Selig family sold the team in 2005, but Bud Selig remains a part of the Milwaukee Brewers' baseball culture and currently serves as the commissioner emeritus of Major League Baseball.

In 2005, Major League Baseball approved the Selig family's sale of the Milwaukee Brewers to Mark Attanasio for $223 million. Attanasio is a co-founder and senior executive of a private equity firm, Crescent Capital Group. He is also part-owner of the Milwaukee Admirals, an affiliate team of the NHL's Nashville Predators.

While Mark Attanasio and his wife Debbie reside in Los Angeles, they also maintain a residence in downtown Milwaukee. The couple is actively involved with the Milwaukee community, and were major sponsors of bringing the Andy Warhol exhibition to the Milwaukee Art Museum. Attanasio has continuously voiced his commitment to keeping the Brewers in Milwaukee, and believes the fan base is amazingly supportive.

During the 2016 season, the Brewers openly discussed being in a period of rebuilding. Attanasio's open letter to fans in December 2015, demonstrated his desire to compete while remaining transparent with those who support the Brewers. While the team's payroll has dropped significantly, he continues to assure fans that the money is there should they need it. Under Attanasio's ownership, the Brewers have done well with six of 11 winning seasons, a .499 winning percentage.

World Series Appearances: 1   Wins: 0
Forbes 2017 Valuation: $925 Million

Minnesota Twins

Year	Owner(s)	Purchase Price
1919-1955	Clark Griffith	NA
1955-1984	Calvin Griffith	
1984-2009	Carl Pohlad	$32 Million
2009-	Jim Pohlad	

In the legend, lore, and mythology of baseball, the Washington Senators are a team consigned, more or less, to the dustbin of history. The popular perception of the franchise as perennial losers and also-rans was forever engraved in the public's imagination with the classic Broadway musical comedy "Damn Yankees" (1955). A clever retelling of the Faust legend, the play revolves around a star player for the Washington Senators who sells his soul to the devil for just ONE season in which the Senators overtake the dreaded New York Yankees and win the American League Pennant.

In fact, the Washington Senators were for a time, in the 1920s and '30s, a very good and competitive baseball team featuring a host of future Hall of Famers including, among others, Joe Cronin, Bucky Harris, Heinie Manush, and the immortal Walter Johnson. Their well-earned and justifiable reputation for mediocrity would not commence until the 1940s. The Washington Senators' manager, and for a brief time, player-manager, was Clark Griffith, who first came to the team in 1912, and then became the owner in 1920.

A venerable franchise, the Senators, founded in 1901, were one of the eight original American League teams. It was at a Washington Senators season-opening game in 1910 that President William Howard Taft threw out the ceremonial first pitch (to Walter Johnson), establishing that time-honored tradition. Despite winning only one World Series (as owner, not manager) in 1924, Griffith, and his family, are synonymous with Washington, D.C., baseball, and owned the franchise until 1984. Upon Clark Griffith's death in 1955, he was succeeded by his nephew (and adopted son), Calvin.

In 1960, when MLB granted the city of Minneapolis, Minnesota, an expansion team, Calvin Griffith was granted approval to move his franchise there, with a brand-new Washington Senators team replacing his old team of the same name in Washington.

Prior to the 1972 season, this second iteration of the Washington Senators would relocate to Texas, going forward as the Texas Rangers. Griffith, needing to equally pay deference to (and gain favor with) both markets in his new location -- the so-called Twin Cities of St. Paul and Minneapolis -- would name his team the Minnesota Twins. Unlike many other expansion teams of relatively recent vintage, the Minnesota Twins have already called three different stadiums home: Metropolitan Stadium (1961 to 1981); Hubert H. Humphrey Metrodome (1982 to 2009); and Target Field (2010). Perhaps a testament to their baseball-rich fan base, the Minnesota Twins were the first American League team to draw three million fans, in 1988.

In 1984, Calvin Griffith sold the franchise to Carl Pohlad, a multibillionaire from the banking and finance industry. Upon Pohlad's death, the franchise passed on to his son, Jim. As befits a franchise the history of which dates back to the turn of the 19th century, baseball purists consider the seventh game of the 1991 World Series, which the Minnesota Twins won 1-0 in extra-innings (beating the Atlanta Braves), one of the greatest professional baseball games ever played.

World Series Appearances: 6   Wins: 3
Forbes 2017 Valuation: $1.025 Billion

New York Mets

Year	Owner(s)	Purchase Price
1961-1975	Joan Payson (Group)	$1.8 Million
1975-1980	Joan Payson (Estate)	
1980-1986	Doubleday and Company	$21 Million
1986-2002	Nelson Doubleday & Fred Wilpon	$81 Million
2002-	Fred Wilpon	$391 Million

The only city with three major league franchises -- the New York Yankees of the American League, and the Brooklyn Dodgers and New York Giants of the National League -- New York City was, from the 1920s into the mid-1950s, the epicenter of major league baseball. It is important to note that despite the marquee value and glamour of the Yankees, New York has always been (and remains) a National League town, due to this legacy.

Walter O'Malley, principal owner of the Brooklyn Dodgers, needed a new ballpark for his team given the disrepair of Ebbets Field, and of course wanted it to be built in Brooklyn, the iconic home of his franchise. This ran afoul of Robert Moses, the autocratic urban planner of mid-20th century New York City, who insisted the new ballpark be built in Flushing, Queens. Rather than acquiesce, O'Malley, after the 1957 season, moved his team to Los Angeles.

Horace Stoneham, principal owner of the Giants, facing the same situation -- an old ballpark, the Polo Grounds in upper Manhattan, and a need for a new one -- fared no better with the omnipotent Moses and followed O'Malley's lead, moving his team to San Francisco. The one minority owner of the Giants who strongly opposed the move was Joan Whitney Payson.

Outside of the organization, at the behest of New York City Mayor Robert Wagner, an influential lawyer named William Shea headed a committee formed to bring a National League franchise back to New York City.

After being rebuffed by the Cincinnati Reds, Philadelphia Phillies, and Pittsburgh Pirates, Shea enlisted Branch Rickey to co-found a third major league, the new Continental League, which he and Rickey publicly introduced with great fanfare in 1959. It was this action that forced and leveraged Major League Baseball to reconsider -- thus the reason for expansion: two American League teams in 1961: The Los Angeles Angels and the Washington Senators; and in 1962, the Houston Colt 45s and the New York Mets -- whose team colors are a combination of Brooklyn's Royal Blue and New York's 'Giants Orange.' The neophyte New York Metropolitans even adopted the Giants' distinctive script for the lettering on their uniforms and interlocking NY logo on their baseball caps (worn to this day).

Joan Whitney Payson, an heiress known for her love of sports (baseball and horseracing) as well as for her patronage of the arts and philanthropy, headed a group that was awarded the expansion New York Mets in 1961. Upon her death in 1975, the team passed to her husband, Charles Shipman Payson, who installed their daughter Lorinda de Roulet as president, and, soon after, chairman of the board. In 1980, the Payson family sold a controlling interest of the team to Doubleday & Co., Inc. for $21 million. Publishing scion Nelson Doubleday, Jr. became chairman of the board.

Joan Payson's greatest investment in New York turned out to be the 1969 "Amazin' Mets" winning the franchise's first World Series championship. The Mets played their first two years in 1962 and '63 in the Polo Grounds where the NY Giants baseball team had played until moving to San Francisco. They shared it with the upstart newly formed AFL's New York Titans (Jets) until both teams moved to Shea Stadium in Queens.

Payson hired retired Yankees manager Casey Stengel as manager. The team also opted to sign older players, like Gil Hodges and Richie Ashburn, in the 1961 expansion draft instead of younger players with growth potential. The reasoning was to attract former Giants and Dodger fans who remembered those guys from bygone years. The result was a losing team that became laughable. They lost their first nine games and ended the season with a 40-120 record. Then in 1966, the Mets, often referred to as the "lovable losers," lost less than 100 games for the first time.

The team was on the rise and got lucky by winning a three-team lottery for the right to sign pitcher Tom Seaver, who won Rookie of the Year in 1967. In 1968, Gill Hodges was named manager. The team had nourished its new recruits and won the '69 World Series, upsetting the highly-touted Baltimore Orioles 4-1. The Mets' only other World Series title came in 1986, the year Nelson Doubleday sold the team to minority owner Fred Wilpon.

Fred Wilpon, chairman of Sterling Equities, Inc., was a Jewish kid from Brooklyn who had been a high school baseball teammate of Sandy Koufax. Fred made his fortune in real estate. In 1986, Nelson Doubleday, Jr. sold all the assets of Doubleday & Co., Inc. (excluding the Mets) to the behemoth German multinational mass media corporation, Bertelsmann, for $475 million. Doubleday and Wilpon then formed a 50-50 business partnership and purchased the team from Doubleday & Co., Inc.

Finally, in 2002, the patrician Doubleday and self-made Wilpon, whose relationship had always been fraught and somewhat contentious, went their separate ways, with Wilpon assuming sole ownership, buying out Doubleday's 50 percent interest in the team. Most recently, Wilpon's personal and business relationship with Bernard Madoff, and the entanglements and comingling of his finances, along with those of the Mets, in Madoff's Ponzi scheme, has been newsworthy and a source of controversy.

Nevertheless, the Mets did make the 2015 World Series, losing to the Kansas City Royals 4-2. Since then, the Mets, plagued by injuries to their highly-touted pitchers, have drifted into mediocre seasons.

World Series Appearances: 4   Wins: 2
Forbes 2017 Valuation: $2 Billion

New York Yankees

Year	Owner(s)	Purchase Price
1922-1939	Jacob Ruppert	$1.5 Million
1939-1945	Ruppert heirs	
1945-1948	Dan Topping, Del Webb	$2.8 Million
	Larry McPhail	
1948-1964	Dan Topping & Del Webb	$2.2 Million
1964-1973	CBS	$11.2 Million
1973-2009	George M. Steinbrenner, III	$10 Million
2010-	Hal & Hank Steinbrenner	

If only one American professional sports franchise could lay claim to the title of most iconic brand in the world, it would be the New York Yankees. By any metric the winningest professional sports franchise in history -- 40 American League Pennants and 27 World Series championships, with 44 players and 11 managers presently enshrined in the Baseball Hall of Fame -- the New York Yankees dominated baseball for four and half decades, from the Babe Ruth/Lou Gehrig "Murderer's Row" teams (1923 to '35), to the Joe DiMaggio teams (1936 to '51), to the Mantle/Berra/Ford teams (of the 1950s), to the "M&M Boys" (Mantle and Maris) teams of the early 1960s.

As with all franchises of a certain vintage, interspersed amongst the "dynasties" are long periods of futility as well: from '65 to '75, from '82 to '95, and '02 to 2015 (with one exception, the 2009 championship). This well suits those who passionately root against them with the same fervor as those who root for them.

By 1920, the start of what we call the modern era, the team had already moved from one city to another and had several names. Upon arriving in New York City in 1903, the Baltimore Orioles (not *those* Orioles) were christened the New York Highlanders. As was in vogue at the time, sportswriters often referred to all American League teams as "Americans," and all National League teams as "Nationals," and so the Highlanders were soon affixed with the nickname "Yanks," which was short for "Yankees," which was short for "Americans."

It wasn't until 1913 that this latest version became official; the New York Highlanders were forevermore called the New York Yankees. In 1922, co-owner Jacob Ruppert, who'd purchased the team with partner, Tillinghurst L'Hommedieu Huston, for $1.2 million back in 1914, bought out Huston's 50 percent interest for $1.5 million and assumed sole ownership. Ruppert, whose family fortune was made in the brewery business, would own the team until his death in 1939, leaving it to his heirs, who would sell the team in 1945 to the trio of Del Webb, Dan Topping, and Larry McPhail -- all celebrated figures of varying degree and temperament.

Webb, a major presence in Arizona and especially Las Vegas, was a real estate developer and construction contractor. An associate of Howard Hughes, and friends with entertainment luminaries such as Bob Hope and Bing Crosby, Webb's Las Vegas roots ran deep. In fact, he built the first casino in what would become modern-day Las Vegas, the Flamingo Hotel and Casino, for notorious gangster Bugsy Siegel and would later build and run his own casino, the Sahara. Topping, whose family fortune was in the tin industry, was a well-known raconteur and sportsman, who fathered nine children and was married six times to various actresses, an heiress, a model, and Olympic figure skating gold medalist Sonja Heine.

And then there was Larry McPhail -- a legendarily volatile drinker and baseball executive whose innovations included night baseball, regularly televising games, and the use of airplanes to transport teams from one city to another. It was McPhail who, in one particularly epic drinking session with Boston Red Sox owner Tom Yawkey, agreed to trade Joe DiMaggio for Ted Williams, straight up. The next day, upon sober reflection, both men rescinded their offers. In 1948, Topping and Webb would consolidate their ownership by purchasing McPhail's stake in the club.

By the mid-1960s, a confluence of three factors precipitated the Yankees' 10-year descent into a losing and second division club: their star players all got old at the same time; the first amateur draft was instituted in 1965 -- the so-called "Rule 4 draft" created specifically to prohibit the Yankees from signing all the best players -- and the abrupt ending of the team's longtime practice of trading cash for talent, both young prospects as well as past-their-prime veterans, to the Kansas City Athletics, whose owner, Alan Johnson, shared various business interests with both Webb and Topping.

In 1960, Johnson sold the Kansas City Athletics to Charles O. Finley, who had no interest in maintaining that cozy relationship with the New York Yankees. And so, in 1964, Topping and Webb sold a controlling interest of 80 percent of the New York Yankees to CBS, which would presage nine years of losing -- one of the lowest points in the history of the franchise. That would change, forever, when in 1973 the child of a shipbuilding family from Cleveland, Ohio, purchased the New York Yankees.

Ringmaster of the "Bronx Zoo," George Steinbrenner's resume reflects the duality of his legacy. He was banned from baseball two times -- once for illegal campaign contributions and once for consorting with a known gambler -- and was also known for hiring and firing and rehiring managers, general managers, and coaches with unprecedented regularity; building a new stadium; publicly feuding with his players; creating a regional sports network, and signing free agent stars to exorbitant contracts.

Yet within just three years of his buying the team, the Yankees were back in the World Series, losing to the Cincinnati Reds in 1976, and then winning back-to back World Series in 1978 and 1979. Steinbrenner's impact on the New York Yankees, as well as on the economics of baseball, is unarguable. Upon his death in 2010, Steinbrenner's sons, Hal and Hank Steinbrenner, assumed ownership and operational control of the New York Yankees.

World Series Appearances: 40   Wins: 27
Forbes 2017 Valuation: $3.7 Billion

Oakland Athletics

Former names: Philadelphia Athletics -1954; Kansas City Athletics 1954-1967

Year	Owner(s)	Purchase Price
1913-1922	Ben Shibe and Connie Mack	
1922-1946	Tom and John Shibe and Connie Mack	
1946-1950	Tom and John Shibe and Connie, Connie Jr., Earle, and Roy Mack	
1950-1954	Connie, Earle, and Roy Mack	$1.75 Million
1954-1960	Arnold Johnson	$6.7 Million
1960-1980	Charlie Finley	$3.78 Million
1980-1995	Walter Haas, Jr.	$12.7 Million
1995-2005	Stephen Schott and Ken Hofmann	$85 Million
2005-2016	Lewis Wolff and John Fisher	$180 Million
2016-	John Fisher	Undisclosed

Ben Shibe and Connie Mack owned the Oakland Athletics, then the Philadelphia Athletics and now commonly referred to as the Oakland A's, when the modern era of baseball began. In fact, the Shibe and Mack families were a part of team ownership for five decades with the Shibes involved from 1901 to 1950 and the Macks from 1901 to 1954.

After Shibe's death in January 1922, Connie Mack owned the team with Shibe's heirs, Tom and John Shibe. In 1946, Mack gave each of his sons, Connie Jr., Earle, and Roy, 10 percent of his shares. Earle and Roy Mack bought out other minority owners for $1.75 million in 1950, including Connie Jr. and Tom and John Shibe's heirs, leaving Earle and Roy with a 60 percent controlling interest in the team.

When the American League awarded the Philadelphia franchise to Connie Mack, he quickly identified Ben Shibe as the ideal partner who had credibility and capital. Shibe had a 50 percent share, Mack, 25 percent, and the remaining 25 percent was held by two sportswriters but Mack held their voting rights. It was agreed that Shibe would run the business side and Mack the baseball side.

It did not matter to Ben Shibe that he did not have an education or that he wore a steel brace on his leg due to a childhood accident. He worked hard on the railroad and volunteered for the Confederate Army of Northern Virginia. After the war, he joined his brother and nephew in their company that made cricket balls and baseballs. Shibe eventually left that business to partner with his friend, Alfred Reach, in what became an enormous manufacturing company of baseballs and bats. The company invented the cork-centered baseball that was introduced in 1910 and ignited the offensive part of the game. Shibe is also known for building the first concrete and steel stadium, Shibe Park. However, he is most fondly remembered for his generosity, taking care of his ballplayers, and always thinking in terms of what was best for the game of baseball.

Connie Mack, also known as the "Tall Tactician," lived and breathed baseball most of his life and accumulated 71 years in organized baseball. He played professional baseball for 10 seasons as a catcher then began his more than 50-year tenure of owning and managing the Athletics. Mack didn't have the capital to own a team but it was his baseball mind that intrigued the American League president, Ban Johnson, and which was largely why Shibe agreed to partner with him.

In addition to his 50 percent voting rights, he had full control of baseball operations, including managing the team. Although this is not permissible today, it was not uncommon at that time. What was uncommon, however, was his approach to managing players. He was kind, soft-spoken, and never criticized others in public. While there were many years with over a hundred losses and last-place finishes, he also accumulated 3,731 wins as a manager.

From 1929 to 1931, the team won an unprecedented 313 games, three pennants, and two championships. The Depression hit and the Philadelphia area suffered many losses, and that didn't bode well for baseball. In the later years, his sons Earle and Roy took on more of the daily ownership responsibilities but Mack retained the role of president.

The other American League owners were not happy with their share of the gate receipts and urged them to sell or move the team. They agreed to sell the team to Arnold Johnson in 1954 for $6.7 million. During the Shibe and Mack modern era of ownership, the Athletics had five World Series appearances and three wins. Connie Mack was inducted into the Baseball Hall of Fame in 1937.

Arnold Johnson was a Chicago native and made his fortune as a banker and stockbroker. In 1953, a year before he purchased the Philadelphia Athletics, he bought Yankee Stadium and the Blues Stadium in Kansas City. The Kansas City Blues were the top farm team of the Yankees. To resolve the conflict of interest, at least on the surface, after buying the Athletics in 1954, he sold Yankee Stadium back to the team and sold Blues Stadium to the city of Kansas City, which named it Municipal Stadium and renovated it to major league standards.

Johnson then moved the team to Kansas City and renamed them the Kansas City Athletics. The team attendance was 1.39 million its first year in Kansas City, the first time the franchise surpassed the million mark. However, the team was never competitive, and most believed there was collusion between Johnson and the Yankees to use the Athletics as their high-end farm team. Year over year, Johnson traded their best players to the Yankees for seemingly poor trade decisions, and the Yankees rarely traded with anyone else. By 1961, the Yankees were one of the best teams ever in baseball and 10 of the players on their roster were former A's.

Johnson's life ended suddenly at age 53 when he suffered a brain aneurysm while driving home from a spring training game.

Following Johnson's death, his estate sold 52 percent of his shares in 1960 to Charlie Finley for $1.975 million. Over the course of the next year, Finley purchased the rest of the shares for around $1.8 million. Finley was born in Alabama but also lived in northern Indiana, just east of Chicago. He became wealthy in the insurance business by writing group medical insurance policies for those in the medical field.

In his first steps to shift the franchise into the win column, Finley stopped making deals with the Yankees and made substantial investments to finally build the Athletics' farm system. Finley was an effective marketer and tried a wide variety of tactics to increase attendance in Kansas City. Nothing was off limits. Probably his most famous promotion was getting the Beatles to play at the Kansas City Municipal Stadium in 1964. To say he was involved in every aspect of the team might be an understatement, as he wanted his prints on every piece of team history, and many resented him for his over-involvement.

After the 1967 season, Finley received league approval and moved the team to Oakland, California, renaming them the Oakland Athletics. The farm system was starting to pay off and the team began performing over .500. Finley loved to reward player performance in a generous manner but it had to be on his terms. He was just the opposite when it came to player contract negotiations, as he became stubborn if a player would not accept his contract offer. Finley traded and tweaked his club to get it exactly where he wanted it. By 1971, they won the division and in 1972, 1973, and 1974 the Oakland Athletics won three consecutive World Series championships. But there was continuing drama around Finley and much unrest with the team and leadership. Their manager, Dick Williams, walked out after winning the 1973 World Series. Within two years of winning consecutive titles, they had plummeted to sub .400 ball. In 1980, Finley's divorce forced him to sell the team to Walter Haas Jr. for $12.7 million.

Born in San Francisco, Walter Haas Jr. was born into the Levi Strauss family. After attending Berkeley and Harvard, he served in the army during World War II and then went to work at Levi Strauss & Co. and eventually became president, CEO, and chairman, succeeding his father. Haas initially wasn't a fan of baseball and primarily bought the franchise to keep it in Oakland; however, he grew to love the game and discovered it was a profitable investment.

Haas brought in his son-in-law, Roy Eisenhardt, to serve as club president. The leadership style and culture of the franchise was drastically different than with Finley. Eisenhardt was empowering to his managers and Haas was considered a beloved owner during his 15 years. Attendance immediate rose above the million mark, reaching 2.28 million in 1988, and stayed above two million for six years while averaging 1.83 million over 15 seasons. The team won the division title five times, appeared in the World Series three consecutive years, and won the championship in 1989.

Haas passed away in September 1995 after a battle with prostate cancer. An honorary jersey was retired in his honor.

After Haas's death, Stephen Schott and Ken Hofmann purchased the Athletics for $85 million. Schott was born in Santa Clara, California, attended college on a partial baseball scholarship, served in the Army, and later formed a real-estate development company, Citation. His company is one of the largest homebuilders in California.

Hofmann was born in Oakland, CA, graduated from the United States Merchant Marine Academy, then founded the Hofmann Company – also a residential real estate development company. It was during the Schott and Hofmann ownership that Billy Beane's strategy of "Moneyball" was created. They owned the franchise for nine seasons, realized a .540 win-rate, won three division titles, and had an average attendance of 1.71 million. However, there were no pennants or championships achieved. Schott and Hofmann sold the team in April 2005 to a group led by John Fisher and Lewis Wolff for $180 million.

Lewis Wolff was born and raised in St. Louis, Missouri. After college, he became a real estate appraiser and relocated to Los Angeles where he formed a real estate consulting firm to help develop the San Diego market. He then managed real estate for 20th Century Fox before forming his own firm, Maritz, Wolff & Co, that owned high-end resorts and hotels around the world. He had previously owned a share of the Golden State Warriors and a Major League Soccer franchise. Stadium issues with the Coliseum have been a thorn in his side but they are currently only two years into a 10-year contract. Team performance has not changed much under his ownership. The team is at a .510 win-rate, has three division titles, no pennants or championships, and an average attendance of 1.75 million.

In late 2016, Wolff sold his shares to entities controlled by John Fisher, giving him total control of the team.

World Series Appearances: 11   Wins: 7
Forbes 2017 Valuation: $880 Million

Philadelphia Phillies

Year	Owner(s)	Purchase Price
1913-1930	William Baker	N/A
1930-1931	Mrs. Baker and Mae Mallen	N/A
1931-1942	Gerald Nugent	N/A
1942-	National League	$350,000
1942-	William Cox	$250,000
1943-1972	Robert R. M. Carpenter, Jr.	$400,000
1972-1981	Robert R.M. Carpenter, III	
1981-1997	Bill Giles and David Montgomery	$30 Million
1997-2014	David Montgomery	
2014-	John S. Middleton	

In pro sports, there are tough towns, some really tough towns, and then there is … Philadelphia. Doesn't matter if we're talking about the Phillies, Eagles, 76ers, or Flyers (even though we do not include ice hockey in this volume, we would be remiss writing about Philadelphia and not mentioning the "Broad Street Bullies"), there is a special quality in Philadelphia's relationship to its teams, for both the fans and the media, which is unique in the pro sports landscape.

The city itself is big enough (none more venerable and historic) to have all four pro sports, each with long and storied histories, yet just small enough to foster an emotional intensity and glare amongst its fans that does not exist in other cities.

The veneer of epic losing streaks and championship droughts can become almost emblematic of a city's defiant pride, obstinacy, and resolve -- Boston's beloved Red Sox and their 86-year "curse,' or Chicago's adored Cubs and their 108-year championship drought (which just ended but existed nonetheless), for example. So too, in other cities, the historic futility and epic losing records of one team, in one sport, are mitigated by periods of sustained excellence (and championships), by other local teams,

236

in other sports. Generations of Bostonians consoled themselves with the championship pedigrees of the Celtics and Patriots and Bruins; Chicagoans had "Da Bears" of Halas and Butkus and Sayers, and later of Ditka and Payton, and, of course, Michael Jordan's Bulls, to counterbalance their lovable Cubbies. Wherever one cares to look, this is always the case: the woeful Detroit Lions share the same city with the Redwings (Hockeytown, USA), the "Bad Boys" champion Pistons, and the '84 champion Tigers, and so on.

Except in Philadelphia. Philadelphia, the City of Brotherly Love: visiting teams dread playing there, visiting fans (who travel to "away" games) feel physically unsafe there, and even Philadelphia players can count on unusually harsh and vocal treatment -- not to mention the occasional battery thrown from the upper deck. If, as the saying goes about Oakland that, "there is no there, there," then in Philadelphia, "there is too much there, there."

Factually, the Philadelphia Phillies are the "losingest" franchise in the history of American professional team sports (they lost their 10,000th game in 2007). While indisputable, it is also somewhat understandable -- they are, after all, the oldest continuous, one-name, one-city franchise in all of American professional sport. There is a certain logic to the team competing the most and losing the most -- even if 77 consecutive losing seasons is a bit much. And, although they were the last of the 16MLB franchises in 1901 to win a World Series, they have indeed won two World Series (in 1980 and 2008) and appeared in four others (1950, 1983, 1993, and 2009).

As for the Philadelphia fan in general, they'll find no respite from all the losing by looking to the Eagles, who have never won a Super Bowl (though appearing twice in 1980 and 2004). However, the 76ers have won three NBA titles: by Moses Malone's famous, "Fo, Fo, Fo" team of 1983, along with two more (in 1955 and 1967). And in the Flyers' heyday, there were back-to-back Stanley Cups in 1974 and '75. What, then, accounts for Philadelphia's hurtful relationship with its teams? After all, there is no shortage of teams and cities in the "big three" sports, with similarly sporadic resumes, a few scattered championships separated by decades of mediocrity.

Which is worse: "Phold of '64," the single greatest collapse in baseball history (and perhaps sports), where on September 20th, the Phillies' record at 90-60 was good for a 6 ½-game lead with 12 to play when they proceeded to lose 10 in a row, finishing one game behind the St. Louis Cardinals; or their still-standing record of a 23-game consecutive losing streak in 1961; or maybe Joe Carter's gut-wrenching 1993 game-winning, World Series-winning, walk-off home run for the Toronto Blue Jays?

Founded in 1983 as the Philadelphia Quakers, who then became the Philadelphias, and finally the Phillies (1890), the team was owned in

1920 (our demarcation of the "modern era") by William Baker, whose frugal nature was both legendary and comical. He was said to regularly release a herd of sheep to trim the grass in the Phillies ballpark, the Baker Bowl. Upon his death in 1930, Baker left half the team to his wife and half to his secretary, Mae Mallen, who was married to Gerald Nugent.

In 1933, upon Mrs. Baker's death, Mae and Gerald Nugent assumed full ownership of the team. The team's continuing financial distress and mismanagement would come to a head in 1943 when Nugent, needing a cash advance simply to bring the team to Florida for spring training, would sell the team to the National League who would quickly sell it to William Cox, whose fortune was made in the lumber business.

There is an oft-repeated (and written) alternate version of these events in which Nugent had a deal in place to sell to Bill Veeck -- who intended on bringing in black ballplayers from the Negro League to revitalize the stagnating franchise. However, the MLB commissioner at the time, Judge Kennesaw Mountain Landis, a staunch opponent of integration, imposed on NL Commissioner Ford Frick to negate the Veeck deal, with the National League buying the franchise only to quickly sell it to William Cox. This version was put forth by Bill Veeck himself and retold and rewritten so many times as to assume historical veracity. The story may or may not be true and is still contested and unresolved to this day -- with supporting evidence claiming authentication from both sides.   What is not disputed by anybody is that Cox would be banished for life from baseball by Commissioner Landis for betting on the Phillies.

In a matter of months, the National League would find a much more credible buyer in the person of Robert Ruliph Morgan Carpenter of Delaware. Carpenter had married into the du Pont family – Pierre S. du Pont, the brother of his wife, the former Margaretta Lammot du Pont, was the president of the DuPont company. Mr. Carpenter would immediately turn over the day-to-day operations of the team to his 28-year-old son, Robert Ruliph Morgan Carpenter, Jr. This new ownership would signal a sea change for the franchise that had always been run by either miserly or relatively impoverished individuals who never adequately invested in scouting, player development, minor leagues, etc.

Although not immediately, this new approach would pay dividends with the "Whiz Kids" of 1950, a totally homegrown roster of star players (including Richie Ashburn and Robin Roberts) from the Phillies' farm system, which would win the NL Pennant, only to be swept by the New York Yankees in the World Series. But what was thought to be a harbinger of success and prosperity going forward never materialized. The Phillies would revert to form and be a losing franchise for the next 25 years.

An unfortunate though necessary aspect of the Phillies' story is their troubling history regarding integration and racism. While we might never know if the aborted Bill Veeck sale story is true, there is no doubt that at least a partial determinant for the teams' continual losing was the

Carpenter family's resistance to integration. The "Whiz Kids" had been an all-white roster, and it would take a full 10 years after Jackie Robinson's debut for the Philadelphia Phillies to sign a black ballplayer. Indeed, there are documented accounts of Robinson's mistreatment by Phillies' players -- verbal abuse from the dugout in Ebbets Field as well as pointing bats at him and making shooting noises when the Dodgers played in Philadelphia.

The year 1950 would also be the year that the other baseball team in town, the Philadelphia Athletics, would lose the great Connie Mack to retirement. Five years later, the Athletics would be sold to the Johnson brothers and relocate to Kansas City. As part of that deal, the Phillies would purchase Shibe Park (by then renamed Connie Mack Stadium), the ballpark they'd shared with the A's since 1938. The Phillies would continue playing in Connie Mack until moving into the new Veterans Stadium in 1971.

Upon Carpenter's retirement in 1972, the franchise would pass to his son, Robert Ruliph Morgan Carpenter III, known as "Ruly."

Ruly would oversee the Phillies' return to respectability and more, winning NL East Pennants in 1976, '77, '78, and finally their first World Series in 1980. Carpenter would sell the team in 1981 to a group headed by two Phillies executives, Bill Giles and David Montgomery.

The Phillies would remain a good team through 1983 (a World Series loss to the Baltimore Orioles) before slipping back, yet again, into a cellar-dwelling ball club for five straight years. They would also in that same year sell a 15 percent stake in the club for $15 million to Herbert Middleton, whose family wealth derived from a Philadelphia tobacco company that later became a cigar company.

After returning to the World Series in 1993, the Phillies would again experience a losing period until their latest "golden era" of 2005 to 2012. Upon moving into their new Citizens Bank Park in 2004, the Phillies would reel off five consecutive N.L. East Divisions (2007-'11), and appear in two World Series, claiming their second World Series victory in 2008. Since then, the team has been in serious decline.

Presently, Bill Giles remains as chairman emeritus of the Phillies while partner David Montgomery, dealing with serious health issues, has given over control to John Middleton, who inherited his interest in the team from his father and who over the years has amassed more and more stock in the Phillies, now at 48 percent.

Regardless of what has been said about Philadelphia and its fans, it has always been a great sports town. Unruly fans like to be unruly. It's their way having fun.

World Series Appearances: 6   Wins: 2
Forbes 2017 Valuation: $1.65 Billion

Pittsburgh Pirates

Year	Owner(s)	Purchase Price
1901-1932	Barney Dreyfuss	
1932-1946	Mrs. Dreyfuss	
1946-1950	Frank E. McKinney	$2.25 Million
1950-1983	John Galbreath and Tom Johnson	$950,000
1983-1985	John Galbreath and Warner Communications	Unknown
1985-1996	Pittsburgh Associates	$22 Million
1996-2007	Kevin McClatchy	$95 Million
2007-	Bob Nutting	Unknown

Barney Dreyfuss and movie star producer, Kevin Costner, had one theme in common: "If we build it, they will come." In Costner's classic film, "Field of Dreams," he imagines legendary baseball players who emerge from the depths of the cornfields to play baseball on his field. Barney Dreyfuss imagined the same thing, but his vision became reality when he took a chance, with financial help from Andrew Carnegie, to build Forbes Field in 1909, the first all-steel baseball park featuring an upper deck. His critics thought he was nuts to spend on such an extravagance, but he proved them wrong as fans poured through the gates to see one of the best teams in baseball at the time.

Pittsburgh, once the "Gateway to the West," was a city in contrast during the beginnings of baseball. Many of the country's early fortunes and brand names were born and made in Pittsburgh: Carnegie, Mellon, Heinz, Westinghouse, Alcoa, Phipps, Frick, Forbes -- and let's not forget Barney Dreyfuss, owner of the Pittsburgh Pirates.

As industry flourished immigrants poured in from Britain, Germany, Poland, Italy, Ireland, and other countries to provide the labor that worked the mills and factories that sprang up in and around this growing industrial city. It was this ethnic mix of people, who lived primarily in their own neighborhoods, who came together as *one* whenever the Pirates took the field.

Today's PNC Park isn't that far from where Fort Duquesne guarded the city in 1754 during the French and Indian War (Seven Years' War). It is also within walking distance of the Andy Warhol Museum, a lesser-known distinction for Pittsburgh, which boasts of its most famous artist.

Barney Dreyfuss was a German immigrant who got his start in business working as an accountant for the Bernheim family in Paducah and Louisville, Kentucky. They owned the distillery that made I.W. Harper bourbon. (Barney's father, Samuel, was said to have made a fortune selling spirits to the Native Americans). Barney rose through the ranks and with the financial help of his cousins, the Bernheims, acquired controlling interest in the Louisville Colonels of the American Association in 1890. When that league folded in 1899, he borrowed from the Bernheims again and bought the Pirates. He brought 14 players to Pittsburgh with him, including legendary Hall of Famer Honus Wagner, regarded by many as one of the greatest players ever.

Today, Honus Wagner is better known for his baseball card than his record as a player. In 2011, his 1909-1911 card sold at auction for $1.2 million and in 2013 it sold for $2.1 million. On October 3, 2016, the Wagner card sold for a record $3.12 million, keeping it the most valuable card in baseball history. Trading cards in those days were inserted into the American Tobacco Company's cigarette packs to promote the brand. What made his card so valuable? According to one version, Honus refused additional production of his card because he didn't want to promote smoking to kids. This refusal limited production to the few hundred that had already been produced before he objected. The other version of an explanation for his reluctance: he wasn't paid enough.

Barney Dreyfuss owned the Pittsburgh Pirates from 1900 to his death in 1932 when his wife took over. She maintained control until 1946. He was one of the most important men in the "pre-modern" era. He created the first World Series in 1903 by challenging the upstart American League's best team (Boston) to a game to show which league was king. He was generous to a fault and popular with players, fans, and other owners.

In that first World Series, he gave his share of the money to his players, taking none for himself. The Pirates lost the game, making it the first time the losers received more money than the winners. During his reign, the Pirates won six NL pennants and two World Series, 1909 and 1925.

Being a numbers man, Barney made the schedules for the league and was known for keeping statistics and using them to evaluate and recruit talent. His influence helped create the position of a single league commissioner rather than a group. In 1921, Judge Kenesaw Mountain Landis assumed that role, which he kept until his death in 1944. Barney also chipped in and helped form the commission to investigate the 1919 Black Sox scandal.

He wasn't inducted into the Baseball Hall of Fame until 2008. This might seem surprising considering his contributions to the game of baseball, but owners never were given their due credit compared to the players and managers.

In 1946, the Pirates were sold to a group headed by Frank McKinney for $2.25 million. McKinney, a banker from Indianapolis who was also active in politics, was hand-picked by President Harry Truman to be chairman of the Democratic National Committee in 1950-1951.

In 1950, John Kenneth Galbreath, who was a minority owner (along with crooner Bing Crosby), and Tom Johnson bought out McKinney and the other owners for $950,000. From 1950 to 1984, under the leadership of John and his son Dan, who took over in 1969, the Pirates won the World Series three times: 1960, 1971 and 1979. Galbreath, who made his fortune as a real estate developer, was best known for his accomplishments in the world of thoroughbred horseracing. He won the Kentucky Derby with Chateaugay in 1963 and with Proud Clarion in 1967. Another Galbreath horse, Little Current, won the Preakness and the Belmont Stakes in 1974. In 1972, he won the Epsom Derby in England with his horse Roberto, named after Roberto Clemente.

Branch Rickey, who was GM during much of Galbreath's ownership, was not an owner of the Pirates, but was as big a name in major league baseball as anyone. But, as the Pirates general manager, it was Branch Rickey who drafted the first Afro-Hispanic player, the great Roberto Clemente.

In 1983, the Galbreaths sold 49 percent of the team to Warner Communications for an undisclosed amount. Two years later, Warner and Galbreath sold 99 percent of the Pirates to a consortium (Pittsburgh Associates) that included many of Pittsburgh's major companies, all of which were determined to keep the Pirates in Pittsburgh.

In 1996, a group led by Kevin McClatchy purchased the team for $95 million. He is a director of the McClatchy Group, a newspaper publishing company owned by his family. As CEO, the Pirates never had a winning season in the 10 years of his leadership.

In 2002, one of the minority owners, G. Ogden Nutting, along with his son Bob, kept buying available shares (for undisclosed amounts) until they became the majority owners in 2007. The Nuttings and the McClatchy Group were not well liked by Pirate fans, and no wonder: The Pirates had twenty consecutive losing seasons (from 1992 to 2012), which was the longest losing streak in North American sports at the time.

When Bob Nutting took over as CEO, he promised to improve the team's performance. He did. He invested in some good players and finally, beginning in 2013, the team made the playoffs in three consecutive years. He also developed the Pirates Training Academy in the Dominican Republic and spruced up their spring training facility in Bradenton, Florida. Nutting also serves as CEO of Ogden Newspapers, Inc. and owns the Seven Springs Mountain Resort.

The Pirates have been an institution in Pittsburgh since the 1880s. During that time, they have gone from sugar to shit to sugar to shit. Looking forward, being a team in a "small-market-city" with no local TV contract to bolster their balance sheet, they won't have the resources to compete for star players, and may be consigned to compete with their in-state-rival Phillies for control of the NL cellar.

Despite being an institution in Pittsburgh, the Pirates had to play second fiddle to two storied Pittsburgh franchises: the NFL's Steelers and the NHL's Penguins.

World Series Appearances: 7   Wins: 5
Forbes 2017 Valuation: $1.25 Billion

San Diego Padres

Year	Owner(s)	Purchase Price
1968-1974	C. Arnholdt Smith	$12.5 Million
1974-1984	Ray Kroc	$12 Million
1984-1990	Joan Kroc	Inherited
1990-1994	Tom Werner	$75 Million
1994-2012	John Moores	$85 Million
2012-	Ron Fowler	$800 Million

C. Arnholdt Smith initially purchased the Padres in 1955 for $300,000 when they were still a minor league team in the Pacific Coast League. Smith did not come from a family of wealth; in fact, his family fled to San Diego in 1907 to help his father avoid prison time in a political perjury case. Smith dropped out of high school to become a grocery clerk and later started as a bank teller who quickly moved through the ranks of what is now the Bank of America. His brother helped him purchase the U.S. National Bank in 1933, which grew to have $1.2 billion in assets. His entrepreneurship took off from there. Smith became known as the rainmaker of San Diego and controlled interests in real estate, transportation, silver mines, and the tuna industry. His wealth brought him connections, including becoming a friend and donor to President Richard M. Nixon.

Major League Baseball selected four expansion teams in 1968 to start the 1969 season. They included the Kansas City Royals, Seattle Pilots, Montreal Expos, and San Diego Padres. A group Smith led was then awarded the expansion and paid the franchise fee of $12.5 million. It is thought that Smith's decision to hire Buzzie Bavasi to be the president of the club was one reason that San Diego was successful in landing a franchise. Bavasi had experience as the general manager for the Los Angeles Dodgers. The other factor was that the San Diego Chargers had a new 50,000-seat stadium available for use by the Padres. San Diego

Stadium became Jack Murphy Stadium in 1980 and Qualcomm Stadium in 1997.

Like many expansion teams, the Padres floundered and finished in last place in each of its first six seasons in the National League West, losing 100 games or more four times. The bright spot in those years was expansion draftee and first baseman Nate Colbert. As of 2016, Colbert still holds the Padres' home run record with 163.

In 1973, Smith attempted to cut his losses and hoped to sell the Padres for $12 million to someone desiring to put a franchise in Washington, D. C. It appeared to be a done deal; bags and equipment were packed, player baseball cards in the new Washington Stars' uniform were printed. At the last moment, McDonald's founder Ray Kroc stepped in to buy the team and keep them in San Diego.

Smith's bank failed in 1973 due to excessive bad loans to Smith's own companies. The I.R.S. ultimately sued Smith for $23 million and he was convicted of an $8.9 million embezzlement and tax fraud. He served seven months in federal prison, with a reduced sentence due to poor health. He died 12 years later at the age of 97.

In 1974, the team was sold to Kroc for $12 million. He is known as the man behind the McDonald's fast food empire, but to baseball fans in San Diego, Ray Kroc will forever be remembered as the man who saved the Padres. Kroc grew up in Oak Park, Illinois, and was an enormous fan of baseball and attempted to buy his hometown Chicago Cubs. He sought to make the Padres a team the city would be proud to call its own. His passion for baseball coupled with his desire for satisfied customers led to one of the most infamous announcements over a public-address system in sports history.

It was opening night in 1974, the crowd was nearly 40,000, but the play on the field was deplorable. The starting pitcher only lasted one inning. A player was doubled off on a simple pop-out because he lost count of the outs. The Padres were down 9-2 in the eighth inning. Kroc asked the announcer for the mic to address the crowd.

"Ladies and gentlemen, I suffer with you," he said. Suddenly, a male "streaker" bolted onto the field, further angering Kroc. "Get that streaker off the field," his voice boomed throughout the ballpark. "Throw him in jail!" Kroc went on. "I have good news and bad news. The good news is that the Dodgers drew 31,000 for their opener and we've drawn 39,000 for ours. The bad news is that this is the most stupid baseball playing I've ever seen." The crowd suddenly erupted in cheers, appreciative of Kroc's frankness. Not amused, however, were the ballplayers themselves, both the Padres and Astros. Major League Baseball fined Kroc and demanded a public apology.

Many believe that Kroc's impassioned remarks helped increase the Padres' attendance that year. The fans seemed to believe that they finally had an owner who cared, someone who also wanted to see great baseball in

San Diego. Despite finishing in last place for the sixth straight time, the Padres drew over one million fans in 1974 after never drawing more than 650,000.

Ironically, the same day as the microphone debacle, there was a debut of a mascot – the KGB Chicken. He was later known as the "San Diego Chicken" and then the "Famous Chicken," but most fans refer to him simply as The Chicken. The innovative entertainment of the KGB Chicken was the forefather of future mascots in pro sports.

Kroc finally saw a winning season in 1978. However, he found frustration with the team and MLB operations in general, and relinquished the reigns to his son-in-law, Ballard Smith. The Padres were on the verge of success when Kroc died in January 1984. The Padres wore a special patch saying "RAK" in 1984 to honor Kroc, and they would go on to win the NL Pennant that year. Ray Kroc was inducted posthumously as part of the inaugural class of the San Diego Padres Hall of Fame in 1999.

Following Ray Kroc's death, the team's ownership passed to his widow, Joan. She tried to donate the team to the city of San Diego but Major League Baseball rules do not allow public team ownership. Although she wasn't a baseball aficionado, she had incredible enthusiasm and passion as an owner. As a philanthropist at heart, she wanted the team to be all it could be for San Diego.

When Joan Kroc assumed ownership, the Padres were on the verge of success with two consecutive .500 seasons. In her first year as owner, 1984, nearly two million fans came to Jack Murphy Stadium and the Padres won the National League West and defeated the Chicago Cubs for the National League pennant. In celebration, the team's star reliever, Goose Gossage, celebrated by throwing Mrs. Kroc into a swimming pool. The team was unable to hold back the ferocious Detroit Tigers who won the World Series four games to one.

In 1986, 2.2 million fans attended home games and were hoping for a repeat performance, but witnessed a losing season. By 1987, the Padres returned to last place and just missed having a 100-game loss season. The team rebounded a bit with winning seasons in 1988 and 1989, so Kroc decided it was time to sell the team so she could spend more time with her family and support her philanthropic endeavors.

Once Joan Kroc decided to sell the team, there was no shortage of interested buyers. Ultimately, the team was sold in 1990 for $75 million to a syndicate of 15 investors led by Tom Werner. He was best known for being a television producer of shows such as "Roseanne," "The Cosby Show," and "That '70s Show," to name a few. His first notoriety came when he invited Roseanne Barr to perform the national anthem. Her now infamous performance was a disgrace that ended with her grabbing her crotch and spitting on the ground. The debacle became known as the "Barr-Mangled Banner."

Werner purchased a team that was performing well, coming off two winning seasons and nearly missing the National League West title in 1989. After winning records in 1991 and 1992, the Padres fell to last place in 1993 with 101 losses. This did not happen by accident, and many call the events of 1992 and 1993 the biggest fire sale in Padres history. When completed, the Padres payroll had been reduced by $10.3 million and was the lowest in the major league. Nearly all the stars were unloaded for very little in return. One exception was in keeping San Diego's hometown hero, Tony Gwynn.

Werner sold the team in December 1994 to John Moores for a reported $85 million. Moores earned his fortune through BMC Software, which he founded in 1980 in Houston, Texas. His estimated $400 million net worth was needed to continuously fund a team that was not making money. Moores spent extensively on free agent signings in 1995. This seemed to have paid off in 1996 when the Padres surprised everyone by passing the Dodgers on the last day of the season to win the National League West title.

Moores was seeking ways to increase attendance and hired a director of Hispanic marketing. They created the "Domingos Padres Con Tecata" program that provided Mexican fans with bus transportation from the border and a game ticket, all for less than the cost of a regular ticket. This program, plus better in-game performance doubled the Padres' attendance from 1.1 million in 1995 to 2.2 million in 1996. Even so, the team still lost money that year.

1996 marked the beginning of the quest for a new ballpark. With Mayor Golding's task force finding in favor of the development project in 1997, the club and the city began outlining a vision for a baseball-only ballpark in downtown San Diego. The Padres won 98 regular season games in 1998, and took the National League pennant before falling to the New York Yankees in the World Series, four games to none. Still, this performance rallied the city and the San Diego voters approved a $400 million ballpark to be built on a 26-block downtown redevelopment area. Although construction began in 1999, it was halted and delayed with numerous lawsuits. Finally, in 2004, the Padres had Petco Park. Season tickets sales were up as was overall attendance.

Moores entered into a rather public and messy divorce that led him to seek buyers for the team in 2009, and Jeff Moorad stepped up to the plate. Moorad, with a group of 12 investors (including Troy Aikman), offered approximately $500 million to purchase the team over five years. At the same time, the group also bought the Padres' Triple-A team, the Portland Beavers. Moorad served as the club's CEO and vice-chairman from 2009 to 2012. The San Diego Business Journal named Moorad one of San Diego's "Most Admired CEOs" in 2010.

Most notable during his non-ownership tenure, Moorad negotiated a substantial TV contract that would bring $1.2 billion to the Padres over

20 years, and led to the creation of Fox Sports San Diego. Even though he sold his 12 percent interest in the Arizona Diamondbacks and owned 49 percent of the San Diego Padres, the MLB ownership group deferred voting on his approval to complete the sale and, in March 2012, Moorad withdrew his group's application for full ownership. Moores stepped back in long enough to select the next ownership group.

Selling the team was a bittersweet moment for Moores but he had much to be proud of in his 18 years of ownership. He served on the "Blue Ribbon" panel that outlined competitive challenges for small-market teams. Moores also helped to write the debt-service rule that restricts clubs from borrowing money to pay down operational debt. From San Diego's perspective, he got a ballpark built and saw the Padres win four National League West titles, make one World Series appearance, and expand the fan base, including Mexico.

After the deal to sell to Jeff Moorad fell through, John Moores sold the team in 2012 to a syndicate headed by Ron Fowler for $800 million. Approximately $200 million of the sale price included the Padres' 20% holdings in Fox Sports San Diego and the $1.2 billion, 20-year contract previously negotiated by Moorad.

Ron Fowler serves as the executive chairman and represents the ownership group at all league meetings. Fowler is the first San Diego-based person at the helm of the Padres since C. Arnholdt Smith. His group includes a rich history of baseball in the O'Malley family, owners of the Los Angeles Dodgers for five decades. Kevin and Brian O'Malley are sons of Peter O'Malley and grandsons of Walter O'Malley. The senior O'Malley was responsible for moving the Dodgers from Brooklyn to Los Angeles following the 1957 season. The other group members are the Seidler brothers (Peter and Tom), nephews of Peter O'Malley.

Fowler was a minority partner in the group assembled by Moorad in 2009 to purchase the Padres. He also serves as chairman and CEO of Liquid Investments, a distributor for Miller, Coors, Heineken, and other beer brands. Many believe that this connection has fostered the increase in beer offerings throughout Petco Park. He has stated numerous times that he wants to see the San Diego Padres win a World Championship in his lifetime and he isn't getting any younger.

Through 2015, the San Diego Padres have had 14 winning seasons and have appeared in two World Series Championships (1984 and 1998). The Padres are the only team remaining to have never thrown a no-hitter in the duration of the franchise. The question remains as to whether this ownership group will be able to drive the Padres to success. At this writing, it doesn't look like it.

World Series Appearances: 2   Wins: 0
Forbes 2017 Valuation: $1.125 Billion

San Francisco Giants

Former name: New York Giants -1958

Year	Owner(s)	Purchase Price
1919-1936	Charles A. Stoneham	$1 Million
1936-1976	Horace Stoneham	Inherited
1976-1993	Robert A. Lurie	$13.5 Million
1993-2008	Peter A. Magowan	$100 Million
2008-2011	William H. Neukom	
2012-	Charles Johnson	

Charles Stoneham was the majority owner of the New York Giants starting in 1919 during the start of the modern era of baseball. Stoneham purchased minority shares from Francis McQuade in 1928 and acquired John McGraw's shares following his death in 1934, giving him full ownership.

While what Stoneham initially paid for the franchise is not confirmed, several accounts indicated it was $1 million, while others say he gained control of the team from Harry Hempstead in a poker game. Stoneham earned his fortune on Wall Street and had his own brokerage firm at one time. He also owned the Sierra Nevada mine in Nevada.

The team found great success during Stoneham's 17 seasons of ownership with a .576-win rate, five pennants, and three World Series championships (1921, 1922, 1933). However, amidst that success on the field was a lot of drama and intrigue off the field. Stoneham was indicted twice related to fraud, perjury, and mail fraud of former clients but was cleared of charges. He was a chronic gambler and owned racetracks and casinos, including the Havana Casino in Cuba. Although the baseball commissioner forced him to sell his casinos, he maintained his horse track. Stoneham was also close with an infamous organized crime boss, Arnold Rothstein, who was connected to the 1919 World Series fix.

Charles Stoneham died in 1936, leaving his ownership of the team to his son, Horace Stoneham. The younger Stoneham began an apprenticeship in baseball at an early age because his father knew he would be a future owner. He learned the business of baseball from the ground up – literally, working with the grounds crew. He did other jobs for the franchise, including working in the ticket office and front office. At age 32, when his father died, he became the youngest National League club owner in history.

Horace took over the franchise at a good time, as they won their league's pennant in 1936 and 1937. Team performance dropped off but rebounded and so did the gate attendance when they surpassed the million mark for the first time in 1945 and kept it above that line for seven consecutive years. They won a pennant again in 1951 but it was 1954 when they won the World Series.

Interest in the team seemed to bottom out after that victory. The Polo Grounds were aging, the neighborhood was not desirable, and the Yankees seemed to be profiting with their newer stadium. Stoneham felt it was time to move and many options were explored. The initial plan was for Minneapolis; however, Walter O'Malley of the Dodgers shared that he would be moving his team to Los Angeles and encouraged Stoneham to also move west. In 1958, the team was moved to San Francisco and renamed San Francisco Giants.

The Giants were welcomed in San Francisco with strong attendance, even at the minor-league park, Seals Stadium, the first two years, where they averaged 1.3 million fans through the gates. In 1960, the team moved to its new stadium, Candlestick Park, and kept playing above .500 ball, with fan attendance in the 1.5 million area. They won the pennant but lost in the World Series in 1962.

The Giants were loaded with talented players like Willie Mays, Juan Marichal, Willie McCovey, Gaylord Perry, and Orlando Cepeda. They innovated major league scouting operations when they were the first to sign a Japanese pitcher in 1964, and started signing players from the Dominican Republic. Stoneham shares the blame for a series of bad trades and the hiring, as manager, of Alvin Dark, who appeared to have difficulty relating to minority players.

The Giants won their division in 1971 but this was also Mays's final season with the team. The next four years were a struggle on the field and financially as well. Gate receipts were plummeting and the Oakland Athletics, who arrived across the bay only a few years earlier, were also struggling for attendance. Stoneham felt he had to put the team up for sale in 1975. In his 40 seasons at the helm, the team boasted a .523-win rate, one division title, five pennants, and one World Series championship. He controlled the team for 22 seasons in New York and 18 seasons in San Francisco and, despite ups and downs with fan loyalty, averaged 1.04 million in average gate attendance.

Stoneham initially had an arrangement to sell the team to Labatt Brewing Company, which wanted to have the team in Toronto. The San Francisco mayor won an injunction to stop the sale. The mayor took things one step further and approached a minority owner to assemble a group that could purchase the team and keep them in San Francisco.

Bob Lurie and Bud Herseth subsequently purchased the team for $8.5 million in 1976. The Lurie name is well known in San Francisco due to the real estate development firm started by his father, Louis Lurie, and later led by Bob Lurie. Lurie bought out Herseth's shares a year later for $5 million. The team's mediocre performance of the 1970s continued, although they had a few seasons where they finished above .500. Then, in 1985, they had 100 losses, the highest number of losses in franchise history.

From that low point, they rebounded and won their division just two years later. In 1989 they won the National League pennant but not the World Series. That said, they achieved over two million in attendance for the first time in franchise history. During this same time, Lurie was trying to get approval for a new stadium. Candlestick Park was big, windy, cold, and fans did not like it. In both of their division winning years, (1987 and 1989) voters rejected stadium proposals even though the Giants were financing most of it. Efforts to pass a proposal to improve the stadium were also rejected and attempts to find a stadium location in neighboring communities also failed. The Giants franchise was losing $2.7 million annually, and Lurie announced in 1992 that he needed to sell the team.

In his 17 seasons of ownership, the team had a .486-win rate, won two division titles, had one World Series appearance, and averaged 1.36 million in annual attendance.

Vince Naimoli led a group that offered to buy the franchise for $115 million but they wanted to move the team to St. Petersburg, Florida. This time the National League stepped in and requested that Lurie secure a bid that would keep the team in San Francisco. Peter Magowan subsequently headed up a group that purchased the franchise for $100 million. The investment group included Charles B. Johnson, Scott Seligman, Philip Halperin, Allan Byer, and David S. Wolff; however, Magowan maintained the role of managing general partner.

Magowan's grandfather was co-founder of Merrill Lynch & Company and his father was chairman and CEO of Safeway. After college, Magowan worked in numerous capacities for Safeway and succeeded his father as CEO in 1979. When Magowan assumed the Giants' leadership role, he set out to accomplish what Lurie could not – consummate a new stadium deal. His plan was for a 42,000-seat ballpark that would be the first privately funded stadium in more than 30 years. The plan was overwhelmingly accepted and the new ballpark, now AT&T Park, opened in 2000. That inaugural year they achieved over three million in attendance for the first time in franchise history and had eight consecutive seasons over three million.

Magowan came under scrutiny during the Mitchell Report scandal regarding the use of steroids in the clubhouse and particularly with Barry Bonds; however, nothing came of it. In Magowan's 16 seasons as managing partner the Giants had a .525-win rate, won three division titles, one World Series appearance, and averaged 2.6 million in annual attendance.

Magowan stepped down as leader of the ownership group at the end of the 2008 season and Bill Neukom took his place. Prior to his role with the Giants, Neukom had a successful legal career that included 25 years as principal counsel for Microsoft and president of the American Bar Association. Neukom only occupied this lead role for three seasons but it included 2010 when the Giants won the World Series for the first time since moving to San Francisco. They also had an overall .547-win rate and 3.1 million in average annual attendance.

After Neukom stepped down at the end of 2011, another partial owner from the 1992 purchase, Charles Johnson, took his place. The ownership group is reported to be quite large, over 30 members, and Johnson owns an approximate 25 percent share. Johnson has a net worth valued at $5 billion and has consistently among the Forbes 400.

He amassed his fortune in the money management business and is the largest shareholder of his family's firm, Franklin Templeton Investments. As a franchise owner, he remains incredibly hands-off and empowers his leadership team – CEO Larry Baer and Senior V.P./G.M. Brian Sabean – to have carte blanche in the daily operations of the team. He does, however, exhibit incredible commitment to the franchise and ensures his leadership team has the funding needed to be successful. Johnson's team has continued the work started with Magowan and Neukom to produce winning results. Four years into his ownership, the Giants have an overall .528-win rate, one division title, 3.4 million in average annual attendance, and World Series championships in 2012 and 2014.

World Series Appearances: 15 Wins: 7
Forbes 2017 Valuation: $2.65 Billion

Seattle Mariners

Year	Owner(s)	Purchase Price
1976-1981	Danny Kaye, Lester Smith, Stan Golub, Walter Schoenfeld	$6.25 Million
1981-1989	George Argyros	$10.4 Million
1989-1992	Jeff Smulyan	$80 Million
1992-	Nintendo of America	$100 Million

One of only three MLB teams that has never won a World Series, or even appeared in one, the Seattle Mariners came into existence as the result of a breach of contract lawsuit brought against MLB by the City of Seattle and State of Washington in 1970. The Seattle Pilots had been purchased by Bud Selig and relocated to Wisconsin as the Milwaukee

Brewers. Selig would later become MLB Commissioner (after divesting himself of the franchise in favor of his daughter).

In 1976, legendary and beloved entertainer Danny Kaye, star of such films as "White Christmas," "Hans Christian Andersen," and "The Secret Life of Walter Mitty," and a highly-esteemed UNICEF ambassador, was part of a group that purchased the Seattle Mariners. Less known about Kaye: he boasted an encyclopedic knowledge of baseball and was a longtime good friend of baseball luminary Leo "The Lip" Durocher.

And so, along with three Seattle businessmen, Walter Schoenfeld (fashion industry), Stan Golub (jewelry wholesaler), and Lester Smith (broadcasting industry), Danny Kaye became the public face of the ownership group that brought major league baseball back to Seattle.

In 1981, this group sold the team to George Argyros, a California businessman and investor who made his fortune in real estate and who would go on, in 2001, to be named the United States Ambassador to Spain.

Argyros sold the team to Jeff Smulyan-Founder, the chairman and CEO of Ennis Broadcasting, the largest privately owned radio broadcasting company in America. With Washington State being an American Pacific Rim locale, it was not surprising that when Smulyan put the team on the market in 1992, Nintendo of America would be the buyer, with Nintendo chairman, Howard Lincoln, representing president and CEO Hiroshi Yamauchi.

Strategically, the Seattle Mariners were the perfect franchise with which to open the Japanese market -- hence the acquisition of the Japanese free-agent superstar right fielder, Ichiro Suzuki in 2001, who would burnish his credentials for enshrinement in Cooperstown over 11 stellar seasons with the Mariners. Upon Yamauchi's death in 2013, Howard Lincoln was installed as the Chairman and CEO of the Seattle Mariners, which is one of three MLB teams under corporate ownership.

World Series Appearances: 0
Forbes 2017 Valuation: $1.4 Billion

St. Louis Cardinals

Year	Owner(s)	Purchase Price
1920-1947	Sam Breadon	
1947-1949	Fred Saigh and Bob Hannegan	$4.1 Million
1949-1953	Fred Saigh	+ $1.5 Million
1953-1996	Anheuser Busch	$3.75 Million
1996-	William DeWitt Jr., Fred Hanser, & Drew Baur	$147 Million

St. Louis is as much a baseball town as any. Its heritage runs deep and its consistently good teams, decade after decade, have forged a fan loyalty that is unequaled in the National League. Perhaps the Dodgers are equally as storied, but they spent their life in two cities, New York and L.A., whereas the Cards have been the St. Louis Cards for nearly 100 years.

Sam Breadon owned the St. Louis Cardinals in 1920 when the modern era of baseball began. He was a self-made millionaire, mostly through his ownership of Pierce-Arrow auto dealerships. He was a minority investor in the team before acquiring a majority to become the principal owner of the franchise in1920. Breadon was financially conservative and did not like the debt that came with the team. He negotiated with Phil Ball, the owner of the St. Louis Browns, (the other baseball team in St. Louis), to share Sportsman's Park so they could sell Robinson Field and clear their debt. In what turned out to be a wise decision, Breadon moved Branch Rickey into the front office. Rickey focused on scouting, player development, and truly invented the minor-league farm system. This move essentially created a winning foundation that made the National League as competitive as the American League.

Growing tired of renting from the Browns, Breadon earmarked $5 million to build a new ballpark but was unable to secure land. This created an unfavorable tax situation. He was terminally ill with cancer and sought to sell the team. A tax attorney, Fred Saigh, wanted to purchase the team along with Robert Hannegan as a minority partner. Breadon passed away 18 months later.

His 28 years owning the Cardinals produced an amazing record. Only in four of those years did they not achieve at least a winning record. Amassing nearly 2,500 wins, they earned an overall win rate of .569. The Cardinals appeared in the World Series nine times and won the championship six times.

Fred Saigh and Bob Hannegan officially acquired the franchise late in 1947 for $4.1 million. This was a challenging time for the Cardinals as Rickey had been forced out five years prior and was using his knowledge with the Brooklyn Dodgers. Bill Veeck had purchased the St. Louis Browns and wanted the Cardinals gone. A mere two years into ownership, Hannegan took ill and sold his shares to Saigh for $1.5 million. During Saigh's brief ownership, he led the other owners to refuse to renew Happy Chandler's contract as the Commissioner of Baseball. He also proposed revenue sharing derived through local television revenues and had a .553-win rate. Unfortunately, the tax dodge that Breadon created, along with some other problematic practices, returned to haunt Saigh, He was indicted on federal tax evasion, pleaded no contest in 1953 and was sentenced to 15 months in prison. These events resulted in the team being put up for sale. The team nearly went to Houston but Anheuser-Busch stepped in at the last moment to keep it in St. Louis. After prison, Saigh later became the largest shareholder in Anheuser-Busch outside of family members.

Gussie Busch, the Anheuser-Busch president, paid $3.75 million for the Cardinals franchise. Although it was less than the Houston syndicate offered, he persuaded Saigh that it was the right thing to do by ensuring the Cardinals were not relocated to Texas. Busch had lifelong ties to St. Louis though his grandfather who was born in Germany and the founder of Anheuser-Busch.

Gussie Busch worked his way through the family business and became CEO in 1946. Within 10 years, he had led the company to become the largest brewery in the world. After securing the Cardinals franchise, Busch quickly moved to purchase Sportsman's Park from the Browns and renamed it Busch Stadium. Most importantly, this shifted leverage and convinced the St. Louis Browns (controlled by Bill Veeck) to relocate rather than compete for attendance with the beer baron. The Browns left at the end of the season to become the Baltimore Orioles.

Busch served as either the president, CEO, or chairman of the Cardinals from 1953 until his death in 1989. A multi-purpose stadium, Busch Memorial Stadium, was opened in 1966 and served as home to the baseball and football Cardinals (until they moved back to L.A. in 2016). They surpassed the two million mark in attendance the following year and won the World Series. The first year with three million in attendance was later achieved in 1987.

Busch turned daily operations over to Fred Kuhlman in 1984 and he assumed the president role following Busch's death. In the 43 seasons that Anheuser-Busch owned the Cardinals, they had a .513-win rate, won seven division titles, appeared in the World Series six times, and won the championship three times. The Cardinals retired the number 85 in honor of Gussie Busch, his age at the time, and inducted him into their 2014 inaugural Hall of Fame class.

In 1996, the team was sold to a syndicate headed by William DeWitt Jr., Fred Hanser, and Drew Baur, for $147 million. DeWitt was the chairman and managing partner and oversaw all league, financial, and operational matters for the franchise. DeWitt grew up in St. Louis and was always immersed in baseball since his father owned the St. Louis Browns and Cincinnati Reds. After earning a Harvard MBA, Dewitt co-founded the Reynolds, DeWitt & Co. investment firm. Their holdings include many Arby's franchises and the U.S. Playing Card Company. He was also part of the syndicate, with George W. Bush, that purchased the Texas Rangers.

To have tighter control of their farm system, the Cardinals purchased three of their minor-league affiliates. DeWitt also opened a baseball academy in the Dominican Republic and placed scouting representatives in six foreign countries. In 2006, the current Busch Stadium (III) was opened. It is one of the few privately funded (mostly) major league ballparks. The Cardinals won the World Series that same year, the first time since the 1923 New York Yankees accomplished that in a brand-new stadium.

Under DeWitt's tenure, the Cardinals have an impressive .550-win rate, 10 division titles, four World Series appearances, and two championships. 17 of 20 years, they have exceeded the three million mark in attendance and have an impressive 3.22 million in average attendance.

World Series Appearances: 19   Wins: 11
Forbes 2017 Valuation: $1.8 Billion

Tampa Bay Rays

Year	Owner(s)	Purchase Price
1998-2005	Vince Naimoli	$130 Million
2005-	Stuart Sternberg	$200 Million

It was March 1995 when Major League Baseball owners voted 28-0 to grant expansion teams to the Tampa Bay Devil Rays and the Arizona Diamondbacks. Vince Naimoli headed a syndicate that purchased the Tampa team for a $130 million franchise fee in 1998.

However, the desire and effort to bring a team to the Tampa Bay area had been alive since the early 1990s. Naimoli originally had a minor share in a group that attempted to get the Seattle Mariners to Tampa Bay. That deal, and others, fell through and the city of Tampa Bay began to feel they were merely a stick used to prod new stadium deals for other franchises.

Becoming impatient, Naimoli crafted a deal that would bring the San Francisco Giants to Tampa Bay but the National League president vetoed that arrangement. It was Naimoli's flood of lawsuits that seemed to get attention and seal his fate. He had learned to play hardball even before owning a baseball team. The son of an Italian immigrant subway worker, he believed that life was about hard work and competing every day.

Naimoli attended the University of Notre Dame for his undergraduate studies and later earned a master's in mechanical engineering and MBA and even completed a management program at Harvard University. He built his fortune in the finance industry as a turnaround specialist. Naimoli became quite adept at taking over companies that were on the brink of total disaster, implementing massive cost cutting, improving efficiencies, and then selling for a large profit. This philosophy and strategy for amassing wealth did not translate well into owning a Major League Baseball team.

It wasn't long before Naimoli became a feared bully who made questionable decisions due to his obsession with money. Although it was not uncommon for ballparks to ban outside food, Naimoli ensured the Devil Rays policy was enforced to the fullest. Gate attendants and ushers were under strict scrutiny to uphold the policy. To make sure his policies were followed, Naimoli would sit in the stands and watch for fans that might be eating outside food. He never hesitated to ask if they brought it in or which gate they entered. It is not surprising that he would immediately fire the gate attendant who allowed the contraband into the stadium. This created a culture of fear while developing snack detectives throughout the organization.

All in all, this did not ingratiate fans or promote attendance. From 1998 to 2004, the Tampa Bay Devil Rays had some of the lowest attendance records in Major League Baseball, often barely exceeding that of the Montreal Expos who, for that reason, were later relocated to Washington, D.C.

Another concern was Naimoli's lack of interest or investment in technology. For nearly four years, the Devil Rays did not use email or any form of internet service. This was in a time when more than 60 percent of U.S. households had internet access, as did all MLB teams. He didn't trust it, believe in it, or want to spend money on it. Employees were forced to find a work-around to deal with clients and vendors, typically by creating personal email addresses. Many outside the organization questioned if they were communicating with someone who truly worked for the Devil Rays because of all the AOL and Yahoo addresses.

While the details of the arrangement between Naimoli and Stuart Sternberg are not fully known, it was reported that Sternberg originally planned to take control of the team in January 2007, but the timetable was accelerated to 2005. Naimoli sold him controlling interest in the team for $200 million.

During Naimoli's eight-year tenure as owner of the Tampa Bay franchise, the team had no winning seasons and an overall record of .401. Vince Naimoli was diagnosed with a rare brain disorder, progressive supranuclear palsy, in 2014, and his health has been on the decline.

Born and raised in New York, Sternberg has maintained a passion for baseball all his life. A true fan of the game, a favorite memory of his is from 1965 at Shea Stadium with his father, watching Sandy Koufax pitch when attending his first major league game. Sternberg has enjoyed playing organized baseball throughout the years as well as coaching his son's Little League teams, and being a season ticketholder for the New York Mets.

Sternberg attended St. John's University and earned a degree in finance. He used that degree to eventually become a partner in Goldman Sachs, and retired in 2002. He still serves on several advisory boards in the financial securities industry. In 2015, Sternberg became more involved with the governance aspects of Major League Baseball. He serves as chair of the MLB diversity oversight committee and was named to the Major League Baseball Executive Council, the eight-member panel that advises Commissioner Manfred on major issues.

In 2007, Sternberg shortened the team's name to Tampa Bay Rays. Under Sternberg's first 10 years of leadership, the team has enjoyed six winning seasons, five 90-plus win seasons, and a .514 overall winning percentage, has advanced to the post-season four times, and had a 2008 World Series appearance. Even with such a positive performance on the field, the attendance continues to be an issue for the Rays at Tropicana Field. The team has been unable to draw two million since the 1998 inaugural season and has ranked last recently in American League attendance. Sternberg invested some $20 million in capital improvements to the stadium and ticket prices are reasonable, but Tropicana Field remains undesirable and will not draw fans.

New stadiums typically bring a substantial jump in attendance and season ticket sales. The importance of working with local government officials to bring new stadium plans to fruition cannot be overstated. Since 2007, Sternberg has been exploring options. The first proposal was for a covered ballpark on the St. Petersburg waterfront but it had too much opposition. In 2009, they explored other possibilities but the St. Petersburg mayor, Bill Foster, remained steadfast on requiring the Rays to honor their lease through 2027 and not to enter into discussions with other communities. This stalemate has fostered many rumors, including some about relocating the team to Montreal and/or selling it. None of these rumors have been verified and Sternberg remains firm that he is keeping the team and staying in the Tampa Bay area for the foreseeable future.

World Series Appearances: 1   Wins: 0
Forbes 2017 Valuation: $825 Million

Texas Rangers

Former name: Washington Senators 1960-1971

Year	Owner(s)	Purchase Price
1960-1963	Syndicate led by Pete Quesada	$2.1 Million
1963-1968	James Johnston & James Lemon	$5 Million
1968-1974	Robert E. Short	$9.4 Million
1974-1980	Bradford G. Corbett	$10 Million

1980-1989	H.E. Chiles	Unknown
1989-1998	Edward W. Rose & George W. Bush	$89 Million
1998-2010	Thomas O. Hicks	$250 Million
2010-	Rangers Baseball Express LLC	$593 Million

The Texas Rangers were founded as the Washington Senators in 1960 when Pete Quesada led a syndicate and paid a fee of $2.1 million. His bid for the franchise was not without challenge. A New York financier and a Washington lawyer each sought ownership. One of the bidders, Edward Bennett Williams, went on to own the Baltimore Orioles and Washington Redskins.

Prior to bidding on the franchise, Quesada had a successful career in the U.S. Air Force and reached the rank of Lieutenant General. Following military service, he transitioned into civilian life as an executive for Lockheed Aircraft prior to becoming President Eisenhower's special adviser for aviation. He was later among the first appointees to the Federal Aviation Administration (FAA). He resigned to head up the syndicate that purchased the expansion franchise.

They selected the same name the prior team was known for, the Washington Senators (1901 to 1960), before they moved to Minnesota to become the Twins. For their first season of play, 1961, the Senators used the existing Griffith Stadium. Quesada collaborated to get a new stadium built, RFK Stadium, which had the capacity to seat 45,000 and housed the Washington Redskins NFL team. It was initially called D. C. Stadium but was renamed in 1969 in honor of the late senator, Robert F. Kennedy. Quesada's ownership was short-lived due to low attendance (663,531 average) and poor performance (.375 average over two seasons).

Quesada's syndicate sold the team in 1963 to a group led by Washington stockbrokers James Johnston and James Lemon for $5 million. They suffered extensive financial losses; Johnston died in 1967. This, combined with continuing attendance below the million mark for six seasons, the lowest in the majors, and lack of performance (.414 average), prompted Lemon to sell the team.

In 1968, Robert (Bob) Short, a wealthy trucking executive, purchased the franchise for $9.4 million after outbidding comedian Bob Hope. The decision was somewhat surprising since Washington was insistent on keeping a major league team in the capitol city. Short lived in Minnesota and had previously bought the Minneapolis Lakers and moved that team to Los Angeles in 1960.

In his first season of ownership, he hired Ted Williams as manager. The team improved; it recorded its first (and only) winning season in Washington, D.C., and nearly doubled attendance to just under the million mark. Unfortunately, performance and attendance plummeted once again and the team was suffering $3 million in losses. Overall, the

Washington Senators, in 11 seasons, had an average win rate of .417 and an average attendance of 665,000. Short concluded the team was not sustainable in that market.

He was ready to relocate the team and liked what he saw in Texas, with the state's long-standing desire to have a major league team in the Metroplex, and another stadium already in Arlington, Texas. Short petitioned the American League to move the franchise to Arlington and his request was granted commencing with the 1972 season.

Turnpike Stadium had been built in 1965 to attract a major league team. Its 10,000-seat minor league capacity was designed to major league specifications with the ability to expand to 50,000 seats. Thus, it only required minimal renovations to be game-ready for the 1972 season.

It was renamed Arlington Stadium, with a new seating capacity of 44,000. The team was renamed the Texas Rangers in honor of the famous Texas law enforcement agency. After a year in Texas, Ted Williams resigned as field manager and Whitey Herzog briefly assumed the role, but was quickly replaced by Billy Martin.

In 1974, after five seasons with monetary and performance losses (.413 overall), Short decided to sell the team to a local group.

Born in the Bronx, Bradford Corbett made his initial fortune in the oil business selling PVC piping after parlaying a $300,000 Small Business Administration loan into millions within two years. He was later part owner of S&B Technical Products of Fort Worth, Texas. In 1974, Corbett purchased the Texas Rangers from Bob Short for $10 million. Like Short, he served as his own general manager, but he spent a considerable amount on acquiring free agent players. The team certainly improved under Corbett's ownership. Even so, he was passionate, emotional, and rather mercurial about the team.

In 1977, he employed four different field managers in an eight-game period, yet the team finished with 94 wins that year. The Rangers finished above .500 four of six years and at .518 overall. Annual attendance consistently exceeded the million mark, averaging 1.28 million overall. Regardless, Corbett decided to sell the team in 1980 because he said it was "killing" him.

After 20 years, the Rangers were ushering in their fifth ownership group. In April 1980, Corbett sold the team to a syndicate led by H. E. (Eddie) Chiles for an undisclosed amount. A native Texan and a self-made millionaire, Chiles made his fortune in the oil industry with Western Company of North America. His organization provided technical services that were needed to discover and produce oil and gas. Chiles's company grew to have annual revenues over $500 million.

Chiles put his proven work ethic and corporate control into the management of the Rangers. There was also a new focus on player procurement and development, including an emphasis on Latin American players. Team performance was up and down over the nine years under

Chiles's ownership, but they never garnered a post-season berth. Chiles's company's revenues plunged in 1989 when the oil market tanked. He was forced out as CEO and could no longer afford to own the Rangers franchise.

In March 1989, Edward "Rusty" Rose and future President George W. Bush headed a group that purchased majority ownership of the team for $89 million, including Arlington Stadium. Although Bush led the drive to purchase the franchise and began as the general partner, his initial investment was only $500,000, but he increased it to $600,000 the following year. Meanwhile, Rose, the majority owner, was the managing financial partner.

Rose appreciated the intellectual and strategic aspects of baseball. A brilliant man and owner of an investment firm, Cardinal Investment Co., he was well respected among the MLB ownership group due to his ability to analyze financial situations in baseball. Rose improved the team's financial stability by refinancing $25 million in long-term debt and renegotiating the television contract.

When Bush stepped down in 1994 to fulfill his newly elected role as Texas Governor, J. Thomas Schieffer succeeded him as general partner. Schieffer was the architect for the construction of a new ballpark, to replace Arlington Stadium and shift the perception of the Rangers from a small-market franchise to a big-market club.

The new ballpark opened in 1994 and was host to the All-Star Game in 1995. Currently known as Globe Life Park, it is the fourth name for this stadium. Together, the ownership group was credited with making the Rangers relevant. They won their division in 1996, which sent them into their first post-season play with an average win rate of .508. Attendance reached two million for the first time in franchise history, and averaged 2.3 million during their nine-year tenure.

In June 1998, the ownership group sold the franchise to Thomas Hicks for $250 million, the second-highest price (at the time) paid for a Major League Baseball team. Hicks, born in Houston, Texas, became interested in leveraged buyouts and venture capital after earning his MBA. He teamed up with Robert Haas to form Hicks & Haas in 1984. They purchased a communication company and several soft-drink makers and took Dr. Pepper and 7-Up public less than two years after merging them. Together, they turned $88 million in investor funding into $1.3 billion.

The Rangers had momentum when Hicks purchased the franchise. They won the division his first two years of ownership but lost the league division series. In addition to the Rangers, Hicks owned the Dallas Stars and the Liverpool Football Club (English Premier League).

In December 2000, Hicks negotiated a $252 million, 10-year contract with Alex Rodriquez, making it the largest in MLB history. Rodriquez was traded to the Yankees in 2004 but they supplemented a portion of his remaining contract.

In a move that foreshadowed the future ownership, Nolan Ryan was hired as team president in 2008. Throughout his ownership, the team performed reasonably with a 12-year .493 average with attendance averaging 2.45 million.

In early 2010, Hicks was ready to sell the club to an ownership group, Rangers Baseball Express, led by Chuck Greenburg and Nolan Ryan, but several issues delayed that deal. In May 2010, Hicks Sports Group filed for Chapter 11 bankruptcy. The court ordered a public auction to be held in August; and the Greenburg/Ryan $593 million bid won. Less than a year later, Greenburg resigned as chief executive and sold his shares.

In 2011, the 30 major league owners unanimously approved Ryan as controlling owner of the club. Previously, Ryan was best known for his pitching prowess during a 27-year Hall of Fame career. In the fall of 2013, Ryan announced he would step down from the Rangers to spend more time with family. However, in February 2014, he moved into the role of special assistant to Jim Crane, owner of the Houston Astros.

The Rangers' co-chairman, Ray Davis, assumed the role of controlling owner. During the first six seasons of ownership by the Rangers Baseball Express, the team flourished. In 2010 and 2011, they not only won their division but made consecutive World Series appearances. In four of the six seasons they earned postseason berths. In 2012 and 2013, they broke the three million attendance mark and had a 2.88 million average.

World Series Appearances: 2   Wins: 0
Forbes 2017 Valuation: $1.55 Billion

Toronto Blue Jays

Year	Owner(s)	Purchase Price
1976-1991	Labatt's Breweries, Imperial Trust Limited, and (CIBC) Canadian Imperial Bank of Commerce	$7 Million
1991-1995	Labatt's Breweries and CIBC	$60.3 Million
1995-2000	Interbrew and CIBC	Acquisition
2000-2004	Rogers Communications/ Interbrew	$168 Million
2004-	Rogers Communications Inc.	$45 Million Additional

How different would the baseball landscape be today if the sale of the San Francisco Giants for $13.25 million to a Toronto group had gone through in 1976? The plans were in the works and Exhibition Stadium had been renovated to accommodate Major League Baseball. Fortunately for the Northern California fans, a U.S. Court upheld an injunction filed by the city of San Francisco and the move to Toronto was halted. The sale later went to Bob Lurie, who kept the team in San Francisco.

Don McDougall, president of Labatt Brewing Company, led the charge to get Major League Baseball in Toronto. His primary competitors were aligned with hockey and Canadian football and Labatt was not gaining ground. McDougall sensed a great opportunity to align his beer brands with baseball. The Labatt board of directors was not as enthusiastic but agreed to ownership on the conditions that Labatt could own a maximum of 45 percent, would have advertising rights for 20 years, and that their interests would be sold in five years. (McDougall would turn out to be correct in his hypothesis; and Labatt became the top brewery in Canada within four years of owning the Blue Jays).

The American League kept Toronto at the forefront of the 1977 expansion and the winning bid went to Metro Baseball Limited (MBL) for the $7 million expansion fee. The ownership group (MBL) was comprised of Labatt Brewing Company (45 percent), Imperial Trust Limited – Howard Webster (45 percent), and CIBC (10 percent).

The team held a "name the team" contest and received over 4,000 submissions. Labatt Breweries selected a name linked to the color of its brand – Labatt Blue – and the Blue Jays were hatched. Paul Beeston was hired as the team's first employee and Peter Bavasi was hired to be president and general manager. Beeston went on to be president from 1989 to 1997 and 2008 to 2015. In between, he was named president of Major League Baseball (1997 to 2002). Exhibition Stadium got additional renovations and 45,000 fans endured a snow-covered field for the team's first game in April 1977.

Canadian weather can be challenging for fans in an uncovered stadium. Heavy rain and snow often made fans miserable and the push for a domed stadium gained momentum. It was the Canadian National Railway (CN) that stepped up in 1984 with a donation of seven acres for a new stadium. It was a perfect location, with the CN Tower, convention center, and public transit all adjacent. Naturally, public squabbles broke out, forcing the province to establish the Stadium Corporation of Ontario to evaluate alternatives. After all the fuss, the CN location won out after all, and the Blue Jays played their first home game in June 1989, in the new Skydome in front of 50,000-plus fans. Baseball was alive and well (and warm) in Toronto.

In 1991, Webster/Imperial Trust sold its 45 percent to Labatt Breweries for $60.3 million, pushing them to 90 percent ownership. The previous restriction of only owning 45 percent was out the window when they saw how much beer was being sold.

The following season, the Blue Jays won their first World Series, defeating the Atlanta Braves. The following year, the team boasted seven

All-Stars and won back-to-back World Series Championships, defeating the Philadelphia Phillies. Two years later, in 1995, the Belgium-based brewing company Interbrew, acquired Labatt Breweries and the 90 percent share of the Blue Jays. CIBC continued to hold a 10 percent share. This was the second team to be owned by a company outside of North America. The other was their sister expansion team, the Seattle Mariners, owned by Nintendo.

In 2000, Rogers Communications purchased 80 percent control of the team for $168 million. Interbrew reduced its share to 20 percent as CIBC relinquished its 10 percent share. Rogers Communications paid an additional $45 million to Interbrew in 2004 to own 100 percent. At the same time, they acquired the Skydome and renamed it Rogers Centre.

World Series Appearances: 2   Wins: 2
Forbes 2017 Valuation: $1.3 Billion

Washington Nationals

Former name: Montreal Expos 1969-2004

Year	Owner(s)	Purchase Price
1968-1991	Charles Bronfman	$1.8 Million
1991-1999	Charles Brochu	$86 Million
1999-2002	Jeffrey Loria	$12 Million
2002-2006	Expos Baseball, LP	$120 Million
2006-	Ted Lerner	$450 Million

The Washington Nationals were originally founded as the Montreal Expos in 1968 when Charles Bronfman headed a group that paid a franchise fee of $1.8 million. When Montreal's mayor, Jean Drapeau, initiated the campaign to bring Major League Baseball to Montreal, Bronfman, president of his family's business, the multinational Seagram's corporation, was the person who stepped up and became the principal owner of the new team.

Locating a suitable ballpark was a top priority and the city and team eventually settled on Jarry Park. Previously only used for amateur teams, the 3,000-seat capacity, municipally owned ballpark was to be a temporary solution while a modern, baseball-only park was being built. However, Montreal won the bid for the 1976 Olympics, which required the construction of an Olympic multi-use stadium. The Expos played at Jarry

Park through the 1976 season before they would move into Olympic Stadium.

Bronfman needed solid baseball leadership at the helm. He selected John McHale to serve as president. At the time, McHale was serving as assistant to the Commissioner of Baseball, William Eckert. McHale had previously been the general manager for the Detroit Tigers and Milwaukee Braves and was well respected in baseball circles. Bronfman left baseball decisions to McHale but was personally involved with many aspects of team ownership and leadership. Once the Expos moved into Olympic Stadium, attendance picked up and so did the win/loss record. The team enjoyed seven consecutive years over .500 (1978 to 1984) and made the postseason in 1981, losing in the NLCS. Bronfman was inducted into the Canadian Baseball Hall of Fame in 1984.

By the conclusion of the 1989 season, Bronfman was ready to sell the team but wanted it to stay in Montreal. To ensure that outcome, he loaned money to Charles Brochu, who had been club president since 1986, so he could create an ownership syndicate of local business owners and keep the Expos in Montreal. The sale was finalized in 1991 for $86 million. Prior to working with the Expos, Brochu had a career in the distillery industry, including a stint as executive vice president of Seagram's.

Although Brochu was committed to the Expos, the other dozen investors made it clear that they would not contribute any additional funds to run the team. This left Brochu in a predicament as the Expos had to operate on a minimal budget. Even so, they acquired some top talent and were poised to take the division in 1994 with an amazing .649-win record, but a strike brought it all to an abrupt halt. The off-season brought a fire sale and the 1995 season reflected that with a sub .500 record. Brochu believed a new ballpark would save the team from bankruptcy; however, when funding attempts failed, he resigned and sold his shares to Jeffrey Loria.

On December 9, 1999, New York art dealer Jeffrey Loria, with a 24 percent stake, headed a group that finalized the purchase of the Expos for $12 million. Over his two years of ownership, he put in a series of cash calls with other owners and they went unanswered. This resulted in his 24 percent stake climbing to 94 percent, and a new team valuation of $50 million. Like his predecessor, he demanded a new ballpark, to no avail. Loria was also unsuccessful at negotiating an English-speaking radio and television agreement for the 2000 season, which further alienated fans.

In February 2002, Baseball Commissioner Bud Selig, orchestrated a deal that sold the Expos to the commissioner's office for $120 million: John Henry sold the Marlins to Loria for $158.5 million (with a $38.5 million no-interest loan from MLB), and the path was cleared for Henry to buy the Boston Red Sox. Selig had all the owners in agreement before contracts were signed.

Loria's former partners in the Expos ownership group filed a RICO lawsuit again him and Major League Baseball but the arbitration panel found in favor of Loria.

Major League Baseball hired Frank Robinson to manage the team and made minimal improvements to Olympic Stadium. The Expos' average attendance increased in 2002, but MLB dictated that the Expos would play 22 of their home games in San Juan, Puerto Rico, for the 2003 season. The team was welcomed and successful in Puerto Rico and the Expos drew over a million fans (at combined locations) for the first time since 1997.

For 2004, the Player's Union tried to prevent play in Puerto Rico but later conceded the arrangement. MLB considered new locations for the team, including Puerto Rico, Mexico, Oregon, Virginia, New Jersey, and Washington, D.C. On September 29, 2004, MLB announced that the franchise would move to Washington, D.C., and the team played its final home game later that night. Ironically, the game was before the season's largest crowd of over 31,000 fans. Their final game was played at Shea Stadium against the New York Mets on October 3, 2004.

Baseball was going to be back in Washington, D.C., but they needed a ballpark. As is typical, much controversy surrounded getting the ballpark financed, but after negotiations an agreement was reached.

The team was renamed the Washington Nationals, which had been the official name of the American League Washington Senators from 1905 to 1956. Although they finished last in their division that first year, they had a .500 record and attendance of 2.7 million.

In July 2006, MLB sold the team to the Lerner Enterprises group, led by real estate developer Ted Lerner, for $450 million. Lerner came from humble beginnings. To start his real estate company in 1952, he borrowed $250 from his wife and grew it to become the largest private landowner in the Washington, D.C. area. The family is also a partner in Monumental Sports & Entertainment, which owns the NBA Washington Wizards, the WNBA Washington Mystics, the NHL Washington Capitals, and the Verizon Center.

The first five years of MLB ownership were challenging and the wins came sparingly; however, the most recent five years have averaged a win record of .548, including two second-place finishes and two division titles, although they lost in the division series. Nationals Park was opened at the start of the 2008 season. The new ballpark boosted attendance to 2.3 million but the two million mark was not broken again until their first winning season in 2012.

World Series Appearances: 0   Wins: 0
Forbes 2017 Valuation: $1.6 Billion

End Zone

What do we glean from this history of professional sports team ownership? For one, we see the collective power and influence the owners wielded through nearly a century. Professional sports leagues are a form of monopoly with all the power and advantage thereof. Mainly, control. The leagues control which cities qualify for a team, which owners qualify for membership in their group; and they control a significant segment of the population by controlling their time and their eyeballs ... if not on television, then on today's handheld devices.

According to a 2017 Forbes article, the average value of an NFL, NBA or MLB sports franchise is more than $1.7 billion. The NFL, the reigning sports-ratings king, has an average team value of $2.388 billion; the NBA $1.355 billion; and MLB $1.537 billion. These valuations have increased dramatically over the last three years, a period of relatively low inflation. I'm not suggesting these increases are undeserved. Quite the contrary. Sports are a key segment of our culture. We fans should thank the owners for bringing us this exciting form of entertainment, albeit at a hefty price. Today, we not only get to go to a ballgame, we get to go to a fancy state-of-the-art venue and sit in comfortable seats.

The owners as a group have had a dramatic effect on America's major cities and their local economies. Look at the array of mega-stadiums and arenas that dot the American landscape. Cities flourish when pro teams relocate to their town. I watched the transformation of Jacksonville, Florida, after the expansion Jaguars put the city on the map in 1995. I relocated my family and business from New York to Jacksonville in 1993, and helped the civic leaders sell enough season tickets (required by owner-to-be Wayne Weaver) for the deal to go through. We bought four Club Seats on the 50-yard line. In 1995, they were only $1,500 each.

Finally, there was something to talk about besides the college rivalry between the Florida Gators and Florida State Seminoles. Jacksonville has always had high school and college football fever. Even so, the excitement of getting a pro team was over the top. For such a relatively small southern city to qualify for an NFL expansion franchise seemed like a pipe dream to most locals, but the community banded together and made it happen. When it finally came true, the city stuck a pin in its hat and prospered ever since. Wayne Weaver became a local hero and, despite owning one of the worst performing teams in the NFL, made a capital gain of approximately $630 million when he sold the Jags to Shahid Kahn in 2012.

A pro sports team gives a city a sense of pride and recognition. People, as fans, gain a common denominator for communicating with other people. All ethnic groups, rich or poor, forget their differences when it comes to being a fan and rooting for their local team. After all, the success or failure of an owner ultimately lies in the hands of the viewing fans.

Which owners were the winners? If we look at the numbers, they all were. Very few lost money selling their teams. Some may not have been able to make ends meet here and there (especially in the early days), but most (probably 98 percent) made a very handsome gain on the sale of their team. Most made huge gains. That does not infer that the teams were profitable all the time. Quite the contrary. If an owner didn't have deep pockets, sustaining a team was a challenge, especially in smaller markets.

I couldn't help but notice the abundance of owners who were in real estate development of one kind or another. More interesting was learning how many owners stemmed from immigrant beginnings, especially from Jewish immigrant families.

This book could have been divided by two eras of ownership: pre- and post-TV. But many owners or their heirs experienced both eras. Baseball dominated as the country's favorite sport for the first fifty years until television brought basketball and football into our homes. Baseball franchises were selling in the multi-millions in the 1950s while pro basketball teams were just getting started. Gradually the NBA and NFL gained viewership and fan loyalty from the 1960s to present. Looking at the Forbes team valuations, baseball, once the most valuable league, has been replaced by football for first place... in riches.

Credit should be given to the early pioneers of professional sports. Men like George Halas, Jerry Colangelo, Barney Dreyfuss, Art Rooney, Branch Rickey, Tim Mara, the Biddle clan, Ben Kerner, Lamar Hunt, William Wrigley, Bill Veeck, Al Davis, and many, many other notables who took the financial risk to invest in a sports business. The record shows how difficult it was to sustain a franchise before the television era. But, owning a sports team had a distinct advantage over most businesses: it was fun and exciting.

Which teams had the best ownership over time, evidenced by a winning tradition? My top franchises that were or are dynastic (in random order): Pittsburgh Steelers, New York Giants, San Francisco Giants, Boston Celtics, San Antonio Spurs, Chicago Bulls, L.A. Lakers, L.A. Dodgers, St. Louis Cardinals, San Francisco 49ers, Dallas Cowboys, New England Patriots, New York Yankees, and Green Bay Packers. Each of these teams had an owner or owners who instilled a tradition of winning championships. Each has had their down periods. All teams do, but these franchises have distinguished themselves over time with multiple championship periods.

Forbes has done an incredible job of analyzing and reporting on the business of pro sports. Their valuations are based on "Enterprise Value (Equity + net debt) adjusted for stadium economics and recent purchase prices." Owning a major sports team is a "trophy" investment, which deserves a premium valuation.

But wait a second. Can pro team valuations keep growing to the sky? That seemed to be the consensus until TV ratings suddenly tanked, slipping 8 percent for the 2016/17 NFL season. I suspect the owners are in a huddle about how to survive this dangerous symptom.

If TV ratings decline, so will advertising rates, which will eventually cause a trickle-down effect, limiting or reducing player salaries and owner profits. Add to that potential catastrophe, the reduction in youngsters signing up for Little League football, and the rise in popularity of a less dangerous sport, Major League Soccer, the NFL's rising team values may not continue. Meanwhile, the NBA and MLB valuations, with their looming lucrative broadcasting contracts are closing in on the NFL's financial supremacy.

And, what about the NBA? How will they keep us engaged when only two or three teams out of thirty are so far superior to the rest of the league?

Nothing goes up forever…except the ball.

Hall of Fame Owners

NBA

Biasone, Danny	Syracuse Nationals/Philadelphia 76ers
Brown, Walter A.	Boston Celtics
Buss, Jerry	Los Angeles Lakers
Colangelo, Jerry	Phoenix Suns
Davidson, Bill	Detroit Pistons
Gottlieb, Eddie	Philadelphia Warriors/76ers
Irish, Ned	New York Knicks
Krause, Jerry	Chicago Bulls
Reinsdorf, Jerry	Chicago Bulls
Zollner, Fred	Detroit Pistons

NFL

Bell, Bert	Philadelphia Eagles
Bidwell, Charles	Arizona Cardinals
Brown, Paul	Cincinnati Bengals
Davis, Al	Oakland Raiders
DeBartolo, Ed Jr.	San Francisco 49ers
Halas, George	Chicago Bears
Hunt, Lamar	Kansas City Chiefs
Lambeau, Curly	Green Bay Packers
Mara, Tim	New York Giants
Mara, Wellington	New York Giants
Marshall, George P.	Washington Redskins
Reeves, Dan	Cleveland/ LA Rams
Rooney, Art	Pittsburgh Steelers
Rooney, Dan	Pittsburgh Steelers
Wilson, Ralph	Buffalo Bills

MLB

Comiskey, Charles	Chicago White Sox
Dryfuss, Barney	Pittsburgh Pirates
Griffith, Clark	Washington Senators/Minn. Twins
MacPhail, Larry	New York Yankees
O'Malley, Walter	Brooklyn/LA Dodgers
Rickey, Branch	Brooklyn/LA Dodgers
Ruppert, Jacob	New York Yankees
Selig, Bud	Milwaukee Brewers
Veeck, Bill	Chicago White Sox/Cleve. Indians/St. L. Browns
Yawkee, Tom	Boston Red Sox

Roster of Current Owners

NBA

Atlanta Hawks	Ressler, Antony
Boston Celtics	Boston Basketball Partners, LLC
Brooklyn Nets	Prokhorov, Mikhail
Charlotte Hornets	Jordan, Michael
Chicago Bulls	Reinsdorf, Jerry
Cleveland Cavaliers	Gilbert, Dan
Dallas Mavericks	Cuban, Mark
Denver Nuggets	Walton, Anne Kroenke
Detroit Pistons	Gores, Tom
Golden State Warriors	Lacob, Joe; Guber, Peter
Houston Rockets	Fertitta, Tilman
Indiana Pacers	Simon, Herbert
Los Angeles Clippers	Ballmer, Steve
Los Angeles Lakers	Buss, Jerry (Children of)
Memphis Grizzlies	Pera, Robert J.
Miami Heat	Arison, Micky
Milwaukee Bucks	Lasry, Marc; Edens, Wesley
Minnesota Timberwolves	Taylor, Glen
New Orleans Pelicans	Benson, Tom
New York Knicks	Madison Square Garden Corp.
Oklahoma City Thunder	Bennett, Clayton
Orlando Magic	Weide, Bob Vander
Philadelphia 76ers	Harris, Joshua
Phoenix Suns	Sarver, Robert
Portland Trail Blazers	Allen, Paul
Sacramento Kings	Ranadive, Vivek
San Antonio Spurs	Holt, Peter M.
Toronto Raptors	Maple Leaf S&E, Ltd.
Utah Jazz	Miller, Gail
Washington Wizards	Leonsis, Ted

NFL

Arizona Cardinals	Bidwell, Bill
Atlanta Falcons	Blank, Arthur
Baltimore Ravens	Bisciotti, Steve
Buffalo Bills	Pegula, Terry & Kim
Carolina Panthers	Richardson, Jerry
Chicago Bears	McCaskey, V. Halas
Cincinnati Bengals	Brown, Mike
Cleveland Browns	Haslam, Jimmy
Dallas Cowboys	Jones, Jerry
Denver Broncos	Bowlen, Pat (Trust)
Detroit Lions	Ford, Martha
Green Bay Packers	Green Bay Packers, Inc.
Houston Texans	McNair, Robert
Indianapolis Colts	Irsay, Jim
Jacksonville Jaguars	Khan, Shahid
Kansas City Chiefs	Hunt, Clark
Los Angeles Rams	Kroenke, Stan
Miami Dolphins	Ross, Stephen
Minnesota Vikings	Wilf, Zygi
New England Patriots	Kraft, Robert
New Orleans Saints	Benson, Tom
New York Giants	Mara, John; Tisch, Steve
New York Jets	Johnson, Robert Wood
Oakland Raiders	Davis, Mark
Philadelphia Eagles	Lurie, Jeffrey
Pittsburgh Steelers	Rooney, Art, Jr.
San Diego/L.A. Chargers	Spanos, Alex
San Francisco 49ers	York, M. DeBartolo & York, John
Seattle Seahawks	Allen, Paul
Tampa Bay Buccaneers	Glazer, Malcolm (Children of)
Tennessee Titans	Smith, Tommy
Washington Redskins	Snyder, Daniel

MLB

Arizona Diamondbacks	Kendrick, Ken
Atlanta Braves	Liberty Media Corp.
Baltimore Orioles	Angelos, Peter
Boston Red Sox	Henry, John
Chicago Cubs	Ricketts, Thomas
Chicago White Sox	Reinsdorf, Jerry; Einhorn, Eddie
Cincinnati Reds	Castellini, Robert
Cleveland Indians	Dolan, Larry
Colorado Rockies	Monfort, Dick & Charlie
Detroit Tigers	Ilitch, Mike
Houston Astros	Crane, Jim
Kansas City Royals	Glass, David
Los Angeles Angels	Moreno, Arturo
Los Angeles Dodgers	Guggenheim Baseball Mgmt.
Miami Marlins	Mas, Jorge
Milwaukee Brewers	Attanasio, Mark
Minnesota Twins	Pohlad, Jim
New York Mets	Wilpon, Fred
New York Yankees	Steinbrenner, Hal & Hank
Oakland Athletics	Fisher, John
Philadelphia Phillies	Middleton, John S.
Pittsburgh Pirates	Nutting, Bob
San Diego Padres	Fowler, Ron
San Francisco Giants	Johnson, Charles
St. Louis Cardinals	DeWitt Jr., William
Seattle Mariners	Nintendo of America
Tampa Bay Rays	Sternberg, Stuart
Texas Rangers	Rangers Baseball Express LLC
Toronto Blue Jays	Rogers Communications Inc.
Washington Nationals	Lerner, Ted

About the Author

William F. (Bill) Beermann is an entrepreneur and author who merges his passion for business and sports through his writing. A Pittsburgh native, he excelled in sports (baseball, basketball, and volleyball) and went to Davidson College on a basketball scholarship.

His business career began in the advertising and graphic design business in New York City. In 1973, he co-founded an international stock photography agency which grew from scratch to become one of the largest agencies in the world. After selling the business, he turned his attention to small business consulting and writing.

An avid sports fan, Beermann was drawn to the business side of sports and became enamored with the people who became owners of professional sports franchises which resulted in the writing and publication of this book.

He also wrote and published, *POUNCE – How Not To Lose Your Ass Betting Pro Football (My 50 Years Betting the NFL)*. His first novel, *The Odd Hour*, is scheduled for publication in 2018

He has three children and resides in Long Island, New York with his Maltese dog, Gracie. When not writing, he spends time reading, playing golf or bridge, and wagering on pro football. He sits on the Board of Visitors of Davidson College and recently served as Executive Director of the Fibrolamellar Cancer Foundation in Greenwich, CT.

For more information and to order books by Bill Beermann, please visit the author's website: www.billbeermann.com